The
Depression
Workbook

A Guide for Living With Depression and Manic Depression

MARY ELLEN COPELAND, M.S.

with contributions by

MATTHEW McKAY, Ph.D.

NEW HARBINGER PUBLICATIONS, INC.

Publisher's Note

This publication is designed to provide accurate and authoritative information in regard to the subject matter covered. It is sold with the understanding that the publisher is not engaged in rendering psychological, financial, legal, or other professional services. If expert assistance or counseling is needed, the services of a competent professional should be sought.

Originally printed by Peach Press, Brattleboro, Vermont.

Library of Congress Catalog Card Number 92-081725

Copyright 1992 by Mary Ellen Copeland
      New Harbinger Publications, Inc.
      5674 Shattuck Avenue
      Oakland, CA 94609

ISBN 1-879237-32-6 Paperback
ISBN 1-879237-33-4 Hardcover

Distributed in the U.S.A. primarily by Publishers Group West; in Canada by Raincoast Books; in Great Britain by Airlift Book Company, Ltd.; in South Africa by Real Books, Ltd.; in Australia by Boobook; and in New Zealand by Tandem Press.

Cover design by SHELBY DESIGNS & ILLUSTRATES
Front cover original artwork by Rick W. Sams
Back cover author photo by Tom Raffelt, Spiral Shop Studios

1st Printing April 1992 10,000 copies
2nd Printing December 1992, 7,500 copies
3rd Printing July 1993, 7,500 copies
4th Printing February 1994, 7,500 copies
5th Printing June 1994, 10,000 copies

This workbook is dedicated to

my mother, who has served as a beacon of continuing hope and inspiration;

all the members of my support team—family, friends, co-workers, fellow travelers, counselors, and health care providers—who accompany, sustain, affirm, validate, nourish, and uplift me on this continuing journey to enhance my wellness, stability, serenity, and joy;

and the people from all over the country who shared so willingly of their experiences, from the deepest depths of depression to the wild fury of mania, from unspeakable tragedies to glorious triumph, so that their vast store of knowledge can be used to ease the way for others.

Contents

Preface

This journal entry was written by a woman who has been a very close friend of the author for over 30 years. It was written when Mary Ellen was in the midst of what seemed to be an interminable depressive episode.

You were standing in the doorway when I drove into your yard. You'd seen my car go slowly down the road past your house and then double back, obviously lost.

And so we became friends quite by accident. We discovered that we had moved to Vermont within a few months of each other and that our husbands were both in public service professions. That was 30 years ago and we were just beginning to raise our families.

Over the years we have shared the usual (and the unusual) heartaches and pleasures that go with the territory of being wives and mothers. We did the PTA, band mothers, 4-H Club, ballet lessons, Little League route together. We survived our children's adolescence and our husband's midlife crises. We supported each other through our own changes from divorce into new relationships and from housewives into more satisfying (and lucrative) careers.

Our annual New Year's Day sleigh ride became an event that marked the passing of time for us, just as large family gatherings must do for others. Years later I planned a "reunion sleigh ride," despite the fact that my son was in a "don't-call-me-I'll-call-you" phase and your daughter was equally unreachable in New Zealand at the time. Nevertheless, on New Year's Eve, as the full moon rose over fields covered with two feet of new fallen snow, all seven of our children were there, along with their spouses, partners, and children of their own.

The only person who didn't come was you, Mary Ellen. For three years you had been slowly withdrawing from us. Oh, you were there in body, but lost to the world around you—your friends, your colleagues at work, your family, and, ultimately, yourself.

The doctors called it bipolar disease (manic depression as it is more commonly known); we called it by other names, which gave expression to our anguish and bewilderment. They gave you medications and said, "This should ease your symptoms" ("cure" was never a word they used). We gave you love and support, not knowing if anything could halt your quickening slide into deep places of despair and isolation. They put you in institutions where you would be safe from harm (what they meant was safe from yourself). We sat up nights with you, facing together the demons that disturbed your sleep. They organized structures for you to fit into, to give a measure of normalcy to your life. We filled the hollow hours of your days with the familiar structures that were once your choices.

I stood by and watched as the friend I had known slowly disappeared. Gradually I learned to numb my feelings, to lower my expectations, and to settle for "reality." One by one I gave up such simple things as hearing your laughter, going for a walk, meeting for lunch, or carrying on a conversation of any length.

I remember the day I let you go—the vital, creative woman that you used to be—and mourned your death just as keenly as if you had actually died.

Ah, my friend, what does it mean? Could we have known it would come to this? All I know now is that I cannot leave this friendship. For someone must stand at the door, see you approaching on the road, and be there to welcome you back.

— Mary Liz Riddle

Introduction

The Origins of My Own Depression

I was born in 1941 and grew up outside of New Haven, Connecticut. My father worked for the railroad, a job that often took him away from home for extended periods of time and caused him to work very erratic hours, including holidays and other significant times in the life of his family. My mother had a degree in nutrition from Penn State and put her energies into raising five children, each born two years apart. I was the middle child, with an older brother and sister and two younger brothers.

My early years were not easy, marked by several severe traumas including being with a special friend when she was struck and killed by a car. I felt that, since her parents couldn't have any more children and my parents had "plenty," it was I who should have been killed.

To justify my existence, I tried to be the perfect child, always trying to do the right thing. But somehow I never seemed to be good enough. My father and older brother constantly reminded me of my failings; I felt humiliated and rejected by their ridicule and criticism, as well as responsible for everything bad that happened.

Ongoing sexual threats and molestation throughout my childhood by a cousin who lived next door turned me into a fearful child who was constantly on guard and afraid, never feeling safe. My perceptions of myself as a person and a woman were molded by these experiences. I continue to work diligently to overcome the severe damage this abuse caused to every part of my being.

In 1949, when I was eight years old, my mother went into a deep, agitated, psychotic depression. After being unsuccessfully treated with the various tranquilizers that were available at that time, as well as electroshock therapy, she was committed to a state institution. For the next eight years, her moods swung from deep psychotic depression to outrageous and uncontrollable mania.

Every Saturday we went to visit her. Sometimes she seemed fine, almost like her old self. At other times she would be extremely agitated, walking in circles and speaking continually in words we couldn't understand. During these periods she became very thin and made no effort to take care of herself. It was impossible to communicate with her. Sometimes when we went to visit she would take us around the place, introducing us to everyone, talking loudly and laughing uproariously at jokes only she could understand.

During my mother's visits home we couldn't relate to her; she was often completely out of control. I still remember what it was like when it came time to take her back to the hospital. Even though it seemed as if she was out of touch with reality, she resisted returning to the overcrowded, smelly institution that provided her with no support and little care. These horrible, violent scenes, trying to get her out of the house and into the car, shall live in a dark place in my memory forever.

I really missed my mother. And there was no one in those days who recognized the need to help a little girl work through such a profound loss. It was one of those unspeakable situations that everyone avoids talking about. No one ever says, "I'm sorry your mother is in a mental institution." That reality was something I did my best to hide from schoolmates. During the early years of my mother's illness, I was very depressed and withdrawn. I spent much of my time playing alone in the woods behind the house where we lived.

Life for me and my brothers and sister became a morass of sadness, pain, and confusion. Unfeeling caretakers came and went for a while; but before long we were taking care of ourselves while my father worked long hours to pay what must have been over-whelming hospital bills.

This went on for eight years—my mother in and out of the hospital, but mostly in and never well; five lonely children struggling to fend for themselves. The stigma of mental illness was so great at that time that we did our best to hide from others what was going on in our lives.

During this time I always felt that my mother's illness was my fault. I didn't know what I had done, but I was sure that if I could get my mother alone and say the right thing, it would all be over and she would be well again. The guilt I carried around with me was tremendous. My self-image and self-esteem dropped off the bottom of the scale.

Then I hit puberty. I suddenly became outgoing, gregarious, the "belle of the ball." But there was really no one around to notice and applaud this change. Although low self-esteem and issues related to my mother's illness continued to be a problem, I made my way through high school, experiencing some intermittent lows, but mostly flying high, getting good grades and having lots of friends.

After high school I studied home economics at the University of Connecticut for a couple of years. It was at this time that my mother got well. Her extreme mood swings ceased. She came home from the hospital and began her life over again. Her children were mostly grown by this time. Despite much disappointment and rejection caused by the stigma of her long hospitalization, she got a wonderful job as a dietician for a large school system. She revitalized and managed a hot lunch program, a job that she kept until her retirement 20 years later. Her story is one that gives us all hope. Through careful monitoring and management of all aspects of her life, she has maintained an enviable level of wellness.

I left college to get married to my high school sweetheart and had, in rapid succession, four children. In raising them I was determined that they would not have the kind of childhood I had. So we played, hiked, visited museums, read stories—whatever struck our fancy. I introduced them to the world. I had the childhood that I had missed. Although the marriage was not going well, this was mostly a delightful time. I had bouts of depression, but still managed to be a "super mom."

I had a compelling concern for less fortunate kids and an overwhelming conviction that I had to make everything in the world right for everyone. This led me to adopt an older child, take in foster children, and finish college with a degree in special education. I founded a private school for adolescents with learning disabilities and behavior problems and for four years directed that school and avoided addressing any of the feelings that had been bottled up inside me for so long.

Then the long festering wound burst, and in 1976 I suffered a bout of severe depression. I had experienced other depressive episodes, but I was able to "successfully" work through them by completely filling my days with taking care of others and not dealing with myself. I visited a psychiatrist when I couldn't bring this latest depressive episode under control by using all my usual evasion techniques. It was becoming impossible to get out of bed, much less to meet my overwhelming load of obligations to others. Based on my history and symptoms, the psychiatrist diagnosed me as manic depressive. On his recommendation I began what turned out to be long-term treatment with lithium and various antidepressants.

Through the next 10 years my life took various twists and turns. My children grew up and moved on. During a hypomanic episode, I left my husband of 20 years (the marriage had been over long before that). I quickly remarried someone who I felt was going to solve all my problems by giving me the attention and understanding I had longed for all my life, something I couldn't give myself.

This new marriage was a disaster. When my husband began drinking heavily and being emotionally and physically abusive, I started seeing a good therapist. With her help I began addressing important issues, including emotional, physical, and sexual abuse; my mother's illness; my father's absence; my very low self-esteem; my inability to do anything nice for myself or to see myself as worthy; my need to always be taking care of someone else, allowing others to define who I am and what I should be like; my inability to experience pleasure and intimacy, my workaholism, and on and on.

Thanks to the work of this therapist, I was able to leave my second marriage. I got my master's degree, had several very good, high-powered jobs, and was thankful for the hypomanic state that, although occasionally interspersed with deep depressive episodes, propelled me through those years.

The Beginnings of Recovery

In 1986 I found myself working in a space with no outside light, in a bleak classroom setting, trying to rehabilitate five high school boys whose emotional and educational needs had been neglected for years. As winter came on, I sank into a deep depression. This was the beginning of three years of severe, rapid cycling, during which I lost my job, was hospitalized many times, and made several suicide attempts. In short, my life was totally out of control. I was unable to concentrate or focus. My short-term memory was nonexistent. Friends drifted away or left abruptly. Some family members suggested that I "pull myself up by my bootstraps" and became extremely annoyed when I failed to do so. Life became a living hell; although I kept searching for answers, prospects for my future seemed quite dim.

In December 1988 I was suffering from a severe depressive episode. Somehow I dragged myself to a workshop on light therapy presented by Dr. Wayne London, a psychiatrist with a holistic and alternative view of mental illness. I listened intently and asked him afterward if light was safe for use by manic depressives. He suggested that I have a complete battery of thyroid tests. I was quite overweight at that time, my skin and hair were dry, my face was puffy, and I moved slowly.

I ignored his suggestion about the thyroid tests, erroneously assuming that they had been done during a previous hospitalization. I went home and tried the lights. The depression lifted somewhat, but the fog in my brain persisted. I kept meeting this doctor every time I walked down Main Street or at the local food cooperative. He kept saying, "When are you going to get your thyroid tested?" So finally I did, to satisfy him as much as anything.

Both Dr. London and the endocrinologist to whom he referred me were shocked at the test results. I was suffering from severe hypothyroidism, an illness that can cause mood swings. The screening tests that are routinely given in hospitals did not show this problem. A complete thyroid battery was necessary for diagnosis.

They started me on a very low dose of thyroxine, with the understanding that they would increase the dosage as my body got used to this amount. Within days of the onset of hormone replacement treatment, my mind started to clear. And then, very gradually, I got better and better. The severity of the mood swings decreased, until now they are a minor irritant in my life rather than a major crisis.

A Program for Wellness and Stability

I feel that I finally have my life back. I'm happier and healthier than I've ever been; and it has now been over three years since I've had any severe symptoms of manic depressive illness. Through close personal monitoring of symptoms, and with the help of my support system, I've dealt effectively with the milder mood swings that are typical of anyone with a sensitive system and an active life.

I work constantly on a healthy lifestyle, cutting down on and dealing more appropriately with stress. I use many of the coping techniques suggested in this book. I've educated a wonderful group of people to be my support system. I meet with them regularly, keeping them honestly informed of how I'm feeling. I meet with several members of my support team for peer counseling on a weekly or as-needed basis. I'm an active member and regular participant in two support groups. I constantly monitor myself—my support team helps me with that—and take appropriate action when necessary. I have intervention plans for use by my support system in case my extreme mood swings return.

I've worked hard at developing positive attitudes and reducing the stress in my life. Through study and practice of various relaxation and meditation techniques, I enjoy deep relaxation which I use to feel better in general, to help me through the hard times, and even to put myself to sleep.

I do my best to eat right, get outside, and use a light box to get adequate light—like so many other manic depressives, I've noticed a seasonal pattern to my mood cycles. Exercise is a critical part of my daily routine. Exposure to electromagnetic radiation from electric blankets and video screens seems to cause me to feel anxious: I've replaced my electric blanket with a fluffy comforter that I love, and gotten a radiation screen for my computer.

With a fine therapist, I continue to work intensively on issues that still plague me and limit my life potential and my enjoyment. I read every self-help book that looks like it might enhance my wellness, making regular visits to the library to check out new additions to the collection. I continue to search for and explore ways to maintain and increase my mood stability and overall health—ways that are safe, noninvasive, and financially feasible. Currently, for me, these include acupuncture, homeopathy, and body work.

For the past three years I have been intensively involved in a vocational rehabilitation program, working to develop a career that takes advantage of my talents and allows me to take good care of myself. I have completed a study of coping strategies for 120 volunteers from around the country who have mood disorders, compiled the data, and sent it out to the project participants. In the spring of 1990 I began giving all-day and evening workshops based on the findings of the study. The workshops continue to be overwhelmingly successful. In addition, I am continuing to develop educational resources for people with mood disorders.

This workbook is my gift to others who are experiencing depression or manic depression, and to those people who love and care for them. It is my sincere wish that through this work, and the sharing of my own story, others may find the key to increased stability, long-term wellness, and happiness.

I know I will be working on maintaining and enhancing my wellness for the rest of my life; but it is the only path I can take. It is a gift I must give myself.

—*Mary Ellen Copeland*

Getting Started

At the present time, my mood has been stabilized for over a year. It would be unrealistic to think that I'll never have symptoms again; but at the same time, I don't want the anticipation of another episode to stop me from living and functioning right now. I just live with the security that if and when it happens again, I will handle it.

How To Use This Book

This workbook was born out of a study I made of the coping strategies and experiences of 120 depressives and manic depressives from around the country (only 25 percent of the surveyed participants had depression rather than bipolar illness).

As I began compiling the results of the study into a book, I found myself wanting to write personal notes to myself in the margins, compare my own experiences to those of the study participants, and commit myself to taking some action based on what I was learning. It became immediately clear to me that an interactive workbook format would be much more appropriate and useful than a merely factual report. To confirm the validity of my opinion, I shared drafts of the workbook with people in my support group, including others who have experienced mood swings, and with mental health professionals. There was a general consensus among us that an interactive format would work best. I hope you'll agree.

When depressed or manic, we are either going so fast or so slow that memory function is often impaired. Writing down your responses in the workbook will increase your ability to remember your thoughts, reinforce them, and subsequently allow you to take more effective action on your decisions. A written record allows you to refer back to your decisions at times when you are feeling less than decisive, or when your judgment is skewed.

I recommend that you own your own copy of this book so that you can write in it. Some people may prefer to type or use a word processing system to print out their responses on a separate sheet of paper; this is also very effective. When you have completed all the exercises, save the book for handy reference when you are making decisions, and for periodic review.

Each one of you who has a mood disorder is in a different place in your quest for achieving stability and wellness. You may have just experienced your first extreme mood swing or have just been diagnosed as having a mood disorder. Or perhaps you have been living and coping with these problems for years.

This workbook is designed to be used as a guide to achieving the maximum level of stability possible for you at this stage in your life, and to enhance your wellness in the years to come. Reading this book will also increase the level of understanding among your family members, friends, co-workers, counselors, and the health care professionals you deal with.

The material in this book is based on the findings of a study of 120 volunteers who have experienced depression or mania and depression. They come from all over the country, having responded to letters of appeal placed in several mental health newsletters and magazines. The response to the appeal was overwhelming, with over 1,000 people volunteering. Finances limited the study to the first 120 people who came forth. It's important to note that I made no effort to screen the volunteers. They comprise a random selection of people who felt comfortable responding to a study of this kind. They came from a wide variety of backgrounds and of experiences with mood disorders.

The thoughts, feelings, ideas, successes, and frustrations of the participants are quoted or summarized throughout this workbook, and provide the basis for a unique chronicle of wellness and stability. Whenever possible, I've quoted the responses of survey participants exactly as they were written. In some cases it was necessary to make slight changes for clarity, but I have made every effort not to change meanings.

I developed the three extensive questionnaires used in the study in consultation with mental health professionals, Vermont Vocational and Rehabilitation Services, the Vermont Alliance for the Mentally Ill, and, most importantly, other people who have experienced extreme mood swings.

Funds for implementing the study were secured from the Social Security Administration, through their Plan to Achieve Self-Sufficiency program. These funds are made available to people who receive Social Security disability payments and have developed a plan for becoming self-supporting.

The premise of this workbook is that by following a wellness program that includes simple, safe, noninvasive and inexpensive self-help techniques, combined with treatment strategies appropriate to the severity of the problem, extreme mood swings can at least be alleviated, and in many cases eliminated. This is not to say that any of this is easy. Nothing about this program is easy. It takes a lifelong dedication, persistence, and vigilance. But the payoff is well worth the effort.

Some parts of this workbook will be more relevant to you than others. But by working your way systematically through the various exercises, you'll discover new ideas and perspectives, gain a new respect for yourself and how you've handled your experiences, and come up with various plans for enhancing the quality of your life. Your goal in using this resource might be to discover the next most appropriate step or steps in your particular journey to physical and mental health.

Parts of this book will seem very appropriate to you right now. Other parts can wait until later. I recommend that you read through to the end before you begin writing. Then start from the beginning and do all the exercises (in writing) that seem most appropriate to you. Review your responses from time to time to remind yourself to keep up and to see how far you have come. When the time feels right, go back and complete those exercises that you left undone.

Be gentle with yourself. Don't rush the process. Just do what you can when you can. Don't forget to give yourself a pat on the back for everything you accomplish.

Many people lose hope when they are diagnosed as having a mood disorder. They may have been told by many health professionals that there is no cure for their problem and that they just have to learn to live with it.

In fact, there is hope. The majority of people in the study have been well for many years. My mother has had no significant mood swings since she was 45; she is now 78. After she got well, she worked at a wonderful job as a dietician until she retired. Since her retirement she has been doing volunteer work and enjoying her many grandchildren and great-grandchildren. However, she continues to work very hard to maintain and improve her wellness.

I have not experienced any serious manic-depressive episodes in the last three years. In those years I have compiled the data from the study, written this book, presented workshops, lectured all over the country, started a support group and a mood disorders hotline, and enjoyed wonderful times with family and friends. My health and sense of well-being have continued to improve. I know much more about mania and depression now. If I do have another episode, I am confident that by working with my support team, using the strategies in this book, and getting appropriate medical care, I can get through it with flying colors.

Your answers to these questions are for you alone. You may decide to share your responses with members of your support team or your therapist, but this is a very personal choice. You are not writing these things down for anyone but yourself—so be absolutely honest. This work is not to be judged by anyone; there are no right or wrong answers, just your answers. Don't worry about neatness, spelling, grammar, or composing complete sentences.

Some people find it easiest to do these exercises with their therapist or counselor, or someone in their support team. My mood disorders support group chooses an exercise to do together occasionally. Use whatever method works best for you, or makes you feel most comfortable.

It is advisable to set aside a certain amount of time every day to work on these exercises. I would suggest starting with 15 to 30 minutes per day. Some people prefer to work with the exercises when they first wake up in the morning. Others prefer a time in the early or late afternoon. Whatever schedule you choose, it's important to be consistent.

I plan to work on the exercises in the workbook every day from _____ to _____ o'clock.

Depending on where you are in the workbook, the length of time you spend on a given exercise may vary from day to day. This may also depend on how you are feeling and your ability on a particular day to focus on the work. Be gentle with yourself. If you find yourself feeling upset or very tired, put the book away until next time. Give yourself credit for whatever you do, whether it's a little or a lot.

Some questions—especially those in the sections on diet and light—require that you try something out for a couple of weeks before writing your responses. In those cases, you should continue working with subsequent questions until the experimental time has elapsed; then you can go back and answer the questions requiring a delayed response. You might want to make a note on your calendar of the date when you'll be ready to answer the questions, and the page numbers on which they appear in the workbook.

Using simple relaxation and breathing techniques or exercising after doing this work will help relieve any tension you may feel (refer to the relaxation and exercise chapters).

Fifty people in the study have had times when they felt that their mood swings were over for good. These periods have lasted from one month to twenty-five years. Eighteen people in the study feel that they no longer have a problem with mood swings. I have not had a serious episode in several years.

Describe your own personal experience with mood swings and how they've affected your life. _____

_____

_____

_____

_____

_____

_____

A frustrating aspect of this illness is how many difficulties it can impose on you as you try to meet life or career goals, in spite of an excellent education and exceptional abilities in many areas. The dramatic highs and lows, or the medication and treatment used to regulate them, often raise roadblocks that seem impassable. Although extreme mood swings can certainly make everything harder for you, they do not have to prevent you from doing what you want to in life.

Among the study participants, for instance, the educational backgrounds, interests, areas of expertise and achievements are simply amazing. Of the 120 people who participated in the survey, 12 had associate's degrees or two years of college, 34 had completed four years of college, 3 were doing graduate work, 14 had master's degrees, 5 had doctoral degrees, 2 were doing postdoctoral work, and 13 had completed various types of technical training.

What is your educational background? _____

_____

What are your future educational goals? _____

_____

How do you plan to meet your future educational goals? _____

_____

_____

In spite of having to deal with periods of mood instability, many people with depression and manic depression can boast of amazing accomplishments and lives that are the way they want them to be. Your life can be the way you want it to be. You can dream and you can achieve your goals. You are already on the way to doing just that. I dare you to make your life just the way you want it to be.

People in the study listed a wide range of interests. These included sports and recreational activities; art, including photography, film production, and theater; performing, understanding, and appreciating music; writing on all subjects (several having been published); extensive studying and teaching of the humanities and sciences; handcrafts, including crocheting, knitting, cross-stitch, needlepoint, sewing, carpentry, wood carving, woodworking, macramé), ceramics, calligraphy, paper making and flag making; technical skills, which include engineering, mechanics, and computer science; community service for the environment, children, elderly, disabled, and handicapped; and work in the political arena.

What interests have you pursued? _____

_____

_____

What other interests do you look forward to pursuing in the future? _____

_____

How do you plan to pursue these interests?_____

_____

_____

A sampling of the fields in which survey participants feel they are expert (something often very hard for a depressed person to do) includes:

consumer advocacy	addiction treatment
counseling	alternative counseling
child and adolescent psychology	psychology of women
all areas of education	community relations
public relations	customer service
working with the terminally ill	psychiatric social work
administration	management
negotiation	research
massage therapy	actuarial work
telemarketing	clerical work
plumbing	tool and die work
mechanics	paralegal work
sales and merchandising	political organizing
insurance	nursing
song writing	writing
baking	welding
music composition	computers
English	French
dancing	mathematics
history	library science
tropical fish	microbiology
spirituality	theology
nutrition	horticulture

What do you feel you are really good at? _____

_____

_____

What skills do you plan to develop further? _____

_____

_____

_____

How do you plan to further develop these skills? _____

_____

_____

Study participants feel their most significant achievements relate to long, happy marriages; successfully raising a family; establishing and maintaining long-term personal relationships; maintaining independence; surviving; coping with mood disorders and in many instances maintaining long-term stability; major contributions to the mental illness consumer movement; amazing progress in growth and development in spite of extreme mood swings; mental health advocacy work; achieving major educational goals of all kinds; recovering from other serious illnesses., including strokes and motor vehicle accidents; staying employed for long periods of time; writing and publishing.

I could fill this book with the achievements of the 120 people who participated in the study. The point of all this is that you can do what you want to with your life, in spite of extreme mood swings. Other people with manic depression have done what they wanted with their lives and are continuing to do so. You can, too! It takes hard work, creativity, persistence, and patience. You may have a much harder time convincing others of your ability to meet your goals. But you can and you will if you are determined.

List your most significant achievements.   Take your time. Include everything. Use additional pages if necessary. Be honest with yourself. _____

_____

_____

_____

_____

_____

_____

If your life could be any way that you wanted, what would it be like? Where would you live, who would you live with? What about your career and education? What hobbies and leisure interests would you pursue? Build yourself a dream and then begin working on it.

_____

_____

_____

_____

_____

_____

_____

_____

_____

_____

_____

PART I

A Clearer Picture

1

A Medical Overview
of Mood Disorders

A mood is an emotion that temporarily colors all aspects of your life. Anxiety, elation, melancholy, anger, and peacefulness are only some of the moods within the great range of human emotion. For many people, moods are not problematic. For others, a mood may persist long after the circumstances that triggered it have passed.

When a mood outlives its context, it can become a serious liability to healthy emotional functioning. Individuals whose moods impair their work, relationships, and potential for happiness are said to have a mood disorder. If you are such an individual, this book has been designed to help you understand your moods and bring them under control.

Doctors recognize two main types of mood disorders: depressive disorders and bipolar disorders. Depressive disorders consist of one or more periods of major depression. Bipolar disorders involve a series of moods that include at least one manic period and one or more periods of major depression. A detailed definition of each of these conditions is given in the *Diagnostic and Statistical Manual of Mental Disorders* (*DSM-III-R*), which is prepared by the American Psychiatric Association and available in all public libraries.

Depression and bipolar illness are unnessarily costly in terms of human suffering, wasted potential, and strain on the health care system. Statistics compiled by the National Institute of Mental Health indicate that depression affects over ten million people per year in the United States. Over an average lifetime between 8 and 15 percent of the population experience serious depressive reactions. Two out of three of these people are women. Bipolar illness affects between 1 and 10 percent of the population, and occurs equally in men and women. Fifteen percent of people who are diagnosed as having a depressive disorder end their lives by suicide. This accounts for about half of all suicides in the United States.

The real tragedy, though, is that 80 percent of all depression and bipolar illness is highly responsive to treatment. This workbook gives an overview of some of the medical, psychological, and lifestyle interventions that are currently available. It is estimated that only one out of three seriously depressed people ever seeks treatment. There are no parallel figures for people with other treatable medical diseases, such as diabetes. The pain caused by this situation is needless. Depression and bipolar disorders are treatable and, in many cases, can be cured.

Symptoms of Major Depression

Most people have experienced depression at least once in their life. The predominant effect of depression is a loss of energy. Few things, if any, seem interesting; motivation drops off to zero. Although this feels terrible, people in the grips of such depressions are still able to do the things they need to do in order to survive. They go to work, pay the bills, cook their food, and relate to the people in their life who demand their attention. This normal type of depression feels rotten, but life continues in spite of it.

The line between normal and major depression is crossed when that down, rotten feeling invades every part of your life. Experiences that may seem objectively satisfying to others feel like failure and frustration to you. Eventually you may try to avoid having any experience at all. Communicating with people, even those you love, may seem difficult or intrusive. You may shrink from speaking with people entirely. And when you envision the future—whether it be tomorrow, two months, or two years down the road—you see no light at the end of the tunnel. You have no sense that your gloom and despair will ever lift. In short, a major depression differs from a normal depression in that its symptoms are much more severe, last much longer, and eventually impair a person's ability to function.

The *DSM-III-R* establishes several criteria by which a major depression is clinically defined.

First, a condition must exhibit at least five of the following nine symptoms, and these symptoms must have been present for at least two weeks:

1. Depressed mood most of the day, nearly every day

2. Diminished interest or pleasure in almost all activities of the day, nearly every day

3. Significant weight gain or loss when not dieting, and decreased appetite nearly every day

4. Insomnia or hypersomnia (sleeping too much) nearly every day

5. Abnormal restlessness or a drop in physical activity nearly every day

6. Fatigue or loss of energy nearly every day

7. Feelings of worthlessness or excessive or inappropriate guilt nearly every day

8. Diminished ability to think, concentrate, or make decisions nearly every day

9. Recurrent thoughts of death, or recurrent suicidal thoughts without a specific plan; or a suicide attempt; or a specific plan for committing suicide

The manual stipulates that one of the first two symptoms (depressed mood or diminished interest) must be among the five symptoms present. In order for any one of these behaviors to be considered a symptom, it must reflect a change from that person's ordinary behavior.

In addition to exhibiting the initial five symptoms, the following must also be true:

1. The disturbance is not being caused by another illness. (There are some exceptions, which will be discussed later in this chapter under Biological Causes of Depression.)

2. The disturbance is not a reaction to the loss of a loved one.

Symptoms of Bipolar Disorder

Two separate and opposite states comprise bipolar disorder, in which depression alternates with mania. During the manic phase of a bipolar condition, a person can appear to be positive, excited about life, even euphoric. An unusually high sense of self-esteem may be evident. This person may seem conspicuously active and brimming with ideas, one after the other. Many projects may be started, and many quests launched. Friends or acquaintances may be aware that something is amiss: after all, the person in the midst of a manic phase seems different than usual. But the hazards of the opposite pole—depression—would probably be the furthest thing from a lay observer's mind. Once the manic stage wanes, and the depression stage emerges, the Jekyll-Hyde nature of this disorder becomes apparent.

Switching from one state or pole to the other, from mania to depression and back again, is called *cycling*. Characteristics of cycling vary from person to person. In some, the cycles last for long periods and switch infrequently. Others switch from depression to mania and back relatively often. This quick switching from one emotional state to the other is known as *rapid cycling*. A one-to-one ratio (one period of depression to one period of mania) rarely occurs; usually, one cycle is more prevalent than the other. In general, men tend to experience manic periods more often than episodes of depression, and women have more depressions than manic episodes. Long periods during which the bipolar sufferer feels neither manic nor depressed can exist between cycles. During these times, the person seems and feels all right.

The *DSM-III-R* presents several criteria that must be met before a condition is considered mania.

First, a person's mood must be elevated, expansive, or irritable. This mood must be different from a person's normal personality. The change must be unusually intense, and must last for a considerable period of time. While exhibiting this elevated mood, a person can become very expansive and grandiose. In some cases of mania the mood that is expressed may be irritated and angry, and the person may act with arrogance and belligerence.

The second criterion states that at least three of the following symptoms must have been present to a significant degree:

1. Inflated sense of self-importance

2. Decreased need for sleep (for example, the individual feels rested after only three hours of sleep)

3. Unusual talkativeness

4. Flight of ideas or a subjective feeling that thoughts are racing

5. Distractibility (the person's attention is too easily drawn to unimportant external stimuli)

6. Increase in goal-directed activity (for instance, social or sexual) or physical activity

7. Excessive involvement in activities that bring pleasure but have a high potential for painful or harmful consequences (for example, the person engages in unrestrained buying sprees, sexual indiscretions, or unwise business investments)

These criteria help differentiate mania from other excitable states. Individuals in the midst of mania almost always have an overconfident and exaggerated opinion of themselves or their abilities. They will talk too loudly, too often, and too quickly. Their thought processes are accelerated; many thoughts occur almost simultaneously and are verbalized about as quickly. This rapid train of thought is easily derailed, and the manic person will often find it difficult to follow a single subject for very long. Activity can increase both in terms of multiple projects and physical activity, such as fidgeting, pacing, or exaggerated sexual behavior. Finally, manic individuals tend to pursue their goals with great abandon and almost total disregard for consequences.

The third criterion articulated in the *DSM-III-R* states that a mood disturbance must be severe enough to affect an individual's job performance, participation in regular social activities or relationships with others; or to necessitate hospitalization in order to prevent injury to self or others. This criterion is designed to distinguish full mania, which is potentially very harmful, from hypomania (or "lesser" mania), which does not necessarily have the potential for harm.

How the Brain Communicates

The part of the brain responsible for regulating emotions is called the *limbic* system. This area lies deep within the brain, below the cerebrum, which is the "thinking" part of the brain. In addition to emotions, the limbic system controls such functions as body temperature, appetite, hormone levels, sleep, blood pressure, and behavior.

Information is transferred from one part of the brain to another with the help of a particular group of chemicals called *neurotransmitters*. This communication network is very delicately balanced. For the limbic system to perform properly, it is essential that this balance be maintained.

Two mechanisms within the neural system allow signals to be passed from cell to cell. The first mechanism is *electrical stimulation*. An electrical impulse is generated in one nerve cell, or neuron, and travels down the length of the cell until it reaches a very small space, or gap, between that cell and the next (neurons are not really connected to each other). This gap between neurons is called a *synapse*. For information to be transmitted, the electrical impulse from the first cell must somehow get across the synapse to the next cell. But it can't jump across this space. Another mechanism is needed to transfer the electrical charge to the next cell.

Here a second chemical mechanism comes into play. As the electrical impulse reaches the end of the first cell, it initiates a chemical reaction. Small sacks, or vesicles, containing neurotransmitters fuse with the cell wall. The sacks then open and empty the chemicals they contain into the gap between the cells. These chemicals float over to the second cell, attaching to the cell wall at specific places called *receptor sites*. Each receptor site will only accept a chemical that is the right molecular shape to fit that site. When enough of the receptor sites are filled on the second cell, an electrical impulse is generated which travels down this cell until it reaches the next synapse. There the process is repeated. Electrical impulses, passing from cell to cell, travel in this manner throughout the limbic system and the rest of the central nervous system as well. The hypothalamus, located within the limbic system, serves as a sort of traffic controller.

Exactly what information is transmitted depends on which neurons are electrically activated, and what part of the brain is stimulated by these neurons. For instance, a particular series of neural firings will stimulate the area of the brain that tells you that you're tired. If another series of neurons fire and stimulate a different part of the brain, you may feel that it is time to eat. Still another series will let you know that you're angry at your boss, or delighted with your child's A in math. Each series of neurons that stimulates a different area in the brain is called a *neural pathway*.

A Brief History of Treatments for Depression

Until recently, mood disorders have been shrouded in secrecy and shame. People suffering from these illnesses have consequently been denied the compassion and access to treatment that are normally available for patients with so-called "physical" complaints.

Early treatment strategies rival each other for bizarreness and cruelty. Contemporary accounts from ancient Greece describe a particularly brutal treatment that was perhaps a precursor to electroconvulsive therapy. Temple priests on an Aegean island threw depressed patients into the sea from a high cliff. Other priests waited in boats in the water below to rescue the "patients" from drowning. The accounts say that many of the subjects of this unorthodox procedure recovered, perhaps cured by the shock of the harrowing experience.

In ancient Phoenicia, the mentally ill were sequestered aboard a "ship of fools" and set adrift to roam the seas in search of more hospitable harbors. During the Middle Ages in Europe, exorcists coaxed the "demons" from the bodies of those who acted strangely. "Shock treatments" were administered to eighteenth-century patients by twirling them on stools until their ears bled or by dropping them through trapdoors into icy lakes.

As late as 1806, a prominent 30-year-old attorney from Vermont was treated for depression by having his head held down in a bucket of water. When the first treatments proved unsuccessful, his head was held under for increased lengths of time until he finally drowned.

The Shift in the Twentieth Century to Chemical Interventions

The greater part of the twentieth century in American psychiatry was dominated by Freudian thought. Freud promulgated the belief that depressive disorders are the result of internalizing a lost object or relationship, then turning the anger about the loss against the self. He taught that the environment and early childhood experiences were responsible for all mental disorders, including depression and bipolar illness. If you were depressed, you needed to enter psychoanalysis and talk about past traumas from your infant and childhood periods.

It is now believed that psychoanalysis alone is not a useful treatment for depression or bipolar disorders. Depression and mood instability may be due, in part, to psychological stress; but there are many other possible components to these disorders. In 1937, Freud himself said, "The future may teach us how to exercise a direct influence, by means of particular chemical substances, upon the amount of energy and its distribution in the apparatus of the mind. It may be that there are other undreamed-of possibilities of therapy."

Based on Freud's theories, people generally viewed depression and bipolar illness as if they were the result of a character flaw within the victim, rather than illnesses like diabetes and tuberculosis. In reality, though, mood disorders are also medical illnesses and should be regarded as such. There is no shame involved in having them: consciousness-raising organizations and nationwide educational campaigns are doing much to erase the social stigma of depression and manic depression.

In 1938, electroconvulsive therapy (ECT) was introduced as a treatment for mood disorders. Today this procedure is often considered the treatment of last resort, because it is the most invasive among the various interventions available. Electroconvulsive therapy uses electrodes attached to the patient's head to induce a seizure in the brain. This type of seizure seems to increase the level of certain neurotransmitters, the chemicals that transmit nerve impulses from one cell to another. After a short series of treatments administered during a two-week period, depressed patients are often able to regain a normal range of emotions. Confusion and memory loss are also frequent byproducts of this type of therapy. Although both these effects are usually short term, full memory restoration can take up to two weeks and, in some cases, the loss can be permanent.

Although not a cure for depression, ECT can be an effective treatment for those patients who don't respond to medication. Such individuals have an 80 to 90 percent chance of responding positively to ECT, which also elicits a much quicker response than drug therapy. Research indicates that ECT can reduce the time required for recovery from depression; but the invasive nature of shock treatment, and its possible side effects, still make it an undesirable treatment for most people.

In 1949, John F.J. Cade, an Australian psychiatrist, discovered that doses of the drug lithium given to frightened guinea pigs changed their behavior from severely agitated to calm and docile. Cade then administered lithium to several psychiatric patients with manic disorders. The patients became emotionally stable. Lithium gradually came to be recognized as a highly effective treatment for mania.

In 1952, French psychiatrists Jean Delay and Pierre Deniker tested and used chlorpromazine (*Thorazine*) to calm psychotic agitation. Soon afterwards, the family of drugs known as tricyclics were developed in a further attempt to treat psychotic behavior. Although ineffective when used for psychosis, these drugs did seem to raise the spirits of many people in the throes of chronic depression. The commercial development of tricyclics and other antidepressants soon followed.

The problem of how to medically treat mood disorders was basically solved backwards. Neurotransmitters are difficult to isolate and study, since these chemicals are released in extremely small quantities, and any extra amount released is broken down by enzymes and reabsorbed into the cell. At the time when the first antidepressant was discovered, very little was known about neurotransmitters. In fact, the first antidepressant was discovered by accident in the course of an attempt to manufacture an antipsychotic drug. It was only after the antidepressant had been administered to patients and found to be an effective treatment for depression that the biological changes in patients could be analyzed.

Researchers discovered that when one of several types of neurotransmitters malfunctioned, the patient experienced mood fluctuations. The primary neurotransmitters linked to mood instability were norepinephrine and serotonin. The neurotransmitter dopamine has also been linked to mood disorders. Subsequent research (Beavers, 1969) has found that increasing levels of serotonin cause elevation of mood, while extremely high levels of serotonin cause manic states. Low levels of serotonin have been linked to depression.

Psychological Therapy for Mood Disorders

Mood disorders—especially depression—usually respond to the use of certain kinds of psychotherapy. Interpersonal therapy and cognitive-behavioral therapy are the two types that seem to work best. Instead of focusing on probable causes of the depression, which may have originated in the patient's childhood, each of these therapies deals directly with how depression makes one think and act, and what needs to be done to bring about change. These are often short-term approaches designed to alleviate only the existing depressive episode, not to solve the deep, hidden secrets of the psyche.

Cognitive-behavioral therapy is based on the theory that patients suffering from depressive disorders see themselves, their family and friends, and their surroundings in a negative light. Negative thoughts usually breed negative emotions. More often than not, a depressed person's assessment of his or her situation is inaccurate. Cognitive therapies help depressive patients see the errors in their thinking and recognize the feelings and behavior that result from their distorted view.

Interpersonal therapy is based on the premise that people in the midst of a mood disorder are also having problems with the primary relationships in their lives. A depressed person's relationship with his or her spouse, children, parents, and friends will most likely be strained. It is considered immaterial whether these relationships became difficult because the patient developed a mood disorder, or whether the difficult relationship was the original cause of the depressive episode. The interpersonal therapist helps the patient discover the exact problem and its possible solutions within each troubling relationship.

Drugs Versus Talking Therapies

Various independent studies have shown that psychotherapy can be an effective treatment in dealing with mood disorders. Does drug therapy or psychotherapy work best? Some studies have shown that psychotherapy performs better in the treatment of depression. For example, one National Institute of Mental Health study showed that cognitive and drug therapies had about the same success rate, but fewer patients treated with cognitive therapy relapsed. Other studies have suggested that for severely depressed people, cognitive and drug therapies are most effective when combined. Most clinicians agree that bipolar disorders are rarely responsive to a course of therapy that does not include drug treatment. Psychotherapy is therefore only adjunctive in treating bipolar conditions. The psychological makeup of each individual can also have a bearing on whether a particular patient will respond better to drugs or to talking therapy. For patients who are not particularly self-aware, or who cannot separate themselves from their feelings or actions, drugs are often more helpful.

The important point here is that different types of mood disorders can be helped by different kinds of therapy. If the first therapy tried doesn't work for you, don't give up altogether. Try again with a different therapy, a different therapist, or a different doctor.

Diagnosing Depression and Bipolar Disorders

Like fever, depression and other mood disorders are the final outcome of a range of causes. There are many ways you can contract a fever, such as through bacterial infections, dehydration, and excessive exposure to the sun. There are likewise many ways in which you can become clinically depressed.

It's useful to divide these mood disorder pathways into two main categories. The first category of causes contains those that are psychological in nature. Stress is the key factor in psychologically induced depression, particularly stress that results from some sort of trauma or loss. The second group of causes are those that arise from a biological source. These physical illnesses, hormonal malfunctions, and genetic factors are all capable of generating the symptoms of major depression by themselves or in tandem with a psychological cause. Mood disorders often arise from a combination of causes that are both biological and psychological in nature. Let's now look at the psychological causes of depression and how these factors can contribute to mood disorders.

Psychological Causes of Depresssion

About 25 percent of people with depressive disorders report that they are experiencing some sort of serious stress, while only 5 percent of the general population report a similar phenomenon. Studies also show that people who had a loved one die when they were young are at least twice as likely to suffer from major depression in their adulthood as those who have not experienced a similar grief. Although there seems to be a clear linkage of some sort between stress and mood disorders, these facts fail to provide real evidence that stress is the causal agent.

A study carried out jointly at the University of Oregon and the University of Pittsburgh concluded that stressful life events do tend to precede depression. Each group of researchers interviewed 500 to 800 women at two different times, 8 to 12 months apart.

These women were questioned about major stresses relating to loss, and minor stresses such as job satisfaction and social support systems. The statements from women who did not report depression during the first interview, but who had clearly become depressed by the time of the second interview, were analyzed. Both groups of investigators concluded that the existence of stressful circumstances during the first interview greatly increased the odds that depression would occur by the time of the second interview (Lewinsohn, 1981). The Lewinsohn study clearly suggests a causal link between stress and depression.

One kind of stress that can be particularly debilitating is known as post-traumatic stress disorder. A stressful event may take place at a time when, as a matter of survival, the individual experiencing it must postpone the mental and emotional processing of the event. After the imminent danger has passed, the trauma of the event is free to rise to consciousness, although it does not necessarily do so immediately. The conscious or emotional memory may not become manifest for many years.

Post-traumatic stress disorder is often linked to wartime trauma, natural disasters (such as hurricanes or fires), childhood sexual abuse, and such violent crimes as rape. When emotions from past traumas surface, the feelings may seem to have no cause in the individual's present context, since they are temporally dissociated from the actual causal event.

Fifty percent of all people who suffer from post-traumatic stress disorder also suffer from depression. This type of depression is difficult to diagnose until the traumatic event, and the emotions that it elicits, are remembered and felt.

Biological Causes of Depression

Biological factors contribute to or cause a large percentage of the cases of mood disorder. Emotional stability is closely related to the normal formation and function of a number of vital chemicals that exist in the brain. These chemicals, the neurotransmitters, are an integral part of the system that transmits information from one central nervous system cell to another. When neural cells lose the ability to make the proper amount of a neurotransmitter, store it properly, or bind it efficiently, a chronic mood disorder may result.

Three physiological conditions affect neurotransmitter production and can inhibit chemical functioning. They are:

1. Specific diseases

2. Hormonal imbalances

3. Genetic factors

Specific diseases that affect neurotransmitter production. You seldom feel ill the precise moment when bacteria or a virus enter your body. It takes time for the bacteria to spread or for the virus to multiply until there are enough foreign bodies present to activate your immune system. As many illnesses progress, they can slowly, almost imperceptibly, change the chemistry of your body. The delicate balance of neural chemistry can be altered enough to generate a mood shift, even before physical symptoms are apparent.

It is easy to understand how diseases of the central nervous system can affect brain chemistry since these diseases are actually located in the brain itself. Alzheimer's disease is a common cause of severe mental impairment in older adults. Epilepsy has often been misdiagnosed as schizophrenia. Multiple sclerosis, a degenerative disease of the central nervous system, is thought to be caused by a virus or a defect in the immune system. All of these illnesses are associated with the common symptom of depression.

Many infectious diseases can generate psychiatric symptoms, including mononucleosis and infectious hepatitis. A wide array of mental symptoms, ranging from depression to psychosis, can accompany such illnesses.

Diseases of the immune system can also be the source of a wide array of psychiatric symptoms. Lupus, allergies, and AIDS are just three examples (all three can cause depression).

Various types of cancerous tumors can generate mood instability before the nature of the disease has been diagnosed. Nutritional deficiencies can alter brain chemistry. Chronic overgrowth of yeast, otherwise known as *candida albicans*, may result from eating too much sugar, taking antibiotics, or an imbalance of hormones. Yeast infections have been inplicated in mania, depression, and malfunctions in the thyroid. This condition can be controlled by eating properly, particularly by restricting sugar in the diet.

Hormonal imbalances. Hormones are secreted into the bloodstream by structures throughout the body called endocrine glands. Hormones help keep the body in a state of balance by regulating metabolic processes such as growth, sexual development, reproduction, sexual activity, energy production, heart rate, and blood pressure. The entire endocrine system is intimately linked to the nervous system. For instance, norepinephrine, a neurotransmitter that is crucial to mood stability, doubles as a hormone secreted by the adrenal gland. The hypothalamus regulates the endocrine glands by using the same neurotransmitters that regulate moods.

The thyroid gland, which secretes two crucial hormones, is perhaps the most common biological cause of depression. It is estimated that 10 to 15 percent of depressed patients have some form of thyroid malfunction. The usual tests that are given to check thyroid function often yield a false negative, necessitating the use of a more exhaustive panel in all cases where mood instability is an issue. Hyperthyroidism, or an overactive thyroid, causes an overabundance of the hormones to be produced. Resulting symptoms can include nervousness, sweating, racing pulse, anxiety, and insomnia. Symptoms of mania sometimes result from this condition. Hypothyroidism, or an underactive thyroid, often results in tiredness, weight gain, mental sluggishness, dry and coarse hair, and an intolerance to cold. It can cause either depression or bipolar disorder. If a bipolar condition is produced by hypothyroidism, it is usually of a rapid cycling nature. Lithium, the usual treatment of choice for bipolar disorders, weakens the thyroid and slows down hormone production. If the underlying cause of a bipolar disorder is a low-functioning thyroid, lithium can actually worsen the mood disorder.

Diseases of the adrenal glands are not as common as those of the thyroid, but can produce symptoms that are psychiatric in nature. The entire endocrine system can be affected by malfunctions of the pituitary gland, and psychiatric symptoms are present in three-quarters of all cases. Since this gland is directly linked to the hypothalamus and the limbic system, anything that alters its function is likely to affect one's emotional state in some way.

Sex hormones, particularly the female hormones estrogen and progesterone, are often implicated in depression and bipolar illness. Severe depression is frequently recorded in women during times when their sex hormones are changing radically. Depressive symptoms are common among women who are premenstrual, pregnant, postpartum, or premenopausal. Few studies have actually pinned down the biological interrelation between mood and these hormones. However, it's known that two-thirds of women with significant premenstrual depression have a history of chronic depression, and that women with a history of premenstrual depression are prone to have a family history of chronic depression. Hormones clearly play a major role in depression, but a precise description of this role has yet to be made.

The pineal gland in the brain produces a hormone called melatonin. The function this hormone serves in humans is still a mystery. In animals, melatonin is related to the seasonality of conception and giving birth. Even though humans don't follow these reproductive rhythms—at least not at this stage in our evolution—our bodies still secrete melatonin at night. Bright light suppresses its production. People who become seasonally depressed—who feel down in the winter because there is less sunlight—may be reacting to their increase in melatonin production. Other researchers have suggested that serotonin levels are the real culprit in seasonal depression. Regardless of its cause, this condition, called Seasonal Affective Disorder, is very common and easily treatable. Exposure to full-spectrum light, either natural or artificial, will decrease melatonin levels and raise your spirits. If you suffer from this condition and a three-month winter vacation to the equator is impossible, keep in mind that artificial light used for treatment needs to be five to ten times brighter than normal indoor lighting. A later chapter in this book treats this subject in greater detail.

Genetic factors. The fact that depression and bipolar illness tend to run in families suggests that genetic inheritance for these disorders plays a role. The role is not absolute: not all children of depressed parents contract depression. However, various studies have concluded that the tendency for mood instability is passed from one generation to the next.

Twins have been a prime group of subjects studied in attempts to discern the nature of mood disorders. In these studies, when both twins express a genetic trait, they are said to be concordant for that trait. When only one individual exhibits the trait, the twins are said to be discordant for the trait. Studies investigating the occurrence of both unipolar and bipolar disorders in twins have determined that the concordance for unipolar disorders in identical twins, where genetic material is the same in each individual, is about 40 percent. When identical twins were surveyed for bipolar disorders, that number jumped to 70 percent. The concordance for both types of disorders in fraternal twins, who have dissimilar genetic material, is the same as that for normal siblings, about 0 to 13 percent. These studies show that mood instability is at least to some extent genetically based; the genetic predisposition for bipolar illness is almost twice that for depression alone (Kield and Weissman, 1978).

It is not yet known whether all genes that affect mood are located on one chromosome or on several. Early research suggests that bipolar illness might be a sex-linked characteristic, and that the genes that govern it might be located on the X chromosome (one of the two chromosomes that define our gender). If bipolar illness is determined by a sex-linked gene, and if this type of mood disorder is a dominant trait, this could explain the reason why depression occurs more often in women than in men. Since women are genetically composed of two X chromosomes, they would have a greater chance of contracting a mood disorder; the genes for the condition could be carried on either of the two X chromosomes. It would be less likely for men, who genetically have one X and one Y chromosome, to contract the disease. However, the relationship of depression to sex-linkage has not been firmly established and at present is still a theory.

It needs to be mentioned that separating genetic factors from environmental ones is difficult at best. If depression is observed in individuals belonging to three consecutive generations, does this absolutely mean that the disorder is transferred genetically? Could a child become depressed because the depressed parent is not able to nurture the child adequately? What about conditions such as poverty and other high-stress factors? Could the same factors exist in each generation, thereby contributing to, or causing depression? And where does learned behavior fit in? Could a child learn, for example, poor nutritional habits and carry on the tradition of depression in this way?

No one knows the answers to these questions yet. The strongest evidence points to the source of depression and bipolar disorders being an admixture of inherited traits and environmental factors. Genetic makeup can lend a predisposition for these illnesses; but it may well be that they only come into existence when those so born are exposed to an environment which, for whatever reason, causes the condition to manifest itself.

The Mind-Body Connection

Chronic negative thoughts, guilt, early trauma, post-traumatic stress disorder, deprivation, emotional losses, and the feeling that your life has no meaning are all psychological states that affect brain chemistry and neurotransmitter effectiveness. Conversely, an imbalanced neurotransmitter system can exacerbate negative thinking, guilt, and reactions to trauma, and rob you of the energy you need to meet important challenges and goals.

Drug therapy and psychotherapy are both viable methods of initiating intervention for depressive disorders; each starts at the opposite end of the mind-body continuum. Drugs chemically alter brain cell function in an attempt to "fix" the biological apparatus. Psychotherapy targets thought and behavior in an attempt to initiate similar chemical changes.

There is a constant interaction between your biological and psychological self, between your mind and your body. Either type of treatment can be an effective way to restore emotional health (although, as mentioned before, bipolar illness is much more susceptible to drug therapy than to psychotherapy alone).

Specific Drug Therapies

Antidepressants

Antidepressants are a class of drugs that increase the amount of the neurotransmitters norepinephrine and seratonin. These neurotransmitters act to decrease a certain type of neural cell function called *reuptake*. In reuptake, a cell not only releases the neurotransmitter into the synapse, but also reabsorbs much of the chemical before it is able to link with a receptor on the postsynaptic cell. Antidepressants decrease the reuptake and increase the time that neurotransmitters are in the synapse, thereby increasing the stimulus across the synapse.

Tricyclics. There are two types of antidepressants. The first group is called tricyclics. These work by increasing the amount of either seratonin or norepinephrine in the synapse. Some tricyclics block the reuptake of norepinephrine, and others prevent the reuptake of seratonin. Still other tricyclics inhibit the reuptake of both neurotransmitters. Here is a list of tricyclics and the neurotransmitters affected by them. (Adapted from *Clinical Pharmacology Made Rediculously Simple* by Preston and Johnson.)

Name	Norepinephrine	Serotonin
Imipramine	yes	yes
Desipramine	yes	no
Amitriptyline	slight	yes
Nortriptyline	yes	yes
Protriptyline	yes	slight
Trimipramine	slight	yes
Doxepin	slight	yes
Maprotiline	yes	no
Amoxapine	yes	slight

For most patients, the use of tricyclics improves the likelihood that depression will cease by about 50 percent. In those individuals who respond to tricyclics, every symptom caused by depression is relieved to some extent. Not only do patients regain the desire for food and the ability to sleep soundly, but mental outlook also turns around. Those who previously felt hopeless, guilty, and confused feel more clear and content after adhering to a regimen of tricyclic medication. They find that they are able to make decisions more readily, think more positively, and remember things more accurately than they could when they were depressed.

If you are taking tricyclics, remember that two to four weeks are needed before the symptoms of depression will start to lift. First, the physical symptoms will subside. Your normal appetite and sleeping habits will return. Eventually, your mood will begin to shift. Altogether, it could take up to eight weeks for depression to entirely subside. In most cases, treatment needs to continue for an additional six months or longer. Without further treatment, 50 percent of all depressive patients will relapse within a year. In 15 to 20 percent of patients with depression, the depression is chronic, and medication must always be taken to control it. Antidepressants are not addictive: they will not intoxicate, stimulate, or make you "high" in any way.

However, tricyclics aren't for everyone. One-third of all depressed patients don't respond to tricyclics at all. Still others find that some of the side effects are too onerous to make continuation of the drug desirable. And for those who suffer from bipolar disorder, tricyclics can have the effect of bringing on episodes of mania.

In addition to increasing the synaptic concentration of seratonin or norepinephrine in your brain, tricyclics also block certain acetylcholine synapses. This action is responsible for a group of so-called anticholinergic side effects. These include dry mouth, blurred vision, urinary retention, sexual dysfunction, and constipation. Most of these side effects are not life-threatening, but urinary retention and constipation can be serious.

Tricyclics can also cause various abnormalities to occur in the cardiovascular system. Rapid changes in blood pressure can cause stroke. The heart may display abnormal electrical activity and arrhythmias. Dizziness caused by low blood pressure in the brain (*orthostatic hypotension*) can occur. Sometimes the heart can lose its ability to pump blood, causing cardiac arrest.

Other side effects include fatigue or decreased energy, excessive sleeping, weight gain, tremor, and tinnitus (ringing in the ears); occasionally, seizures occur. Tricyclics that have sedating effects will reduce memory somewhat and inhibit psychomotor performance.

Obviously, no one should undertake drug therapy without careful consideration and the oversight of one or more competent physicians.

MAOIs. The second kind of antidepressant is called *monoamine oxidase* (MAO) inhibitors, or MAOIs for short. MAO is an enzyme that breaks down the neurotransmitters. If a cell malfunction results in an overabundant production of MAO, there will not be a sufficient amount of neurotransmitters in the synapses. By inhibiting production of the enzyme that breaks down neurotransmitters, MAOIs increase the amount of neurotransmitters retained in the synapse.

People who suffer from atypical depression often respond more readily to MAOIs than to other antidepressants. Atypical depression is a condition in which patients, instead of having difficulties with appetite and adequate sleep, find that they are oversleeping and overeating. They also feel extremely fatigued and are overly sensitive to rejection. People who don't respond to tricyclics will also sometimes be helped by the MAOI. Others who cannot tolerate the side effects of tricyclics will more readilty be able to deal with the side effects of MAOIs.

MAOIs cause many of the same anticholinergic side effects as tricyclics, but the MAOIs' side effects are much less severe. Side effects in sexual function also appear while taking MAOIs. However, the most serious side effect involves the MAOIs' effect on metabolism. Just as the enzyme MAO is used to break down certain neurotransmitters, it also breaks down certain compounds in food, specifically the amino acid tyramine. Since the patient taking these drugs cannot metabolize tyramine, if the amino acid is ingested, it will enter the circulatory system. Tyramine releases norepinephrine from the nerve cells that regulate blood pressure, and the result can be a sudden surge in blood pressure and possibly stroke. This amino acid is found in many foods, such as aged cheese, beer, wine, chocolate, and liver. Individuals taking MAOIs must strictly avoid these foods.

For the same reason, nose drops and cold remedies should not be taken with MAOIs. These drugs are chemically similar to the catecholamines that are normally metabolized by MAO. When MAOIs prevent the breakup of cold medications, the drugs' concentration in the blood rises and may dangerously increase blood pressure.

Other antidepressants. Since the discovery of tricyclics and MAOIs, many newer antidepressants have been synthesized. The most popular by far is fluoxetine, more commonly known as *Prozac.* As effective as tricyclics, *Prozac* seems to have an advantage in that it causes fewer and milder side effects. No anticholinergic or cardiac side effects appear at all. Mild bouts of nausea, headache, insomnia, and nervousness may be noticable. All of these symptoms, however, should decrease over time. It has also been suggested that Prozac may be more effective than tricyclics at preventing depressive relapses.

Drug Therapies for Bipolar Illness

Lithium is unparalleled in the treatment of bipolar disorders. Unlike tricyclics, MAOIs, and *Prozac,* lithium is not a complex molecule, but rather a simple metal ion in the form of a salt. Lithium works by inhibiting the production of *second messengers,* molecules that are produced when certain neurotransmitters bond with certain receptors. These molecules activate enzymes that affect the neurotransmitter-receptor bond, perhaps altering the amount of neurotransmitters, or altering the number of receptors that are sensitive to that neurotransmitter, or affecting the electrical charge that builds in the postsynaptic cell. The exact chemical process is not yet understood. It's thought that lithium prevents the manufacturing of a particular second messenger called PIP2, stopping the cell from responding to certain neurotransmitter signals.

The condition of mania is produced when certain neurotransmitter-receptor bonds send signals to various neurons, causing them to become overactive. Likewise, depression can be triggered by cells becoming overactive, but in response to signals sent by a different set of neurotransmitter-receptor couplings. If the second messenger is not produced, the cells' response to signals that elicit mania, and to signals that elicit depression, will decrease. Lithium turns down the response to any stimulus that depends on the presence of the PIP2 enzyme.

The most common side effects of lithium are weakness, tremor, fatigue, nausea, abdominal cramps, diarrhea, weight gain, lethargy, and increased thirst and urination. All of these side effects, with the exception of the tremor, will disappear within a month. No sedating effects occur with lithium.

The problem with lithium treatment is that there is a fine line between therapeutic and toxic levels of this drug. If the prescribed dose is too high, lithium poisoning can occur. Lithium poisoning affects the brain. Symptoms are slurred speech, drowsiness, loss of balance, tumors, vomiting, diarrhea, and, ultimately, coma and death.

In order to find the right dosage, frequent blood tests must be taken to check the lithium concentration in the bloodstream. During the first week of lithium therapy, lithium blood concentration rises rapidly. After the lithium blood concentration stabilizes, the number of tests can be reduced. However, it is important that these tests continue to be steadily administered, as lithium concentration can change when diet, healthiness, or activity levels alter.

Lithium is often ineffective for bipolar disorders that involve rapid cyclers—patients who experience four or more manic-depressive cycles per year. About 25 percent of manic patients don't respond to this treatment. For these patients, the anticonvulsant drugs *tegretol* and *volproic acid* sometimes prove effective. Our understanding of how these two drugs alleviate bipolar illness is still very limited.

Tying It All Together

Don't feel that you have to master the technical information presented in this chapter. We've simply provided it as an overview to the rest of this workbook, in which you'll play an active role in learning as much as possible about practical strategies for coping with a mood disorder. Of course, the more knowledge you have about the medical components of mood swings, the greater your ability will be to fully participate as part of your own medical care team.

References

American Psychiatric Association (1980) *Diagnostic and Statistical Manual of Mental Disorders.* 3d ed. Washington, D.C.: American Psychiatric Association Press.

Beavers, D.J. (1969) "The challenging frontier: Environmental, genetic, biochemical and neurological factors in severe mental illness." *Schizophrenia*, vol. 1, no. 4.

Gold, M.S. (1986) *Good News About Depression.* New York: Bantam Books.

Kidd, K.K., and Weismann, M.M. (1978) "Why we do not yet understand the genetics of affective disorders." In *Depression: Biology, Psychodynamics, and Treatment*, edited by J.O. Cole, A.F. Schatzberk, and S.H. Frazier. New York: Plenum Press.

Lickey, M.E., and Gordon, B. (1991) *Medicine and Mental Illness.* New York: W.H. Freeman and Co.

Preston, J., and Johnson, J. (1991) *Clinical Psychopharmacology Made Ridiculously Simple.*

White, R.W. (1964) *The Abnormal Personality.* 3d ed. New York: Ronald Press Co.

2

Experiencing Depression

*I feel like I am in a grave and someone is continually throwing dirt in to
cover me—there is a small bit of light, but I am smothering.*

The experience of depression varies widely from person to person. Yet there are common
threads that weave their way through this morose tapestry.

Study participants have shared how they feel when they are depressed. Which of
their feelings and symptoms do you relate to?

- ☐ hopeless
- ☐ useless
- ☐ apathetic
- ☐ unresponsive
- ☐ desire only to sleep
- ☐ low energy level
- ☐ sad
- ☐ anxious
- ☐ short-tempered
- ☐ miserable, terrible, horrible, lousy

- ☐ worthless
- ☐ might as well be dead
- ☐ emotionless
- ☐ extremely fatigued
- ☐ no motivation
- ☐ slow
- ☐ down
- ☐ irritable
- ☐ black attitude
- ☐ lonely, alone, abandoned

☐ void, empty, hollow
☐ guilty of everything
☐ scared
☐ low self-esteem
☐ inability to concentrate
☐ ugly
☐ inability to function
☐ inability to experience pleasure
☐ angry
☐ want to be alone
☐ tense
☐ quiet
☐ heavily burdened
☐ sense of futility
☐ wanting to be unconscious
☐ guilty
☐ like a gray, dirty windowpane
☐ as if the world is cloud-covered
☐ as if I'm in hell
☐ heaviness, and it's a burden to move

☐ self-accusing
☐ cry easily
☐ helpless
☐ hoping to die
☐ like a failure
☐ fat
☐ frozen, dead inside
☐ unbearable
☐ inability to sleep
☐ disorganized
☐ silent
☐ paranoid
☐ hateful
☐ obsessed with past mistakes
☐ physically unhealthy
☐ hating my existence
☐ pain so deep it can't be fixed
☐ want to curl up and not exist
☐ deeply buried anger, and knowing it can never be resolved

Other descriptions of depression from study participants include:

"Pain—dark—totally empty—in a fuzzy fog—nothing penetrates."

"Nothing is any good nor is anybody, and I'm trouble—I don't want to do anything or see anybody."

"All will never be right, everyone is not what they appear, and I'm not what others want me to be."

"It feels heavy, slow, hard to move, to do ordinary tasks. I feel fearful and berate myself for past actions."

"The hopelessness of hell. I feel like a nonperson; life feels meaningless. I lose all feeling for my family. I can't make myself do anything. I am alive physically but not mentally."

"Sometimes I feel as though I have two kinds of depressions. One is responsive to adversity in my life, whereas the other one comes even if things are going well for me. Sometimes joyful things will relieve my depressions, whereas sometimes nothing will make depressions go away. The nonreactive depression seems to ruin my appetite and causes sleep problems."

"I feel like someone has clamped a brake on my brain and thrown a thick, gray blanket over it, and everything has ground to a halt. I can't see anything positive anywhere, but at the same time experience constant, overpowering panic."

"Wishing, thinking of bad things happening to me or my family—why do I hate myself so much? The depression curtain is trying to engulf me—I have to fight back! Full of anxiety—I want to run outside with nothing on. Waiting for things to happen—usually bad. Cannot make decisions. Think I am going to die the next day. I have given away too many things in this mood. I become real stingy with money, find fault with all persons and things, cannot close my eyes at night for fear."

"My kind of depression is endogenous, or internal, that is, it arises out of internal, biological mechanisms. Once started, the depression is self-sustaining and does not respond to changes in the environment. I call it depression with a capital D."

"I sometimes sit and stare at the wall for hours while crying. I tell people to stay away, and I vacillate between no appetite and binge eating. I become unkempt."

"I become sure each time that this time it won't go away—that the wonderful part of mania won't return. I am filled with fears and nightmares."

"I put on a mask and act like nothing is wrong."

"Too much daydreaming—all fears, real or not, converge on me. I become self-centered, sloppy in dress, unclean. I don't sleep at night. Too much burping. Tear at fingernails, rub big sores into my face, completely negative. Cannot see anything good or positive. Cannot make positive decisions. Have made costly mistakes at the onset of my depression. No sex drive—want to be left alone, want to divorce the human race. My mind wants to close me down."

One person in the study shared this in-depth experience of depression:

"These depressions feel very much like physical illness. In fact, sometimes I've been coming down with the flu and at first mistaken it for the beginning of a depression—the body/mind sensations are so similar. In endogenous depressions, my moods are lowered. My body is fatigued and exhausted. I have no energy, no drives of any kind, whether sex, appetite, or work. I experience no pleasure in the usual things I enjoy—

everything seems to be a drag. My sleep is disturbed by insomnia or hypersomnia.

"My thoughts seem to revolve around an incessant surging of negative past memories. It's as though the positive experiences of my life aren't available for retrieval at this time. My perceptions of things in my present environment are colored negatively; even on sunny days I see gloom. I have negative expectations and have fears of the future. I can no longer look forward to tomorrow. The blackness ushers in suicidal ideation almost without my needing to give any conscious direction to my thoughts. I didn't choose to think these thoughts; they entered my mind uninvited and unwanted. It wasn't so much that I felt so miserable I wanted to end it all, as that the thoughts of suicide constantly forced their way into my consciousness. And, in fact, I had to work to survive these thoughts.

"For years before I knew my depressions had a name or a treatment, I sensed that they were something constitutional, something beyond my control. My mother, exasperated, used to cry at me: "You don't have anything to be depressed about!" This was true—I didn't have anything to be depressed about. That should have been the clue! This was not a depression with a little d; this was depression with a capital D: a system malfunction, a lack of lower limits on my mood state. I needed to be treated, not rationally talked out of my perceptions. Those of us with depressions most need people who will try and understand us and not label us as lazy or weak-willed or inferior. When I'm in one of my depressions, I have a need to confide in someone that I am down. It helps to have a caring— and a careful—listener."

Describe your experience of depression. Getting in touch with how it feels can be the first step to overcoming these feelings. Use extra paper if you need it. _____

_____

_____

_____

_____

_____

_____

Forty-four people in the study reported that their body physically hurts when they are depressed. This pain can be, and has been for me, absolutely excruciating and totally debilitating. Which of these symptoms relate to how you have felt?

- ☐ aching all over
- ☐ stomach tight
- ☐ nausea
- ☐ chest aches
- ☐ chest feels empty
- ☐ pain deep inside the heart
- ☐ constipation
- ☐ aching limbs
- ☐ jaws clenched
- ☐ eyes feel heavy
- ☐ low blood pressure
- ☐ muscle spasms

- ☐ headache
- ☐ stomachache
- ☐ backache
- ☐ chest feels constricted
- ☐ chest pain
- ☐ arrythmia
- ☐ diarrhea
- ☐ heaviness in limbs
- ☐ eyes ache
- ☐ gums ache
- ☐ fainting spells
- ☐ burning, searing pains

"My head feels like it will explode, and I hope it does so I will die."

"I feel like I'm being electrocuted."

"My heart hurts; it feels like it will stop beating."

"My head feels stuffy and I have no energy."

"My chest aches and I have difficulty breathing."

"Indescribable pain radiates from the center of my being."

"My entire body is wracked with pain. It feels like a thousand knives being driven into me at the same time."

"I have splitting headaches, almost blinding, in the back of the head."

"I have a dull ache in my chest and abdomen, gnawing like hunger that can't be satiated."

"My whole body feels heavy and paralyzed. I feel catatonic."

"As if I have a bad case of the flu, as if a chunk of lead is bearing down on my brow, as if I and my body and the hour and the world weigh tons."

Describe your experience of the physical pain of depression. _____

_____

_____

_____

3

Experiencing Mania

I feel like I am trying to hold back a 400-pound boulder on a 90-degree slope, like every atom in my body is speeding a million miles per hour, trying to escape through my skin.

Note: If you have depression only, rather than bipolar illness, you don't have to read this chapter.

With depression, all is bad and lost. However, the experience of mania is a double-edged sword. While everyone enjoys lifting out of the depression and cycling up, up, up to a place where everything seems possible and all the world is beautiful, at its extreme mania is infinitely dangerous and destructive.

These are feelings and symptoms of mania as described by study participants. **Which ones can you relate to?**

☐ energetic
☐ speedy
☐ pressured
☐ can't be still
☐ talking very fast
☐ financially irresponsible
☐ need little food
☐ insightful

☐ quick movements
☐ hyperactive
☐ need to do something
☐ pressurized speech
☐ compulsive buying
☐ need little sleep
☐ brilliant, wonderful
☐ "know-it-all"

- ☐ very happy
- ☐ optimistic
- ☐ authoritarian
- ☐ grandiose
- ☐ confident
- ☐ perceptive
- ☐ alert
- ☐ creative
- ☐ work very hard
- ☐ overenthusiastic
- ☐ inflated self-concept
- ☐ overtly friendly
- ☐ excessive, loud laughter and giggling
- ☐ full of fun
- ☐ childish
- ☐ socially unacceptable behavior
- ☐ easily infatuated
- ☐ argumentative
- ☐ aggressive
- ☐ haughty
- ☐ racing thoughts
- ☐ dangerous
- ☐ cruel
- ☐ poor judgment
- ☐ impulsive
- ☐ impatient
- ☐ inability to trust others
- ☐ inability to calm down
- ☐ suggestible
- ☐ happy and sad at the same time

- ☐ exalted
- ☐ euphoric
- ☐ domineering
- ☐ invincible
- ☐ super aware
- ☐ clear
- ☐ sharpened thinking
- ☐ more intelligent speech
- ☐ able to accomplish a great deal
- ☐ preoccupied with self
- ☐ outgoing
- ☐ life of the party
- ☐ wild dancing
- ☐ live in a fantasy world
- ☐ poor social interactions
- ☐ bizarre behavior
- ☐ increased interest in sex
- ☐ verbally abusive
- ☐ obnoxious
- ☐ arrogant
- ☐ confused thoughts
- ☐ irresponsible
- ☐ rapid, unpredictable emotional changes
- ☐ destructive to self, others
- ☐ boisterous
- ☐ hallucinations
- ☐ inability to concentrate
- ☐ "flight of ideas"
- ☐ feeling driven

"The flip side of depression is mania and hypomania. They can be kind of fun, especially hypomania; however, they're really a mixed blessing. For me, mania and hypomania last too briefly and are always followed by unpleasant depressions. In mania, I become hyperactive, hypersexual, overly talkative, overconfident, and extremely elated. I cannot remember being down, and I think I am the best person around! I think, speak, and act very rapidly and become impatient with how slow the rest of the world is going. I have been known at those times to start finishing other people's sentences for them—not an endearing quality, believe me! And I have experienced such intense mania that it frightened me."

"I wear makeup, my hair is done up. I'm smiling, laughing, good natured, busy. I make sure my bed is made, pick up after myself, dishes are done, etc."

"I feel that others are less alive and cannot see the correctness of my ideas. I do lots of sweating, am jerky, feel very edgy and uncomfortable."

"I feel like the filters have been removed from my senses."

"I want to be alone and do what I want to do when I want to do it, like an engine that has revved up beyond its highest speed and if left that way will destroy itself by burning out."

If you have experienced mania, **describe what it was like for you**. Use extra paper if you need it. _____

_____

_____

_____

_____

My own personal experience of mania includes extreme pain. I feel unable to stay physically still or to quiet my brain. My body hurts all over. Every cell says I want to rest, but the body and mind cannot and will not cooperate.

Aspects of mania that feel painful or unbearable to people in the study include the following descriptions. **Which of the feelings and symptoms can you relate to?**

- [ ] become s-o-o-o tired but can't slow down enough to rest or sleep
- [ ] wanting to cry with every other person's hurt, feeling angry with others' anger
- [ ] unable to relax
- [ ] skin hurts, even to be touched
- [ ] physically ache all over
- [ ] ache for someone to hold me
- [ ] psychic pain
- [ ] feel like something is eating away at my brain
- [ ] feel like I'm being tortured

"I feel like my whole body is on fire. I can't sit still. I'm terrified."

"Like so many ideas whirling around, like BB's in a #10 can being shook."

"I feel like a high-speed engine that finally self-destructs in a million unrecognizable pieces."

"Sheer hell! Once I got lost in my home town, didn't recognize my father, thought strangers were old friends, saw and heard things that weren't there, forgot my name."

If mania is ever painful for you, **describe what you feel**. _____

_____

_____

_____

Aspects of Mania That People Enjoy

The paradox of mania is that there are aspects of it which people really enjoy, especially after they have been depressed for a long period of time. Often when people sense early warning signs of mania, they like the feeling so much that they don't want to do anything to stop that upward spiral.

Which of these pleasant aspects of mania, as cited by people in the study, are similar to what you have experienced?

- ☐ happiness
- ☐ super-sensitive senses
- ☐ feeling smart
- ☐ excessive energy
- ☐ unleashed abilities
- ☐ sociability
- ☐ self-confidence
- ☐ being alert mentally
- ☐ feeling free
- ☐ increase in synchronicity
- ☐ relief from depression
- ☐ being able to do difficult things with very little effort
- ☐ feeling like nothing can go wrong
- ☐ establishing friendships that get shelved during depression
- ☐ feeling like I am floating in a sea of glass

- ☐ full of good feelings
- ☐ feeling attractive
- ☐ euphoria
- ☐ productivity
- ☐ creative, free-flowing ideas
- ☐ feeling powerful
- ☐ feeling better than everyone else
- ☐ analytical
- ☐ intuitive
- ☐ lose all inhibitions
- ☐ weight loss
- ☐ feels like everybody loves me and I love everybody

Describe the aspects of mania that you enjoy. _____

_____

_____

Negative Aspects of Mania

Looking at the positive aspects of mania, one might say, "What's wrong with that?" Plenty! Mania often gets people in serious trouble with family, friends, the community, and the law. Here are some descriptions from people in the study. **Which of the following negative aspects of mania do you experience?** *My mania sometimes causes*

- ☐ detrimental effect on relationships
- ☐ embarrassment to self, family, and friends
- ☐ physical wear and tear on the body
- ☐ poor judgment
- ☐ incoherence
- ☐ feeling of failing others
- ☐ disruptive behavior
- ☐ me to miss school
- ☐ others to be scared
- ☐ lack of control
- ☐ me to become easily confused
- ☐ inappropriate lusting
- ☐ me to ignore responsiblity
- ☐ lack of sleep
- ☐ professional damage
- ☐ kleptomania
- ☐ me to get into trouble
- ☐ my being called unreasonable
- ☐ loss of support
- ☐ my not knowing how much is too much
- ☐ losing my thoughts
- ☐ hospitalization
- ☐ paranoia
- ☐ carelessness with relationships
- ☐ anesthetized emotions
- ☐ offense to others
- ☐ financial crisis
- ☐ my not knowing what is real
- ☐ stigmatization
- ☐ feelings of anger, rage
- ☐ carelessness with driving
- ☐ me not to take good care of myself
- ☐ lost careers
- ☐ me to be avoided
- ☐ my being called weird
- ☐ being sick and not knowing it
- ☐ friends and family to hate the rages and forcefulness
- ☐ knowing I will come down and not be able to live up to expectations
- ☐ having to correct things done wrong, picking up the pieces afterwards
- ☐ sexual impositions that destroy relationships and are dangerous
- ☐ fear of what will happen: flights, accidents, injuries, hangovers, illness

> "I lost everything—my husband, family, daughter, home, car, possessions, jobs."

> "Manic depression has cost me my career, my kids, and almost my independence. I was a nurse and my two teenage kids are in a foster home. That makes me angry."

"You can't function when you can't filter any stimulation out of your brain. You need help with everything you do, including dressing. Agony—at risk of dying due to delusion-induced accident, cardiac arrest."

"I tried to fly off my twentieth-floor porch knowing I was superwoman."

"I sleep poorly and my head feels bad, like it is moving. I want to bang my head against the wall to relieve the excessive matter in my brain."

Describe the aspects of mania that are negative for you: _____

_____

_____

_____

Describe your personal reasons for wanting to prevent yourself from getting manic: __

_____

_____

_____

_____

_____

4

Taking Responsibility for Your Own Wellness

It became very clear to me in compiling the data from the study that those people who personally take responsibility for their own wellness achieve the highest levels of stability, the highest levels of wellness, control over their own lives, and happiness. Learn all you can about mood disorders.

Resources

Review the Resource List at the back of this book. Check at least five resources that seem most appropriate to you at this time. Some you may want to own, to make them available at any time for reference. These might include *Back to Basics; Full Catastrophe Living; Peace; Love and Healing; Feeling Good;* and *The Feeling Good Handbook*. You can borrow others for shorter-term use from your library. List the resources that you feel are a high priority for you to explore here:

   1. **Reference:** _____

What I hope to learn from this resource: _____

_____

☐ *I plan to purchase it. Where?* _____

Why? _____

☐ *I will borrow it from the library.*
☐ *I will borrow it from a friend.*

Other possible places I will look for it: _____

2. Reference: _____

What I hope to learn from this resource: _____

☐ *I plan to purchase it. Where?* _____

_____

Why? _____

☐ *I will borrow it from the library.*
☐ *I will borrow it from a friend.*

Other possible places I will look for it: _____

3. Reference: _____

What I hope to learn from this resource: _____

☐ *I plan to purchase it. Where?* _____

Why? _____

☐ *I will borrow it from the library.*
☐ *I will borrow it from a friend.*

Other possible places I will look for it: _____

4. Reference: _____

What I hope to learn from this resource: _____

_____

☐ *I plan to purchase it. Where?* _____

Why? _____

☐ *I will borrow it from the library.*
☐ *I will borrow it from a friend.*

Other possible places I will look for it: _____

5. Reference: _____

What I hope to learn from this resource: _____

☐ *I plan to purchase it. Where?* _____

Why? _____

☐ *I will borrow it from the library.*
☐ *I will borrow it from a friend.*

Other possible places I will look for it: _____

Get these resources and read them. Learn and make those adjustments in your life that seem appropriate based on what you are learning. When you finish with these, continue to read and learn. Review the resource list repeatedly for possible choices. Another good source of follow-up reading ideas is the bibliographies of the books you are reading.

Spend some time in the reference section of the library. Take a look at the *Physicians Desk Reference (PDR)*. Learn how to use it. Then when your doctor suggests use of any medication, use this reference to check it out (or you can ask your doctor to make you a copy of the pertinent information from his *PDR*). Then you can make appropriate decisions based on all the facts. Introduce people on your support team to this reference, so they can make decisions for you when you cannot make them for yourself.

Newsletters

The resource section at the back of this book has a list of organizations, many of which put out newsletters with valuable wellness information. Send the organizations a postcard requesting a complimentary copy of their newsletter. Subscribe to the ones that seem most appropriate to you. They can be an excellent source of inexpensive information, and are usually written by people who have experienced mood disorders.

Workshops and Seminars

Watch newsletters and newspapers for workshops and seminars that will be useful to you in your search for stability and wellness. Then go. You will meet other great people with similar problems, and you will come away with useful ideas.

Mental Health Professionals

Your team of mental health professionals will have a wealth of information to share with you. If they don't, you have the wrong team of health professionals working with you. Pick their brains. Ask them questions. That is what they are there for.

Other People With Mood Disorders

Through the study, I have found that other people who have mood disorders are the greatest resource available to any of us. Why reinvent the wheel if someone else has already solved the problem you're facing? The best way to meet these people is through support groups, which are in themselves a rich source of information. Locate support groups through the community calendar in the newspaper or by checking with local mental health organizations. (See the chapter "Support Groups" for information on how to set up a support group if there is none available in your area.)

How It Helps

Knowing all you can about mood disorders empowers you to make good decisions about your treatment, lifestyle, education, career, relationships, living space, parenting style, and leisure pursuits.

Being educated enables you to ask the right questions, leading you to discover the most appropriate treatments.

How have you learned what you know about mood disorders? _____

_____

_____

Do you feel that you take responsibility for your mood swings? If so, give yourself a pat on the back. You deserve it. How do you feel when you take responsibility for your ups and downs? _____

_____

_____

Why do you feel it's important to know all you can about mood disorders? _____

_____

_____

In what ways do you plan to take more responsibility for your mood swings? _____

_____

_____

Educating Others

The next chapter gives instructions for building a strong support system of friends, relatives, and health professionals. It's important to educate other people in your support system so they can make good decisions for you when you are not able to make them for yourself. The people in your support system should learn all they can about mood disorders by reading appropriate literature, visiting with mental health professionals, attending workshops and seminars, and listening to you.

Many family members of people with mood disorders belong to local affiliates of the National Alliance for the Mentally Ill. These groups are an excellent source of information and empathetic understanding. The Alliance is listed in the resource list.

Like anyone else who has a history of mood swings, you need to have several people who can make decisions for you when you are unable to make decisions for yourself. When in a deep depression or an agitated manic state, it may be impossible to concentrate well enough to make appropriate decisions about your own treatment. To avoid having such decisions made by people who don't know you or understand mood disorders, it is essential to have several people whom you trust to make decisions when you're incapacitated. These people might include a spouse, parents, children, siblings, close friends, or trusted health professionals.

People I want to make decisions for me when I am unable to make decisions for myself:

1. _____   2. _____

3. _____   4. _____

Talk to these people about taking responsibility for you when you are unable to take responsibility for yourself. (And make certain that they're willing to assume this responsibility!) Educate them about your illness. Direct them to resources you have found useful. Ask them to attend informational meetings with you. Introduce them to your health care professionals. You may want to include them in a counseling session. Tell them what kinds of treatment are acceptable to you and what kinds are not. Be very clear and precise in making your wishes known: you might want to write them down and review them together.

Hospitals, doctors, and counselors have confidentiality rules that may keep people in your support system from getting the information they need to make appropriate decisions about your treatment. To avoid this situation, have a legal document available which allows health care professionals to consult with, and get permission for treatment from, designated members of your support system. Here's an example of a format you might use:

I give (name) _____ *the authority to consult with my mental health professionals about my treatment and to make decisions about my treatment in the event that I am unable to make these decisions for myself.*

Signed: _____   *Date:* _____

Witness: _____

Witness: _____

Make copies of this document and give them to your health care professionals and the designated members of your support system.

5

Possible Causes of Mood Disorders

I don't believe there is one answer for everyone. Controlling the symptoms must be dealt with first, then each individual must explore his or her own problem. Different people respond differently to different approaches. There's bound to be something that will work—it just takes time to find it.

If you are suffering from a mood disorder, have a complete physical examination with a physician you trust. He or she must come well recommended, be able to communicate clearly, be willing to answer questions, respond to your concerns, and address the possibility of a biological basis for your mood disorder. Your physician must also be open to exploring all possible causes and treatments, particularly those that are least invasive.

My own personal experience yields enough evidence to support this course. I was completely disabled for three years with rapid cycling, inability to concentrate, loss of memory, inability to lose weight, and periodically, extreme fatigue. I was hospitalized for extended periods four times. A local doctor found—through appropriate testing—that I was severely hypothyroid. With hormone replacement treatment, the extreme, rapid-cycling mood swings were eliminated, I regained my ability to concentrate, my memory returned,

I lost weight, and my energy level increased dramatically. This, or some other easily treated problem, may be causing some or all of your erratic moods.

Twenty-three people in the study have had conflicting diagnoses of their mood disorder. Only thirty-nine participants feel that all possible causes of their mood disorder have been explored. Forty-six people are not satisfied that all possible causes of their mood disorder have been explored.

Learn all you can about mood disorders. Then insist that you get the necessary testing. Don't let anyone talk you out of a given test unless the procedure itself has harmful side effects. If your doctor won't order a test that you feel is warranted, then find a different doctor. Your life is too important to miss any clue. You owe it to yourself to be thorough.

If cost is keeping you from getting the testing you need, explore other payment options with your doctor and your medical facility. Many doctors and medical facilities have funds available for people who are unable to pay for testing.

There are no testing procedures that even approach the exorbitant cost of staying in an institution, not to mention the time taken out of your life, time when you could have been well and productive.

Why do I owe it to myself to see that I am tested for every possible condition that may be causing or exacerbating my mood swings?

_____

_____

_____

The following possible medical causes for mood swings were suggested by study participants. Which ones do you feel you need to explore?

- ☐ allergies—food and environmental
- ☐ endocrine system problems, including hypothyroidism—make sure you get a complete thyroid battery, which includes Total T4, Free T4, Total T3 and TSH (this test will cost over $100. If it doesn't, it's the wrong test)
- ☐ anti-candida antibody test
- ☐ chemistry 20 screening test
- ☐ complete blood count with differential
- ☐ seasonal affective disorder
- ☐ PMS
- ☐ medication interactions
- ☐ acute or chronic stress reactions

Other possibilities you plan to explore that you have discovered through your research:

_____

_____

For more information on possible causes of extreme mood swings, see the book *Back to Basics*, which is included in the Resource List. This book describes the testing you need and simple, noninvasive, and inexpensive ways to increase your level of wellness. It will help you understand what the test results mean.

Always ask your doctor for a copy of test results, even if you don't understand what they mean. The results should be in your own file, so that they'll be available to you if you see another doctor. Make sure that all your doctors have a copy of any test results.

Do you feel that all possible causes of your problem with mood disorders have been explored? _____ If not, what are you going to do about it?_____

_____

_____

*A complete physical examination showed that I have the following health problems which may be causing or exacerbating my mood swings:*_____

_____

_____

*Based on these findings, I am going to take the following action:*_____

_____

_____

_____

As a result of the above action, I have made the following changes in my treatment: _____

_____

_____

_____

What are the changes in the way you feel that might be attributable to new treatment strategies? _____

_____

_____

_____

6

The Way Out of Depression

I have developed a program that includes reading anything current on depression, forcing myself into self-help to slowly reverse the depressive cycle, using self-practiced cognitive therapy, and forcing myself to return slowly to life's surroundings and functions. I must use all of these techniques; they work together. I have spent many years developing these techniques and I know how important they all are: it's like being a world-class chef who would never leave any ingredient out of his best recipe.

Early Warning Signs

As you become more aware of the subtleties of your depression through your research and by charting your moods, you will become familiar with your own early warning signs of depression. These may be quite subtle indeed: for instance, an early warning sign of depression for me is that I don't look both ways before I cross the street.

When you notice such signs, there are simple, noninvasive, safe, and inexpensive techniques you can use to slow or halt the downward spiral. By being aware of your early signs of depression and taking action early, you may be able to avoid plummeting to the depths of depression.

What are your early warning signs that you are on a downward spiral?

☐ withdrawal
☐ inactivity
☐ tire easily
☐ excessive sleep
☐ slow speech
☐ premature awakening
☐ poor appetite
☐ irritability
☐ poor ability to concentrate
☐ confused
☐ cry easily
☐ despondent
☐ self-destructive thoughts
☐ inability to experience pleasure
☐ unable to do what I normally do
☐ insecurity
☐ anxiety
☐ agitation
☐ sore shoulders and neck
☐ low back pain
☐ low libido
☐ extreme grief-type emotions
☐ overeating
☐ eat junk foods
☐ inability to show affection
☐ void of emotions
☐ everything seems disorganized
☐ hair becomes wiry
☐ my learning disabilities are more pronounced
☐ eczema
☐ see white spots
☐ have trouble getting dressed
☐ feelings of regret for past decisions

☐ not wanting to do anything
☐ inability to function
☐ low energy level
☐ talk little
☐ insomnia
☐ stay in bed for long periods
☐ nausea
☐ negative attitude
☐ mind slows down
☐ low self-esteem
☐ lack of interest in everything
☐ suicidal ideation
☐ feel no one understands me
☐ feel like giving up on life
☐ boredom
☐ fear
☐ desire to be taken care of
☐ ache all over
☐ headache
☐ trembling
☐ senses shut down
☐ paranoia
☐ eat a lot of salty foods
☐ craving for carbohydrates
☐ easily frustrated
☐ avoid people
☐ feel clumsy, drop things
☐ I start wearing a coat all the time
☐ as my eyesight does not seem right, becoming sure I need new eyeglasses
☐ swollen thyroid
☐ increased consumption of alcohol
☐ skin problems

One study respondent wrote:

> "A sign that depression is imminent is that to my ears everybody speaks to me in a critical tone of voice. 'You're so quiet tonight' is heard by me as 'Thank God you're quiet—you're usually such a loud mouth.'

Everything my husband says seems to be in a fault-finding tone of voice. Strange, because he never criticizes or belittles me."

Other early indications of depression you have noted: _____

_____

_____

Learn what your early warning signs of depression are. Take appropriate action when you notice these signs.

Strategies for Alleviating or Eliminating Depression

Below is a checklist of ways in which the study respondents alleviate their depression. These strategies are divided into five categories: activities, support, attitude, management, and spirituality. Which strategies have you used successfully? Which ones do you feel you should use more often? Which methods have you never used that you would like to try? Remember—what works for someone else may not be the right thing for you. Cleaning is such an example. For some people it is depressing and discouraging. Others are uplifted by it.

Activities	Have tried successfully	Should use more often	Would like to try
Exercise			
Sports (such as basketball, soccer, volleyball)			
Long walks			
Yoga			
Dancing			
Reading			
Listening to music			
Long, hot baths			
Making love			
Gardening			
Long drives			
Needlework			
Working with wood			
Working with clay, pottery			
Drawing, painting			
Journal writing			
Writing poetry			
Writing letters			
Canoeing			
Horseback riding			
Shopping			
Relaxing in a meditative natural setting			
Day trips			
Playing a musical instrument			
Spending time with young children			
Cleaning			
Watching a funny movie			
Watching TV			
Watching videos, a movie, or a play			
Buying something I've been wanting			
Helping others			

What other activities have you used successfully to help alleviate your depression? ___

_____

_____

_____

_____

_____

_____

Support	Have tried successfully	Should use more often	Would like to try
Talking it out with an understanding person			
Getting emotional support from a person I trust			
Talking to a therapist or counselor			
Peer counseling			
Talking to people who validate my feelings			
Spending time with good friends			
Talking to staff at a crisis clinic or hotline			
Arranging not to be alone			
Reaching out to someone			
Being held by someone I love			
Going to a support group			
Spending time with and taking responsibility for a pet			

What other kinds of support have been helpful to you in alleviating your depression?

_____

_____

_____

_____

_____

_____

Attitude	Have tried successfully	Should use more often	Would like to try
Changing negative thought patterns to positive ones			
Waiting it out			
Staying active			
Remembering that depression ends			
Recalling good times			
Being good to myself			
Diverting my attention			
Being gentle with myself			
Refusing to feel guilty			
Focusing on living one day at a time			
Endorsing and affirming my efforts			
Laughter			

What other attitudes have you developed and used to help alleviate your depression?

_____

_____

_____

Management	Have tried successfully	Should use more often	Would like to try
Medication			
Full-spectrum light			
Spending time outside			
Keeping busy			
Eating a diet high in complex carbohydrates			
Eliminating foods that worsen my depression			
Resting			
Forcing myself to get up in the morning			
Forcing myself to go to work			
Doing whatever I need to do to meet my needs			
Maintaining a balance of rest and good times			

Study participants wrote:

> "If my depression gets to be too much to handle, I should have the right to use hospitalization without feeling guilty. I like to try and use the most conservative treatment possible."

> "I use activity and exercise together. Using the body fully stimulates the brain."

What management strategies have you found for alleviating your depression? _____

_____

_____

_____

_____

_____

Spirituality	Have tried successfully	Should use more often	Would like to try
Praying			
Getting in touch with my spirituality			
Meditating			
Keeping up with a 12-step program			

What other spiritual practices help to alleviate your depression?_____

_____

_____

_____

Use Scheduling and Planning To Help Alleviate Depression

A person who is experiencing depression may spend a whole day or many days literally doing nothing. This inactivity and lack of accomplishment can deepen your depression and lower your self-esteem. If you accomplish anything, you may belittle it as "insignificant."

People with whom I talk and work find that the following strategies can help break this cycle and help the depressed person feel better.

- make and stick to simple plans
- break tasks down into smaller componants
- learn to give yourself credit for whatever you accomplished

The success of this approach is corroborated by Dr. David Burns in *Feeling Good* and by Dr. Aaron Beck in *The Cognitive Therapy of Depression*.

Make and Stick to Simple Plans

In everyone's life, there are some things you have to do—such as washing the dishes or vacuuming; and other things you really enjoy—such as going for a walk or listening togood music. When planning the day's schedule, it is important to include some things you "have to do" (so you come out with a sense of accomplishment) and some things you "enjoy doing" (to increase your good feelings about being alive). Referring to the lists on the previous pages, make a list of things you must do on a daily basis and things that you really enjoy doing. These lists will be different for everyone. Before you start your list, take a look at these examples:

Things I have to do	**Things I enjoy doing**
Examples:	*Examples*:
wash the dishes	take a hot shower
vacuum	pet the dog
mow the lawn	pick some flowers
go to work	paint
make my bed	chat with a friend
balance my checkbook	play with a baby
shovel snow	go to a movie
organize my closet	watch TV

What do I have to do?   **What do I enjoy doing?**

_____   _____
_____   _____
_____   _____
_____   _____
_____   _____
_____   _____
_____   _____
_____   _____
_____   _____

Keep these lists in a handy place so you can refer to them when you need to. Build activities from each list into your daily plan. Avoid spending the whole day doing things that "must be done," as that is a recipe for failure.

As you develop your daily plan, assess your expectations of that activity by rating it on a scale of 0 to 5, with 0 being that you expect you could do it or could enjoy it, 3 being that you think you could do the activity and/or would enjoy the activity, and 5 being that you expect to be able to do the activity very well or that you would enjoy it immensely. For instance, if the activity is something you *have* to do, such as washing the dishes, and you think you will be able to do it, you could rate the activity H (for "have to do") 3, meaning that you expect to be able to do the task. If the activity were something you usually enjoy, such as going to a movie, but you don't think you'll be able to enjoy it now, you could rate it E (for "enjoy") 1, meaning that you don't think you'll have a good time. When you complete the activity, rate how well you did it or how much you actually enjoyed yourself. You will discover that your expectations and what actually happens can be very different!

Example of a Schedule for a Person Who Is Depressed But Able To Work
(Note that even on a workday, activities for enjoyment are included.)

Date: Nov. 20   *Mood*: low, depressed

Time	Planned Activity and Expectations	Actual Activity	How It Felt
7-8 a.m.	Get up; shower; make and eat hot cereal **H1**	Got up; took a shower; had tea and toast	Better than if I had stayed in bed **H3**
8-9 a.m.	Walk to work, picking up the mail on the way **H3**	(As planned)	Exercise lifts my spirits **H4**
9-10 a.m.	Open and sort mail; return two phone calls **H1**	Opened and sorted mail; made one phone call	At least it feels better to be doing something **H3**
10-11a.m.	Attend office meeting **H0**	(As planned)	Hard for me to be with a group, but I did it **H2**
11-12 Noon	Write press release **H1**	(As planned)	Glad I got it done **H3**
12-1 p.m.	Have lunch with Jane in the park; take a 15-minute walk with her **E1**	Ate lunch with Jane at park	It felt good to share how I have been feeling **E4**
1-2 p.m.	Watch a management video **H1**	(As planned)	OK, but I fell asleep for part of the time **H0**
2-3 p.m.	Interview a candidate for a data entry position **H1**	(As planned)	Hard, but I did it **H3**
3-4 p.m.	Enter data in computer **H2**	(As planned)	Felt slow **H4**
4-5 p.m.	Walk home from work; stop at store for milk **H3**	Walked home, but did not stop at store	Tired **H3**
5-6 p.m.	Relax, meditate **E2**	(As planned)	Helped me feel better **H4**

6-7 p.m.	Cook frozen pizza and eat **H2**	Had a peanut butter sandwich instead	Wish I had cooked the pizza **H0**
7-8 p.m.	Do the dishes; straighten up the house **H0**	Did the dishes	Fine; the housework can wait **H3**
8-9 p.m.	Watch *Nature* on PBS **E2**	(As planned)	OK **E4**
9-10 p.m.	Call a member of my support team for a talk; read a light novel, go to bed **E2**	Talked to Claire for 15 minutes; read and went to bed	OK **E4**

Example of a Schedule for a Person Who Is Unable To Work

Date: November 20   *Mood*: low, depressed

Time	Planned Activity and Expectations	Actual Activity	How It Felt
7-8 a.m.	Get up, dress; sit in front of the light box and read a light novel **H1**	(As planned)	OK, but mornings are always hard **H4**
8-9 a.m.	Eat a bowl of cereal; make bed; put up load of wash **H1**	Skipped doing wash	OK **H3**
9-10 a.m.	Take the dog for a walk **H2**	(As planned)	Difficult, but I did it **H3**
10-11 a.m.	Sit on sun porch and read **E2**	(As planned)	OK; fell asleep for 15 minutes **E5**
11-12 Noon	Put wash in dryer; clean bathroom **H1**	Put wash in washer; scrubbed sink and tub	OK **H3**
12-1 p.m.	Lunch with Tom (he is bringing Chinese food) **E2**	(As planned)	He did all the talking; I felt weary **E3**

Time	Planned Activity and Expectations	Actual Activity	How It Felt
1-2 p.m.	Nap *E3*	(As planned)	Fine—I was ready for it *E5*
2-3 p.m.	Drive to the store for groceries *H0*	(As planned)	Did not like being in the store, but I got through it *H2*
3-4 p.m.	Put away groceries; meditate with audio tape *E1*	(As planned)	Hard time really relaxing *E2*
4-5 p.m.	Appointment with counselor *H3*	(As planned)	It really helps *H5*
5-6 p.m.	Watch sitcom on TV *E2*	(As planned)	OK *E5*
6-7 p.m.	Cook frozen pizza and eat *H1*	(As planned)	OK *H4*
7-8 p.m.	Peer counseling with Janet *E2*	(As planned)	Helps a lot *E5*
8-9 p.m.	Watch concert on PBS *E1*	(As planned)	OK *E4*
9-10 p.m.	Read light novel; go to bed *E2*	Fell asleep soon after I started reading	Wish I had been able to stay awake longer *E2*

Review these charts after you have completed them. When people are depressed, they often feel quite negative prior to undertaking an activity. Upon completion of the activity, you may realize that you actually had a better time, or did a better job, than anticipated. Being tuned in to this can encourage you to have more realistically optimistic expectations.

Make copies of this form to plan daily schedules for yourself when you are depressed

Date: *Mood*:

Time	Planned Activity and Expectations	Actual Activity	How It Felt
7-8 a.m.			
8-9 a.m.			
9-10 a.m.			
10-11 a.m.			
11-12 Noon			
12-1 p.m.			
1-2 p.m.			
2-3 p.m.			
3-4 p.m.			
4-5 p.m.			
5-6 p.m.			
6-7 p.m.			
7-8 p.m.			
8-9 p.m.			
9-10 p.m.			

How I felt on a day when I was depressed and did not follow a plan: _____

_____

_____

How I felt on a day when I was depressed and followed a plan: _____

_____

_____

Based on my experience, I intend to take the following action with regard to scheduling my days when I am depressed: _____

_____

_____

_____

_____

*(time of day)*_____ *is the best time for me to make plans when I am depressed.*

Breaking Tasks Down Into Smaller Components

When you're depressed, even the smallest and most familiar task can feel overwhelming. By analyzing a task and breaking it down into smaller components, it can be made manageable. Talking through the task with a support team member, and writing down the steps necessary to accomplishing the task, will facilitate the process. Your sense of accomplishment from getting something done—even something very simple—can help lift your depression.

For example, when I'm depressed, doing the laundry seems absolutely impossible. If I break this task down into smaller components, and tackle one component at a time, I can often get it done.

1. Gather all dirty clothes in the laundry room.

2. Sort light colors from the dark. Empty pockets.

3. Set the dials to the right water temperature and agitation speed.

4. Add the detergent, and turn on the machine.

5. When the soap is dissolved, add the light-colored clothes.

6. When the cycle is complete, move the clothes into the dryer. Set the timer on the dryer and turn it on.

7. Repeat this process with the dark clothes.

8. As the clothes dry, fold them or put them on hangers.

9. Put the clothes away.

What tasks do you have a hard time tackling when you're depressed?_____

_____

_____

_____

_____

_____

_____

With the help of a friend, if necessary, break down one of the tasks you listed into smaller, incremental components. This will make the task manageable for you.

Step 1 _____

_____

Step 2 _____

_____

Step 3 _____

_____

Step 4 _____

_____

Step 5 _____

_____

Step 6 _____

_____

Step 7 _____

Step 8 _____

_____

Learn To Give Yourself Credit

"I just can't get anything done!" "I never accomplish anything!" "I have never amounted to anything!" These are the kinds of negative thoughts that hamper people who experience mood swings. By paying close attention to what you do, you can learn to give yourself credit for even the smallest accomplishment. Each accomplishment, in turn, will add to your optimism and self-esteem.

Remember, there is no set rule for what anyone must accomplish in a given day (unless you are working on an assembly line!). Some days you may be able to get a lot done. Other days, you may not accomplish as much. Sometimes you may not get anything done at all.

A bipolar person in the study said, "When I am depressed, I can't get much of anything done. What I do get done, I don't feel very good about. But when I am well or hypomanic, I get a lot done and do it very well."

My doctor told me to give myself credit if all I do on a given day is plant one package of carrot seeds. If you are able to get out of bed in the morning, give yourself credit for that.

You also deserve credit for taking a shower, getting dressed, eating breakfast, walking to work, feeding the birds, petting the dog, encouraging your child, doing the exercises in this workbook, and so on.

Make a list of the things you have done so far today for which you can give yourself credit. This will help you focus on the positive instead of the negative. Include such things as *washed my face, made and ate toast and tea, made my bed, fed the cat, drove to work, walked to the corner to get a newspaper, filled the car with gas, answered the phone and responded appropriately, watered the plants, listened to a friend, encouraged a friend, paid a bill, organized my desk, read a chapter in a book, played a game with a child.*

List of my accomplishments for today:

_____

_____

_____

_____

_____

_____

Other Suggestions on How To Alleviate Depression

"I start in on a new project, clear my mind, and re-program myself—sometimes this works."

"A meal with my husband at a good restaurant with atmosphere helps a little."

"I don't push myself any more than necessary, and I tell those around me what is going on."

"The best way for me to deal with depression is like the old adage, 'Doc, it hurts when I do this.' The doctor replies, 'Then don't do that.' If I am depressed, I am experiencing a problem with my lifestyle. When I was first in recovery, if I went to a party where people were drinking or getting high, I would start to feel sorry for myself because I couldn't drink or get high. I had to quit going to parties where that happened. If my car broke down, I would get depressed, so I learned to work on my car myself. I went to school and studied to get the exact job I wanted. Twelve-step, traditional self-help has been a lifesaver for me, because I learned to recognize my spiritual [component]. I am not religious, but I am spiritual. Spirituality is my relationship to the universe. I am the wounded healer. I help others through my experience, strength, and hope. Two people with similar pain helping each other is a very spiritual matter."

"Don't withdraw from people or activities. Use principles of cognitive/behavioral therapy: change your negative, distorted thoughts to realistic ones (this takes knowledge of distortions and a strong will to fight for your mental health). A typical affirmation is, 'Symptoms of depression are distressing but not dangerous.' With practice, it is possible to function adequately even while enduring a fairly severe 'down.' Belief that the world is basically ordered (by God), as opposed to the chaos that many modern philosophers suggest, has helped me greatly. The meaninglessness of the existential view of life undermined my stability and, I believe, contributed, along with other things, to my depressions."

A technique I have found useful in alleviating depression, and that I know has worked for others, is to block out the day, planning it very carefully, considering every aspect in terms of how it will affect my mood. When very depressed, you may need to ask a support person to help you with this process.

Here is a sample plan for a day that follows some of my early warning signs of depression.

6:45-7:00	Meditation
7:00-7:15	Stretching exercises
7:15-7:30	Write in my journal
7:30-8:00	Warm bath, dress
8:00-8:30	Prepare and eat a breakfast of hot cereal with yogurt, and herb tea
8:30-9:30	Leisurely walk
9:30-10:00	Relax, meditate
10:00-11:00	Meet with counselor
11:00-12:00	Find a good book in the library
12:00-1:00	Lunch with a good friend
1:00-2:00	Relaxation exercises and nap
2:00-3:00	Peer counseling
3:00-4:00	Take the dog for a walk
4:00-5:00	Read something light and humorous
5:00-7:00	Prepare brown rice and vegetable stir-fry for supper, eat it with family
7:00-9:00	Watch a good but light video
9:00-10:00	Read or listen to music
10:00-10:15	Meditation
10:15	Go to bed

Use extra paper to make several detailed plans for a perfect healing day for yourself when you are feeling low. Then, when that day comes, put one of them into action. Refer to the lists above for ideas about activities that make you feel good. Have plans for several days on hand so you can choose the one that feels best. Having these available protects you from needing to make decisions at a time when decision-making is very hard.

Seeking Help for Dealing With Depression

People in the study cited different criteria for when they should seek help for depression. The general feeling seems to be "The sooner the better." Many feel that it's best to seek help at the first warning signs of depression. One respondent said that she seeks help "when all my usual attempts to help myself aren't working." When do you seek help for depression?

☐   as soon as I notice early warning signs of depression
☐   when the depression stays with me for more than a day

☐ when the depression is out of proportion to circumstances
☐ when I need help in prioritizing and sorting out feelings
☐ when I become unable to care for myself
☐ when it lasts a week or more
☐ when suicidal thoughts start
☐ when my thoughts become jumbled
☐ when I start thinking about divorce
☐ when I feel emotionally unstable
☐ when I have extreme feelings of despair
☐ when I feel out of control
☐ when I can't move anymore
☐ when the pain is unbearable
☐ when I can finally cry
☐ when I can't get out of bed
☐ when I notice that I'm spending too much time on the couch
☐ when my sex drive disappears
☐ when I am unable to sleep
☐ when I lose my appetite
☐ when I overeat to feel better
☐ when I am hallucinating
☐ when the depression continues too long
☐ when I want to die
☐ when it overwhelms me
☐ when I become irrational
☐ when I lose interest in things
☐ before I can't function any more
☐ when I can't get motivated
☐ when it is starting to hurt
☐ when I can't work
☐ when I can't relax
☐ when I isolate myself
☐ when I see no colors
☐ when I can't snap out of it
☐ when I sleep poorly

What are some other criteria you use to determine the right moment to seek help? _____

_____

_____

_____

Explain your reasons. _____

_____

_____

These are the kinds of help people prefer. **What is your preference?**

☐ psychiatric—who?_____

☐ medication—what? _____

☐ group therapy—with whom? _____

☐ 12-step program—which one? _____

☐ close friends—who? 1) _____ 2) _____

  3) _____ 4) _____

What do you want from your close friends?
☐ support
☐ someone to do errands
☐ reassurance
☐ lots of love, hugs, touching
☐ affirmation that I am a good person
☐ someone to take me out or do things with me
☐ one-on-one talking

Other things you want from close friends: _____

_____

_____

_____

_____

Other kinds of help you prefer:_____

_____

_____

_____

_____

This is how people in the study feel if others suggest that they get professional help. Check the reactions that apply to you.

☐ I don't like it, but deep down I know I need it.

☐ With those I trust, I want them to tell me; with those I don't trust, I hate it.

☐ If they are real friends, I know they know what is best for me.

☐ I've learned to listen and take their advice.

☐ They don't have to—I do it on my own.

☐ I usually know it first, but appreciate another's caring.

☐ I'm grateful they're watching my symptoms, because I am likely to miss them.

☐ If they see the changes more clearly and earlier than I do, I realize that I need to see the doctor.

☐ I feel down and more depressed.

☐ I appreciate it.

☐ I consider it.

☐ It's fine unless they get too insistent.

☐ I ignore it.

☐ I feel sad.

☐ I feel resentful.

☐ I go into denial.

☐ It depends on who it is.

☐ I feel like all my personal struggles to keep myself alive are being negated—like I am not doing my part.

☐ I agree.

☐ I seek help.

☐ It makes me afraid.

☐ It makes me angry.

☐ It makes me feel helpless.

☐ I feel misunderstood.

☐ I don't like it.

☐ I don't listen.

☐ It depends on what they offer.

How do you think you should feel or respond? _____

_____

_____

How would you like to be encouraged to get help?

☐ with respect

☐ firmly

☐ I don't want people to push too hard

☐ simply and honestly
☐ quickly
☐ gently
☐ with compassion
☐ by not turning against me
☐ lovingly
☐ by offering time to talk and listen
☐ by reaching out to me because I cannot reach out to them
☐ by making suggestions, but letting me make the final decision
☐ by sharing their concerns with family members
☐ by asking me outright if I am having a depression
☐ the same as if I had a physical problem
☐ with concrete ideas of what I can do
☐ by reminding me to stick to the techniques I have found that help me alleviate depression
☐ by telling me directly in a kind, not condescending or patronizing manner about the behaviors that concern them
☐ by letting me decide how dangerous the situation is (I want to make the decision)
☐ by telling me to call my doctor—that I am getting sick
☐ by making the call to my psychiatrist when I can't
☐ by explaining the symptoms and what they think is wrong

In what other ways would you like to be encouraged to get help?_____

_____

_____

How People Want To Be Treated When They're Depressed

How do you like to be treated when you're depressed? These are some of the answers of the study participants:

☐ with love
☐ kindly, gently
☐ with compassion
☐ with respect
☐ I want to be listened to
☐ with patience
☐ with tolerance

- ☐ firmly
- ☐ I want someone to keep me safe
- ☐ I want someone to pray for me
- ☐ I want reassurance
- ☐ I want touching
- ☐ with understanding
- ☐ with caring
- ☐ as a normal person
- ☐ with encouragement
- ☐ with acceptance
- ☐ I want to be comforted
- ☐ with an effort to keep me involved
- ☐ with honesty
- ☐ I want someone to stay with me
- ☐ I want people to let me work it out
- ☐ with nurturing
- ☐ in an uplifting manner
- ☐ with help to take care of my responsibilities
- ☐ I want others to take over if necessary
- ☐ I want people to remind me that it has happened before
- ☐ I want someone to encourage good grooming, help me with clean clothes and housekeeping
- ☐ I want people to include me, but just at the level I can participate
- ☐ quietly, without panic; I want people to come over and visit briefly, but also to give me space
- ☐ I want people to be sympathetic to the pain I go through and understand that it is not just me, it is an illness
- ☐ I want people to be nearby but not watching over me, not to try and cheer me up, just to listen: not to try to have any answers
- ☐ just be there—without talk about how wonderful life is
- ☐ I want people to show extra attention through invitations, especially involving food—there's nothing like good homey food
- ☐ I want people to remind me not to be so hard on myself
- ☐ I want to be allowed more time to complete tasks
- ☐ by people reducing the demands on me
- ☐ with concrete ideas about what to do
- ☐ I want people to be direct and ask if I need to talk
- ☐ I want people to take me out to eat or for some activity

"To know enough about the illness to not be trite, to sense that my depression is automatically imposed from within my brain, that I can no more stop it or dilute it than an epileptic can willfully interrupt a seizure or a heart patient can curb a coronary. There is a naturalness to it which is especially hard for onlookers to understand."

How would you like to be treated when you are depressed?_____

_____

_____

What People Don't Want From Others During Depressive Episodes

These are some of the answers given by people in the study. *I don't want people to*

- ☐ blame me for what I cannot help
- ☐ humiliate me
- ☐ desert me
- ☐ put undue demands on me
- ☐ tell me to get my act together
- ☐ tell me to "pull myself up by my boot straps"
- ☐ pressure me to go out (although being invited is better than not being invited)
- ☐ make fun of me
- ☐ avoid me
- ☐ give me sympathy
- ☐ tell me to cheer up

"I find that people are angry with me because I have difficulty caring for myself. They label me as 'lazy' and wanting to be a patient and playing the sick role. I've been told that I am not busy enough and that I need pets to solve my problems. Many times I am trying very hard to put my life back together and people don't recognize that. Telling me to 'get my act together' or to 'buck up' makes it even more difficult to cope. I feel more hopeless than even before. That is one of the worst things someone can do for me."

What other ways do you *not* want to be treated? _____

_____

_____

_____

_____

You have just explored your experience of depression in an in-depth manner. Based on what you have discovered through this exercise, **what changes are you going to make in the way you cope with depression**?

_____

_____

_____

_____

_____

Photocopy the next page—or rewrite it to suit you own needs; then post it on your refrigerator.

What To Do When You Are Getting Depressed

These are some simple ways to help yourself alleviate symptoms while you're waiting for other help, or trying to keep things on an even keel. They may not solve the underlying problem, but they will provide some relief.

- Get help while you still can: the longer you wait, the harder it gets. Depression is very dangerous. Medications may take from four to six weeks to work.

- Use cognitive therapy techniques to get you out of negative thought patterns (read self-help books: refer to Resource List).

- Plan your day with some activities you have to do and some activities you enjoy. Rate your expectations of these activities, and then reassess how you felt after their completion.

- Break down difficult tasks into smaller incremental parts.

- Give yourself credit for even the smallest things you get done.

- Remember that depression passes. Focus on living one day at a time.

- Get emotional support from a family member, friend, or mental health professional. Get involved in a fun activity with someone you enjoy. Cuddle with your mate. Spend some time with your pet.

- Talk to an understanding, nonjudgmental person for as long as you need to talk (or several people might take turns talking with you). It needs to be okay to talk about anything and to be emotional.

- Listen to or help someone else.

- Use whatever spiritual resources you are comfortable calling on.

- Get some exercise, whatever you can muster—walk, run, bike, swim, etc.

- Get out in the sunlight as much as possible. If you must be inside, sit or work near a window.

- Use full spectrum lighting indoors (read the chapter in this book on full spectrum lighting). Avoid areas lit with conventional fluorescent lights.

- Eliminate sugar, caffeine, and junk food from your diet. Eat three healthy meals a day.

- Buy yourself something you have been wanting and would enjoy.

- Read a funny or light book or watch a funny video. Listen to music that you enjoy.

- Get dressed, putting on something that makes you feel good.

- Take a long, hot bath.

7

Coming Down From Mania

"I never can understand how people can say that mania is good or fun. I suffer with it just thinking about it. It reminds me of what I've gone through."

Note: If you have depression only, rather than bipolar illness, you don't have to read this chapter.

Early Warning Signs

In order to prevent a full-blown manic attack, it is essential to be aware of your early warning signs and to take action. The following behaviors and symptoms were noted by people in the study as signals of impending manic episodes. Which behaviors and symptoms are early warning signs for you?

☐ insomnia   ☐ sleeping much less
☐ surges of energy   ☐ others seem slow
☐ flight of ideas   ☐ speech pressure
☐ writing pressure   ☐ making lots of plans

- [ ] irritability
- [ ] spending too much money
- [ ] unnecessary phone calls
- [ ] wanting to keep moving
- [ ] increased appetite
- [ ] euphoria
- [ ] feeling superior
- [ ] increased creativity
- [ ] overambition
- [ ] taking on too much responsibility
- [ ] nervous and wound up
- [ ] anxious
- [ ] overly self-involved
- [ ] negativism
- [ ] feeling unreal
- [ ] more sensitive than usual
- [ ] out of touch with reality
- [ ] inappropriate behavior
- [ ] poor judgment
- [ ] oblivious
- [ ] increased alcohol consumption
- [ ] dangerous driving
- [ ] increased community involvement
- [ ] tingly feeling
- [ ] friends notice behavior change
- [ ] inappropriate anger
- [ ] money loses its value
- [ ] difficulty staying still
- [ ] restlessness
- [ ] compulsive eating
- [ ] feeling great
- [ ] feeling very important
- [ ] obsessions
- [ ] unusual bursts of enthusiasm
- [ ] very productive
- [ ] doing several things at once
- [ ] inability to concentrate
- [ ] outbursts of temper
- [ ] disorganization
- [ ] ability to foresee things happening
- [ ] noises louder than usual
- [ ] bizarre ideas, thoughts
- [ ] laugh to self uncontrollably
- [ ] thrill seeking
- [ ] more sexually active
- [ ] danger to self and others
- [ ] spotless, energetic housekeeping
- [ ] itching
- [ ] flushed and hot
- [ ] increased sociability

"It begins with waking for a couple of days at 3 a.m. and lining up several days' work or shopping to be done in one day."

"Life feels as clear as fresh air and I am in the middle of my life, ready to act."

"I do so much work that I am exhausted and catch colds or flu easily. I feel much more alive—but it is a ragged and warped vivacity. I begin thinking I can do many things superbly."

"I catch the small signs before my chemistry blows, and take tranquilizers—or I'm gone."

"My doctor told me that insomnia is the very first sign of mania. He said that, when insomnia starts, it forces the sympathetic nervous system into 'overdrive' and, in turn, the rapid racing thoughts begin, along with poor judgment. (This doctor uses 1 mg. of Ativan for two nights at the first sign of insomnia. If it continues past two nights, he adjusts the medication to prevent it [from] going any further.) My therapist also told me it is very difficult to detect early signs, because usually the first thing to go is good judgment. She said that's why seeing a therapist or doctor weekly will help a lot, because they can pick up on signals I may not be aware of."

What are other early warning signs of mania for you? _____

_____

_____

_____

_____

_____

_____

_____

_____

Strategies for Alleviating or Eliminating Mania

Following is a checklist of ways that people in the study use to alleviate mania. These strategies are divided into five categories: activities, support, attitude, management, and spirituality. Many of these strategies are similar to those used for alleviating depression. **Which ones have you used successfully? Which ones do you feel you should use more often? Which methods have you never used that you would like to try?** Remember—what works for someone else may not be the right thing for you.

Activities	Have tried successfully	Should use more often	Would like to try
Exercise			
Long walks			
Yoga			
Reading			
Listening to music			
Long, hot baths			
Gardening			
Needlework			
Working with wood			
Working with clay, pottery			
Drawing, painting			
Journal writing			
Writing poetry			
Writing letters			
Canoeing			
Horseback riding			
Shopping			
Relaxing in a meditative natural setting			
Playing a musical instrument			
Cleaning			
Watching TV			
Watching videos, a movie, or a play			
Helping others			
Turning energy into creativity			

What other activities have you used successfully to help alleviate mania? _____

_____

_____

_____

_____

Support	Have tried successfully	Should use more often	Would like to try
Talking it out with an understanding person			
Getting emotional support from a person I trust			
Talking to a therapist or counselor			
Spending time with good friends			
Talking to staff at a crisis clinic or hotline			
Arranging not to be alone			
Reaching out to someone who understands			
Going to a support group			
Peer counseling			

What other kinds of support have been helpful to you in alleviating mania?_____

_____

_____

_____

_____

_____

_____

Attitude	Have tried successfully	Should use more often	Would like to try
Changing negative thought patterns to positive ones			
Remembering that mania ends			
Focusing on living one day at a time			
Understanding what is happening			
Staying neutral			
Stopping regularly to ask myself, "How am I feeling right now?"; bringing my mind into touch with my body			

What other attitudes have you developed and used to level out mania? _____

_____

_____

_____

_____

_____

Management	Have tried successfully	Should use more often	Would like to try
Consulting with doctor			
Sleeping			
Eating a diet high in complex carbohydrates			
Avoiding caffeine and sugar			
Maintaining a balance of rest and activity			
Avoiding stimulating places and activities			
Using relaxation tapes and exercises daily			
Writing down a list of things to do and sticking to it			
Being in a quiet room with no outside stimuli			
Using self-control as much as possible			
Biofeedback			
Staying away from alcohol and illegal drugs			
Staying home			
Avoiding overextending myself			
Stimulating the left brain (by paying attention to detail)			
Surrendering all credit cards, checks, etc. to a responsible person			
"Tying" self down emotionally to familiar surroundings			
Staying away from groups of people			
Reducing environmental stress			

"If my mania gets to be too much to handle, I should have the right to use hospitalization without feeling guilty. I like to try and use the most conservative treatment possible."

What other ways have you found to manage mania? _____

_____

_____

_____

_____

Spirituality	Have tried successfully	Should use more often	Would like to try
Prayer			
Getting in touch with my spirituality			
Extensive meditation			

What other spiritual practices help you alleviate mania? _____

_____

_____

_____

_____

Use Planning and Scheduling To Help Alleviate Mania

When experiencing a manic episode, a person may have so many ideas and so much energy that fragmentation and a lack of ability to focus can lead to a sense of not getting anything done, or not doing anything well.

The goal in mania is to stay grounded and focused enough to get something done, rather than being very scattered and initiating lots of projects that remain unfinished. A daily plan can help you meet this goal.

Refer to the lists of things you have to do and things you like to do in the chapter called "The Way Out of Depression." When planning your schedule for a manic day, include activities from both lists.

As described in that chapter, rate your expectations of an activity on a scale of 0 to 5. A 0 indicates your expectation that you could do or enjoy a given activity; a 3 indicates that you think you could do an activity and/or would enjoy it; a 5 indicates that you expect to be able to do the activity very well or that you would enjoy it immensely. An "H" in your rating categorizes the activity as a have-to-do; an "E" is the label for an activity you normally enjoy. You might give an H5 to washing the dishes when you stuck to the activity and did a very good job. Lunch with a friend might rate E2 if for some reason your friend seemed distant and preoccupied. When you complete the activity, rate how well you did it or how much you actually enjoyed yourself. This exercise should reinforce the fact that your expectations and what actually happens can be very different.

Example of a Schedule for a Person Who Is Experiencing Mania

Date: Nov. 20   *Mood*: High, manic

Time	Planned Activity and Expectation	Actual Activity	How It Felt
7-8 a.m.	Get up, shower, dress, walk the dog **H3**	(As planned)	Fine, everything feels fine **H5**
8-9 a.m.	Cook and eat breakfast; wash the dishes; start the wash **H4**	Also made bed and cleaned bathroom	Kind of speedy **H4**
9-10 a.m.	Meditate for 1/2 hour; walk to post office and drug store **H4**	(As planned)	Fine **H5**
10-11 a.m.	Peer counseling with Sue **E4**	(As planned)	She is very understanding **E5**
11-12 Noon	Clean hall closet **H1**	(As planned)	Feels good to get things organized **H5**
12-1 p.m.	Buy a grinder for lunch, eat it in the park, go for a walk **E4**	(As planned)	Played on the swings for a while **E5**

Time	Planned Activity and Expectation	Actual Activity	How It Felt
1-2 p.m.	Relax for 1/2 hour with audio tape; read for 1/2 hour *E2*	(As planned)	Hard to relax, but it helps *E4*
2-3 p.m.	Write a list and shop for groceries *H2*	(As planned)	Hard to stick with list; bought a few things I didn't need *H2*
3-4 p.m.	Put away groceries; clean the kitchen *H2*	Also swept the porch and sidewalk	Cycling up at this time of day *H3*
4-5 p.m.	Counseling appointment *E3*	(As planned)	Hard to sit still *E1*
5-6 p.m.	Write in journal; write letters to friends *E5*	Wrote 4 pages in journal along with 2 letters	I want to write and write and write *E5*
6-7 p.m.	Fix dinner of vegetable stir fry and rice; eat dinner *E4*	Also watched PBS News	Ate too fast; want to slow down *E2*
7-8 p.m.	Walk *E3*	(As planned)	Feels good to be outdoors *E5*
8-9 p.m.	Work with clay *E4*	(As planned)	Feels really good *E5*
9-10 p.m.	Relax with audio tape *E3*	(As planned)	Helped me get to sleep *E3*

Make copies of the form on the following page to plan daily schedules for yourself when you're feeling manic.

Date:		Mood:	
Time	**Planned Activity and Expectation**	**Actual Activity**	**How It Felt**
7-8 a.m.			
8-9 a.m.			
9-10 a.m.			
10-11 a.m.			
11-12 Noon			
12-1 p.m.			
1-2 p.m.			
2-3 p.m.			
3-4 p.m.			
4-5 p.m.			
5-6 p.m.			
6-7 p.m.			
7-8 p.m.			
8-9 p.m.			
9-10 p.m.			

How I felt on a day when I was manic and did not follow a plan: _____

_____

_____

_____

_____

How I felt on a day when I was manic and followed a plan: _____

_____

_____

_____

_____

Based on my experience, I intend to take the following action with regard to scheduling my days closely when I am manic: _____

_____

_____

_____

_____

<u>*(time of day)*</u>_____ *is the best time for me to make plans when I am manic.*

Breaking Tasks Down Into Smaller Components

Breaking tasks down into smaller components can be helpful when you're manic. In mania you may be able to get a lot done, but you are moving so fast that the quality of your work may suffer. (I was nicknamed "Smash, Rip, and Ruin" by some friends during one of my manic episodes!) By analyzing tasks, and by having a clear picture of how to accomplish what you want, you can stabilize both your performance and your mood.

Make a list of tasks that are hard for you to accomplish satisfactorily when you're manic:

_____

_____

_____

_____

_____

_____

_____

Take one of the tasks you listed, and break it down into smaller incremental components. This will make it easier for you to do a good job, even if your mood is extremely high.

Step 1 _____

_____

Step 2 _____

_____

Step 3 _____

_____

Step 4 _____

_____

Step 5 _____

_____

Step 6 _____

_____

Step 7 _____

_____

Step 8 _____

_____

People in the study added these thoughts:

> "I shop with credit cards and leave all tickets on items for easier exchange and refunds, but sometimes outsmart myself by removing tickets so I can keep items."

> "I use exercise coupled with warm, soothing beverages and baths—conscious relaxation."

"While ill, I seemed to be more easily influenced—especially by music. After the illness, I learned to use music to gain control of my moods. When my moods or emotions are more in control, my thoughts change and become manageable, too."

"My husband uses my energy to hire for our home's benefit. He rented a jack hammer to tear up a sidewalk. 'Let me try,' I said, so he did. Four hours later he gave me a list of safe things to do. 'No problem,' I said, and three days later my energy was gone—and so was being manic."

Seeking Help for Dealing With Mania

Most people who responded to the study felt that getting help early was important in avoiding mania. **When do you seek help for mania**?

- ☐ when I have difficulty sleeping
- ☐ the moment I'm aware of "going up"
- ☐ when I start getting too busy
- ☐ when I'm very restless
- ☐ when I start to feel high
- ☐ when I'm psychotic
- ☐ at the instant of the switch
- ☐ when I'm out of control
- ☐ when I can't sit still
- ☐ when I'm acting differently
- ☐ when I'm hallucinating
- ☐ before I am out of reality
- ☐ when I feel too aggressive
- ☐ when it becomes stressful
- ☐ when I am using poor judgment
- ☐ when I'm unable to make plans
- ☐ when my therapist confronts me
- ☐ when I become grandiose and paranoid
- ☐ when I am a danger to myself or others
- ☐ when my spending is out of control
- ☐ when I feel the pressure of thoughts
- ☐ when the mania continues for more than two days
- ☐ when I start getting into trouble with other people
- ☐ when I become extremely tired and my body aches but I still can't slow down
- ☐ when the best I can do for myself is not enough to get me through

☐ when I feel like I have to act on a huge decision with real urgency
☐ when I start overdoing and feel irritable to the point of being enraged
☐ when I feel as though something is eating away at my brain and I will go berserk
☐ before I have lost three or four nights of sleep, spent all my money, and seduced half the world

What kind of help do you seek when you feel you need assistance in dealing with mania?

☐ psychiatric care   ☐ psychotherapy
☐ hospitalization   ☐ self-help groups
☐ crisis hotline   ☐ assurance, a hug
☐ self-help books   ☐ medication
☐ counseling   ☐ friends
☐ crisis clinic staff   ☐ 12-step program
☐ family

"I seek out someone who is understanding, has similar problems, knows how to be calm, and will not alienate me."

"My family is well educated and knows my views on the illness. They have my permission to get me the help I need when I am not capable of making decisions for myself."

"My friends have instructions and permission to force neuroleptic medication."

"I let my roommate and parents have open communication with each other and my doctor. There have been times when I didn't notice the change coming on and they did. They were able to alert my doctor and watch me more closely, and some potential situations were stopped before they got out of hand. I had to swallow a lot of pride and let others step in when needed; but over time, we've reached a compromise of restrictions (no overprotectiveness) and extreme trust."

Inducing Mania

Some people who took part in the study have tried to induce mania, usually because of long-term chronic depression. However, overwhelmingly, the people in the study agreed that this is a *very dangerous thing to do and should be avoided under any circumstances.*

How People Want To Be Treated When They're Manic

How do you like to be treated when you're manic? These are some of the preferences described by people in the study. Check the descriptions that match your own feelings. *I want people to*

- ☐ get help for me as soon as possible to save me from having too many pieces to pick up after it is over
- ☐ understand that I am doing my best to cope
- ☐ treat me the same as when I'm not manic
- ☐ give me space, leave me alone
- ☐ treat me gently, calmly
- ☐ be tough, with an eye on reality
- ☐ treat me with respect
- ☐ treat me as a person who needs help
- ☐ treat me with support
- ☐ let me enjoy myself
- ☐ give me guidance
- ☐ support my self-care efforts
- ☐ make me aware
- ☐ treat me with compassion
- ☐ treat me firmly
- ☐ treat me with patience
- ☐ take me seriously
- ☐ treat me with love
- ☐ listen
- ☐ encourage me
- ☐ slow me down
- ☐ be available
- ☐ encourage me to avoid stress
- ☐ go with the mood, yet control my irrational behavior
- ☐ realize that I have a medical problem and it is not just me
- ☐ put me in the hospital to get me regulated on drugs
- ☐ be calm, to smell the edge of sadness emanating from mania, to refuse to be sucked in my garish, warped enthusiasm

In what other ways would you like to be treated when you're manic? _____

_____

_____

_____

_____

_____

What People Don't Want From Others During Manic Episodes

Some friends and family members always know the right things to do and say; others only make things worse! Participants in the study cited many behaviors and attitudes on the part of others that just make things worse. **Which ones can you relate to**?

- ☐ reinforcement of manic behaviors
- ☐ taking advantage of me
- ☐ abandonment
- ☐ being treated coldly
- ☐ being treated with cruelty
- ☐ being stigmatized
- ☐ believing everything I say
- ☐ avoidance
- ☐ reacting with fear
- ☐ blaming me
- ☐ ridicule
- ☐ anger
- ☐ reserve
- ☐ indignation
- ☐ being ignored
- ☐ terseness
- ☐ hatred
- ☐ being rebuffed
- ☐ being teased
- ☐ reacting with disgust
- ☐ being patronizing
- ☐ acting exasperated
- ☐ reacting with confusion
- ☐ impatience
- ☐ expecting all I promise to be accomplished
- ☐ acting like they sense something is wrong with me
- ☐ giving me more things to do
- ☐ raising their expectations of me

"People worry more about me when I am 'high.' In many instances, my depressions are ignored. People want to subdue my behavior and expect me to stay in the background and not deal with my problems. I don't like being treated this way."

Describe what else you don't want from others when you're manic:_____

_____

_____

_____

_____

Handling Inappropriate Treatment

How should you handle treatment by others when you're manic? Here's what people in the study group said:

- ☐ ignore it
- ☐ try to educate others
- ☐ withdraw
- ☐ count to ten
- ☐ thoughtfully
- ☐ keep trying
- ☐ find understanding friends
- ☐ quietly
- ☐ give in more
- ☐ listen to music
- ☐ find the right help for myself
- ☐ address the issue and talk it out
- ☐ avoid people
- ☐ be patient
- ☐ go to the doctor
- ☐ think through their side of the situation
- ☐ apologize
- ☐ forgive
- ☐ maintain my dignity
- ☐ meditate
- ☐ assertively
- ☐ try to be in control as much as I can
- ☐ wait until I am more level and then handle it if the situation still seems unfair
- ☐ with judgment—but that is what is lacking when I'm manic
- ☐ I like to be able to say, "I am out of control and need your help"
- ☐ later educate them and make my preferences known
- ☐ tell them to look at the positive aspects of my behavior
- ☐ tell them what I think about the way they treat me
- ☐ talk specifically about it in *I* and *them* statements when I am feeling in better control

Describe how you would like to change your response to people when they treat you inappropriately during the times when you're manic:_____

_____

_____

_____

_____

_____

Responding to "Slow Down"

When people are experiencing mania, others often tell them to "slow down," "relax," or "take it easy." People in the study responded in a variety of ways to such statements. **Which answers reflect the way you feel when people tell you to "slow down"?**

- ☐ okay
- ☐ I don't listen
- ☐ I don't like it
- ☐ I try to comply
- ☐ I become irritated
- ☐ I call my doctor and check it out
- ☐ I feel insulted
- ☐ I tell them that whatever I am doing is important
- ☐ I tell them I will when things ease up
- ☐ I feel agitated
- ☐ I feel confused
- ☐ I try to take control, and feel frustrated when I can't
- ☐ I feel resentment
- ☐ I ignore them
- ☐ I tell them to hurry up
- ☐ I feel puzzled
- ☐ I agree
- ☐ I feel embarrassed
- ☐ I feel that they have discovered I am sick
- ☐ I try to listen but am unable to
- ☐ I feel hurt
- ☐ I become more vigilant about myself
- ☐ it feels too good to care what others say
- ☐ I feel that they are laggards and spiritless
- ☐ I feel like they don't understand that I can't slow down
- ☐ I've learned about my own behavior from the observations of others
- ☐ I feel like they are in slow motion and should try to hurry up
- ☐ I feel they are wrong—there is nothing wrong with me

☐ they can't realize you have this power to ration things out quickly and accurately

☐ I feel that they are being wet blankets and don't want me to have fun

☐ I accept it from my spouse; from others I do not like it

In what other ways do you respond when people tell you to slow down? _____

_____

_____

_____

_____

Dealing With Embarrassment and Guilt

Many people have a difficult time dealing with the embarrassment and guilt that often follow an acute manic attack. People in the study responded in the ways described below.

Mark which of these reactions reflects how you have handled the embarrassment or guilt when you've realized you've behaved in a bizarre manner when you were manic. Think about which of these reactions seem most appropriate and/or in your own best interest.

When I feel embarrassed and guilty after a manic episode, I

☐ apologize

☐ don't blame myself, I blame the illness

☐ try to erase it from my mind

☐ get up and go on, swallow it, cope, etc.

☐ give matter-of-fact explanations

☐ laugh and let it blow over

☐ forgive myself

☐ try not to make it more than it was

☐ withdraw

☐ make amends

☐ turn it inwards

☐ send homemade "I'm sorry" cards

☐ cry

☐ feel like I hate myself, that I'm dirty

☐ try to pass it off

☐ try to avoid repeating that type of action

- ☐ avoid feeling guilty
- ☐ try to keep my dignity
- ☐ take the punishment
- ☐ make swift corrections of the situation
- ☐ attend Al-Anon meetings
- ☐ sometimes put distance and time between me and the person involved—I withdraw
- ☐ discuss it and face my feelings with a therapist or another understanding person
- ☐ realize that all the important people involved are health professionals or friends who understand the situation

"[I react with] lots of blushing, quivering, stammering, shying away and avoiding people."

"I have made mistakes the same as everyone else. I talk and apologize about them the same as others."

"Depression can be made worse and longer lasting by the things I've done during a manic period. Sometimes I've offended people and then become afraid to rekindle a friendship with them. Sometimes people are also afraid to approach me again. I've lost some good friends because of this. For a number of years my life became stagnant because of my fear of interacting with people. The fear led to mistrust and resentment."

In order to ease the guilt and embarrassment for themselves, people in the study have used the following techniques. **Which ones have you used?**

- ☐ medications
- ☐ exercise to try and release energy
- ☐ therapy
- ☐ "come out" as manic depressive
- ☐ apply as much humor as possible
- ☐ have a strong support system
- ☐ have someone with me wherever I go
- ☐ ride it out
- ☐ cognitive therapy
- ☐ close down emotionally
- ☐ humor and openness
- ☐ effectively manage the illness
- ☐ leave room for unexpected stresses
- ☐ prevention through self-monitoring

☐ avoid stressful activity
☐ progress to control highs
☐ make amends
☐ forgive myself
☐ join a support group
☐ maintain an easy lifestyle
☐ follow doctor's orders
☐ hide it
☐ acceptance of the illness
☐ keep my dignity
☐ go with the flow
☐ avoid overextending myself
☐ catch mania before it gets out of hand
☐ personal training and extensive self-practice
☐ jump back into life and start back up again
☐ be honest with those close enough to care or who want to care
☐ try not to think about it a lot (guilt can paralyze us from relating to others and this relating is vital if you have a mood disorder)
☐ discuss it and face the feelings with a psychiatrist, therapist, or friend
☐ educate others about manic depression
☐ tell myself I'm not responsible, because I was temporarily out of control
☐ try to realize I have never done anything too bizarre and take comfort in that knowledge
☐ move to a new area where I can relate to people in stable ways (using lithium)
☐ I decided it wasn't worth the effort to make most people understand

What other ways of easing guilt and embarrassment have you found to be useful following a period of mania? _____

_____

_____

_____

_____

_____

How can you best handle your guilt and embarrassment in the future? _____

_____

_____

_____

_____

_____

Increased Libido in Mania

Many people in the study have experienced increased libido when manic. These are some of the strategies they've used to manage it.

- ☐ masturbation
- ☐ having frequent sex with mate
- ☐ abstinence in some situations
- ☐ more active sex life
- ☐ going with the flow
- ☐ enjoying it
- ☐ agreeing with partner to extramarital sex
- ☐ flirting heavily but never carrying through
- ☐ multiple partners (dangerous these days)
- ☐ controlling it
- ☐ no problem, spouse loves it
- ☐ fantasizing
- ☐ recognizing the feelings, but not reacting
- ☐ asking assistance from trusted friends
- ☐ staying away from situations that might be overtly tempting or compromising
- ☐ expressing how I feel and looking for someone to fulfill my need

"I have been in counseling for a year with a doctor who helped me understand that it is not me but the disease."

How I plan to deal with the increased libido of mania in the future: _____

_____

_____

_____

_____

Dealing With Psychosis

People in the study reported that they frequently experienced psychosis (being out of touch with reality) when they were manic. Below are some of the ways in which they respond. Check the reactions that correspond with your own experience.

When I experience psychosis in mania, I

- ☐ contact my doctor
- ☐ adjust my medication
- ☐ let it happen
- ☐ call my therapist
- ☐ enjoy it but don't tell anyone
- ☐ seek hospitalization
- ☐ tell people I trust
- ☐ reduce sensory input
- ☐ try to sleep and relax
- ☐ sort out delusion from reality
- ☐ remain calm and don't get frightened
- ☐ travel only with friends or family, not alone

In what other ways have you reacted to psychosis in mania? _____

_____

_____

_____

_____

My plan for dealing with psychosis in the future is: _____

_____

_____

_____

_____

Increased Clarity

Increased clarity is a symptom of mania experienced by many people who participated in the survey. They handle or use this clarity in a variety of ways. **Which of these ways have you used successfully?** *When my clarity increases as a symptom of mania, I*

☐ write a lot
☐ catch up on projects
☐ enjoy it
☐ go with it as long as it lasts
☐ use it to see the bigger picture more clearly
☐ express myself more
☐ get a lot done
☐ try to make changes
☐ take advantage of it
☐ realize that my thoughts are so quick, I am not making rational decisions
☐ set priorities more easily and come up with solutions or compromises
☐ recognize it as a delusion

"I decrease stimuli, regulate my time so I have less time to work on things, increase routine, remind myself that I am high and it is not dangerous."

"At first I doubt if my 'new' perceptions are reliable. Soon I am convinced they are truer and crisper than everyone else's."

"I ride it like a wave, because I know the time is limited. I try to pace myself so I don't overextend. I put together a stigma-busting workshop at a conference, which I thought was very creative and enlightened; but I am not sure whether anyone else did."

What other ideas do you have about ways in which to use this increased clarity? _____

_____

_____

_____

_____

_____

Increase in Intensity of Mania Relative to the Time of Day

Many people experience an increase in the intensity of mania as the day goes on. People in the study use the strategies below for dealing with this increase in intensity. Check the strategies that are relevant to your own experience. *If my mania increases in intensity as the day wears on, I*

☐ use medication
☐ work hard
☐ draw
☐ write in my journal
☐ do relaxation exercises
☐ talk it out with a supportive person

☐ lower my stressful activities
☐ read a good book or write letters
☐ focus on self-care activities
☐ listen to music
☐ try to mentally ride it out

What other strategies have you used? _____

_____

_____

_____

_____

Very few people in the study said that their mania was more intense in the morning; but when this is the case, they deal with it by

☐ getting up and getting busy
☐ trying to accomplish what I need to get done during this time
☐ trying to do things to tire me out

If you experience more intense mania in the morning, what other ways do you have of managing it? _____

_____

_____

_____

_____

At what time of day is your mania most intense? _____

How are you going to deal with that in the future? _____

_____

_____

_____

_____

_____

Increased Intensity of Mania at Different Times of the Month

Thirteen people in the study noticed that their mania is more intense at different times of the month. Women tend to notice that their mania is more intense just before ovulation and menstruation. **When is mania most intense for you**? _____

    Women in the study have developed various coping strategies to deal with the problem of manic surges. If this has been a problem for you, **which coping strategies have you used**?

☐ trying not to make important decisions at that time
☐ increasing certain medications as recommended by my doctor
☐ reminding myself that this will pass
☐ taking PMS medication
☐ taking progesterone
☐ letting someone else handle my business at that time
☐ scheduling activities heavily then
☐ exercising five or six times a week
☐ charting menstrual cycle to maintain awareness and better utilize up-surge of energy in a constructive way
☐ enjoying it, because I am more relaxed at this time (pre-ovulation)

Other:_____

_____

How do you plan to deal with this problem in the future? _____

_____

_____

_____

_____

_____

_____

Seasonal Patterns and Mania

Twenty-eight people noted a seasonal pattern to their mania. Most of them found that they are more likely to be manic in the spring, with summer ranking second and fall ranking third. Only a few people said they had experienced mania in the winter. **If you have noticed a seasonal pattern to your mania, what is it?**_____

Which of these ways of dealing with these patterns has helped you?

☐ be aware
☐ keep the doctor informed
☐ expect the unexpected
☐ save projects to do at this time
☐ channel energy into projects
☐ relax as much as possible
☐ go with the flow

☐ enjoy it
☐ go out a lot
☐ regular medication checks
☐ monitor carefully at these times
☐ rely on family to help me through
☐ try to keep it under control

☐ in the spring I sleep on the west instead of the east side of house to keep morning light from setting it off

How do you plan to deal with the seasonal aspects of your mania in the future? _____

_____

_____

_____

_____

You have just explored your experience of mania in an in-depth manner. Based on what you have discovered through this exercise, **what changes are you going to make in the way you handle mania?**_____

_____

_____

_____

_____

_____

_____

What To Do When You Are Getting Manic

Photocopy this section—or rewrite it to suit your own needs; then post it on your refrigerator.

- Get help before things get out of hand. Do not hesitate to call a doctor if you need one.

- Use your support system. Let your supporters know how you are feeling. Talk with them for as long as you need to, expressing all emotions that come up.

- Stay at home or in familiar surroundings. Steer clear of stimulating environments such as bars or dances.

- Reduce the stress in your environment. Keep away from stressful people.

- Make a list of things to do for the day and stick to it.

- Regulate your activities to avoid overstimulation. Restrict yourself to activities that are quiet and soothing, such as a long, slow walk; a long, warm bath; a relaxing swim; sitting for a while in a steam room or hot tub; listening to quiet music; reading a soothing book; watching a nature show on TV.

- Keep a list of things you can do to use up excess energy, such as washing the floor, weeding the garden, painting, cleaning out closets; but make sure that these activities are not overstimulating.

- Practice relaxation techniques several times during the day.

- Avoid sugar, caffeine, and alcohol. Eat regular meals. Do not skip meals. Do not eat too much of any one thing.

- Do not make any major decisions. Put off decisions until you feel calmer.

- Do not commit yourself to extra activities outside your usual routine (unless they're things that you've chosen for the express purpose of burning up excessive energy).

- Avoid spending money. Give your credit cards and money to a trusted support person.

- Regularly stop what you're doing, bring your focus onto yourself, and ask yourself how you are doing. Keep your mind focused on what you are doing. Don't allow your thoughts to ramble or become obsessive.

- If all of your relaxation techniques are not working to put you to sleep, and you are not sleeping, get help from a doctor right away. Loss of sleep exacerbates mania.

8

Using a Chart To Keep Your Moods Controlled

Develop a chart using the one included here as a guide, listing your own early warning signs that your mood needs attention. While many of these signs are experienced almost universally by people who have depressive episodes, others may be unique to you. That's why it's essential to create a chart that's tailored to you individually.

Check the chart at the same time each day to help you determine how you're feeling. The chart will enable you to respond early, before the situation gets out of hand and is harder to bring back under control.

Even small changes are important and need to be recognized. It's particularly important to use the chart regularly in those seasons when you have had problems before, or in times of acute stress, such as when you are beginning a new job, beginning a new relationship, embarking on parenthood, or suffering a loss or illness.

After you design your chart, make a good supply of copies to have available. I make my charts up with space for checking off moods and behaviors for one week. That way I can get an overview of how I'm doing. If your chart is as long as mine, you may want to use legal-size paper, so you can get it all on one side for easy review.

Save charts after you have used them. This record will allow you and your health care team to analyze patterns in your mood swings.

Get input on developing your chart from your health care professionals and other members of your support system. They may be able to bring to your attention danger signs that you may have overlooked or ignored. The chart will also assist them in understanding and making appropriate recommendations about your treatment. When the chart is complete, give everyone on your support team a copy. This will give them a handy reference for checking in on how you're feeling.

This is the chart that I use. Remember—you have to tailor it to your own needs, based on your knowledge about your own patterns of thought and behavior.

Warning Signs
Daily Checklist

I will be honest with myself in this assessment. When I note signs of mania or depression, I will let my support system know and will take the necessary corrective action.

Month and Year _____

Early Warning Signs of Depression:	Mon.	Tues.	Wed.	Thurs.	Fri.	Sat.	Sun.
Excessive appetite							
Lethargy							
Extreme fatigue							
Difficulty exercising							
Unwillingness to ask for things							
Down on self							
Down on future							
Low self-confidence							
Procrastination							
Avoid crowds							
Irritable, impatient							
Negative attitude							
Insecurity							
Hard time getting up							
Sleep problems							
Poor judgment							
Obsessive thoughts							
Repetitive words, actions							
Unable to concentrate							
Misperceptions							
Destructive risk-taking							
Suicidal thoughts							
Paranoia							
Unable to experience pleasure							

Early Warning Signs of Mania:	Mon.	Tues.	Wed.	Thurs.	Fri.	Sat.	Sun.
Insomnia							
Argumentative							
All-knowing							
Controlling							
Overcommitting							
High energy							
Racing thoughts							
Very talkative							
Obsessive thoughts							
Sexually overactive							
Thrill-seeking							
Irresponsible risk-taking							
Poor judgment							
Change in appetite							
Self-medicating							
Drug or alcohol abuse							

What To Do Every Day (*Check off activities or behaviors that you manage to fit into each day*)	Mon.	Tues.	Wed.	Thurs.	Fri.	Sat.	Sun.
Eat well (high carbohydrate, low fat, no sugar)							
Exercise							
Take good care of self							
Be with positive people							
Get plenty of light							
Spend at least one hour outside							
Talk with support system							
Have fun							

Medications (*Record the medications* *you use each day*)	Mon.	Tues.	Wed.	Thurs.	Fri.	Sat.	Sun.

Use the early warning signs from the previous two chapters, "The Way Out of Depression" and "Coming Down From Mania," as well as input from people in your support system, to help you in developing your personal chart of early warning signs. Make copies of your chart for on-going use (here's a sample of a format you can use).

Early Warning Signs

Month and Year _____

Early Warning Signs of Depression:	Mon.	Tues.	Wed.	Thurs.	Fri.	Sat.	Sun.

Early Warning Signs of Mania:	Mon.	Tues.	Wed.	Thurs.	Fri.	Sat.	Sun.

What To Do Every Day (*Check off activities or behaviors that you manage to fit into each day*)	Mon.	Tues.	Wed.	Thurs.	Fri.	Sat.	Sun.

Medications (Record the medications you use each day)	Mon.	Tues.	Wed.	Thurs.	Fri.	Sat.	Sun.

Comments: _____

_____

_____

_____

Necessary Action: _____

_____

_____

_____

PART II

Support Is Essential

9

Building a Strong Support System

*I know of others who have done research similar to yours. I believe they
found from respondents that the most common reason for recovery is that
someone believed in them. This is most often the catalyst in recovery.*

All people need at least five good friends or supporters they can call on when they need
someone to talk to—people who can count on you when they need a friend as well. Family
members and partners are also candidates for your support network. Choose people whom
you love and trust. They should be people who can

- *Empathize with you*, be able to say, "I understand what you are going through,"
  and "I can see that this is a really difficult time for you."

- *Affirm your individuality and your strengths*; treat you with love, humor, and honesty; validate and encourage your dreams.

- *Play with you*—sing, dance, join you in whatever fun activity you both enjoy!

- *Be open-minded*, let you describe how you are, what you feel, and what you want.

- *Accept your ups and downs* without being judgmental, who can help you as well
  as ask for your help.

- *Work with you* as you decide on your next best step, and support you as you carry through.

List five people on whom you can count in these ways. (These may or may not include the four proxies you named in Chapter 4.)

1. _____
2. _____
3. _____
4. _____
5. _____

This is a very hard exercise for many people. When they realize that they have no one, or only one or two people, it makes them feel very bad and increases their feelings of loneliness and isolation. If this is your reaction, don't give up. There is a lot you can do to change the situation. Changing this situation is very important to your wellness.

☐ *I wish I had more friends and a stronger support system.*

Many people in the study expressed feelings of loneliness and isolation. They feel deserted by family and friends; often these feelings are based in reality. The resulting social isolation further exacerbates their mood disorder.

These are some of the reasons that people in the study gave for the fact that they have a hard time making and keeping friends. **Which attributes apply to you**?

☐ low self-esteem
☐ tend to be very needy and draining
☐ unreliable
☐ unpredictable
☐ have a hard time reaching out
☐ become overly dependent on one or a few people, wearing them down
☐ inappropriate behavior embarrasses and turns off others
☐ lack of social skills

The kind of support people in the study said they wanted from their support system varies. **What do you want from your support system**?

☐ mutual support   ☐ companionship
☐ someone to talk to   ☐ someone who will listen
☐ understanding   ☐ caring
☐ counsel   ☐ empathy
☐ acceptance   ☐ sharing
☐ advocacy   ☐ monitoring

☐ diversion   ☐ activities
☐ time   ☐ correspondence
☐ phone calls

Other ways you would like a friend to be, and things you would like a friend to do: __

_____

_____

_____

Keys To Building and Keeping a Strong Support System

Use all the techniques described in this book to keep your moods as stable as possible. Enhance your wellness every way you know how.

I use the following techniques to keep my moods as stable as possible: _____

_____

_____

_____

Work with a counselor on development of appropriate social skills.

☐ *I am going to work with my counselor on developing appropriate social skills so that I can build a stronger support system.*

Use peer counseling techniques to work on the development of appropriate social skills and to build close relationships with other people (see the chapter entitled "How About Counseling?").

I am going to peer counsel with _____ to work on the development of my social skills.

Become an active member of a support group for people with mood disorders (see "Support Groups"). Check your newspaper, call your mental health center, or ask your counselor for information on support groups. This is the key vehicle by which people in the study found friends and established new family-type groups to replace those that had been lost. Some people even found appropriate partners in these groups.

☐ *I already belong to a support group.*
☐ *I'm going to join a support group for people with mood disorders.*
☐ *There is no support group in my area so I'm going to start one.*

You can do this by finding a place to gather and putting a notice in the newspaper. A community mental health center or your counselor could assist you in doing this (see "Support Groups").

Participate in community activities and special interest groups. Use your local newspaper to keep current with what is going on and then participate in those activities that interest you.

Community activities and special interest groups that I would like to check out include: _____

_____

_____

Do volunteer work. There are many agencies that could use your help. Inquire at churches, schools, hospitals, youth agencies, soup kitchens, the Red Cross, and so on. Some communities have organizations that organize volunteers: these are an excellent resource when you are looking for just the right place to become a volunteer.

I am going to explore volunteering in the following places: _____

_____

_____

This is what people in the study had to say about volunteer work:

> "When you give of yourself to others, your own problems have a way of solving themselves."

> "I volunteer in a local high school filling out financial aid forms—I do a good job for the students, and it makes me feel worthwhile. My experiences have given inspiration to others who are temporarily down. I get and give tremendous support from and to loyal friends and family, and I have never given up on life."

> "I feel much better when I'm doing something for others or that I enjoy. I like to do things for others and not always let them know it was me."

Be mutually supportive. This means being there for others when they need you, as well as expecting them to be there for you when you need them.

☐ *I am going to pay more attention to the needs of my friends.*

Keep in touch with friends and acquaintances. Many of us lose contact with people we enjoy simply because we don't keep in touch. When you meet someone you like, invite him or her out for tea, lunch, or to share an activity. When you're parting, make a plan for the next time you'll get together. Renew acquaintances with old friends by inviting them for tea or lunch, or to share an activity with you. I have several close friends with whom I have a set time every week when we get together for an hour.

I am going to renew contact with the following friends and acquaintances: _____

_____

_____

_____

I am going to schedule regular times to get together with: _____

_____

_____

_____

It's important that you have several friends so you don't put an undue strain on any one of them. Paying attention to their needs is important for you as well as for them. I can't emphasize this too much.

Now, try it again! **List five supportive or potentially supportive friends.**

1. _____

2. _____

3. _____

4. _____

5. _____

10

Finding Appropriate
Health Care
Professionals

*My doctor listens to me and my ideas and perceptions of the illness, gives
me suggestions, involves me in all levels of my treatment, and treats my
mood swings like any other recurring illness.*

Finding appropriate health care professionals who are willing to work with you on alleviating and/or eliminating mood problems is often a difficult task, especially when you are experiencing a deep depression or acute mania. However, locating such people is essential. This is a time when family members and friends who are well educated about mood disorders can be helpful. Ask your proxies for assistance if the task of finding good care is more than you feel you can handle.

Through the self-education process, and individual interviews where appropriate, you will be able to determine which health care professionals can best assist you in working toward wellness and stability.

Those in the study almost unanimously recommend that people with mood swings explore a variety of approaches, including safe and noninvasive holistic or alternative therapies. In addition to my endocrinologist, psychiatrist, and therapist, at various times in the course of my treatment I have worked with a homeopathic physician, an acupuncturist, a chiropractor, a body worker, a movement therapist, and a career counselor. Each of these people has played an important and essential role in my treatment, as well as enhancing my wellness.

Study participants gave the following reasons for exploring a variety of treatment strategies. **Which reasons reflect your feelings, too**?

- ☐ It is the only hope.
- ☐ The more we can learn, the more we can do to control our condition.
- ☐ Any reduction of severity or incidence of mood swings helps.
- ☐ I feel more comfortable with alternative treatment.
- ☐ No one has all the answers to mental health.
- ☐ Medical approaches are very limited, biased, and exclusionary—the surface has merely been scratched.
- ☐ Treatments are so new in this field that much is yet to be accomplished.
- ☐ There is no one answer for everyone; controlling the symptoms must be dealt with first, then individuals must explore their own problems.
- ☐ Anything that can be gently effective is preferable.
- ☐ The action of searching for alternative approaches is a signal of hope and a willingness to try.
- ☐ Misdiagnosis is a possibility.
- ☐ The symptoms can come not just from the genes, but from an inappropriate lifestyle.
- ☐ Lithium is usually not enough for happiness and productivity.
- ☐ Traditional treatments are not working.
- ☐ One has to do so much for oneself; the physicians cannot do it all.
- ☐ Different people respond differently to different approaches.
- ☐ There's bound to be something that will work—it just takes time to find it.
- ☐ We must do whatever we can to feel healthy, safe, and normal.
- ☐ A careful, inquisitive person can benefit in many ways.
- ☐ Any information that is helpful should be gathered to form a personal program.
- ☐ Always be open to suggestions that may help, always be willing to at least try, because you never know what may help until you try.
- ☐ Don't give up trying—you are important; you have a right to seek happiness, and you have a life to live.

Other reasons why you might explore alternative or holistic health care strategies: ____

_____

_____

_____

You have to decide which treatment is right for you, what works best for you, and the treatment strategies with which you are most comfortable.

Cost can be a limiting factor in determining your health care team. Coverage by Medicaid, Medicare, and other insurance is generally limited.

What kind of treatment does your health insurance cover? What are the limitations of your coverage? _____

_____

_____

_____

☐ I plan to advocate for appropriate health insurance coverage.

Health care professionals I want to include on my support team:

☐ medical doctors   ☐ psychiatrists
☐ psychopharmacologists   ☐ endocrinologists
☐ allergists   ☐ pharmacists
☐ therapists or counselors   ☐ social workers
☐ osteopaths   ☐ chiropractors
☐ body workers   ☐ are therapists
☐ nutritional therapists   ☐ occupational therapists
☐ homeopathic physicians   ☐ massage therapists

Others whom you want to include in your health care team:_____

_____

_____

Whom I plan to consult in setting up a team of health care professionals:

☐ other people who have mood disorders
☐ your general practitioner or a highly respected medical doctor
☐ respected mental health professionals
☐ mental health clinic

☐ hospital staff members
☐ mental health organization
☐ support group
☐ psychiatric association
☐ Better Business Bureau
☐ state university
☐ clergy

Others who might give recommendations on finding appropriate mental health professionals:_____

_____

_____

_____

Study participants recommend that you

• shop around

• network

• interview until you find professionals with whom you're comfortable

• keep changing if necessary until you find those who are knowledgeable and interested

Other strategies you are going to use to find appropriate mental health professionals for yourself:_____

_____

_____

_____

What attributes do you want from the health professionals on your team? (Remember, these qualities may differ according to the services you desire.) *I want to work with health professionals who*

☐ monitor my condition and prescribe accordingly
☐ are willing to use minimal medication dosages
☐ use appropriate testing procedures
☐ are willing to use a team approach
☐ are willing to explore and try new approaches
☐ listen well

- ☐ are caring
- ☐ are accepting
- ☐ are compassionate
- ☐ are supportive
- ☐ are perceptive
- ☐ consider individual needs
- ☐ are willing to be flexible
- ☐ are easy to communicate with
- ☐ are optimistic
- ☐ promote mutual understanding
- ☐ are empathetic
- ☐ are friendly
- ☐ are gentle and warm
- ☐ are trustworthy
- ☐ emphasize self-care
- ☐ share religious background
- ☐ are respectful
- ☐ are compatible
- ☐ have a sense of humor
- ☐ know the dangers of mood disorders
- ☐ promote individual growth
- ☐ can be firm and protective when necessary
- ☐ have expert knowledge of mood disorders
- ☐ allow me to make my own decisions about treatment
- ☐ are willing to keep trying until appropriate, successful treatments are found
- ☐ have ample time to provide adequate services
- ☐ encourage development of positive self-esteem
- ☐ are knowledgeable about medications, side effects, and the latest medical advances
- ☐ are willing to educate me and members of my support system about mood swings
- ☐ specialize in working with people with mood swings
- ☐ are usually available and have appropriate people to cover at other times
- ☐ have personally experienced mood disorders
- ☐ are able to admit the possibility of being wrong or not knowing what to do
- ☐ understand and adjust to my personal financial constraints
- ☐ know me and can quickly access my moods

☐ only resort to hospitalization when a danger exists to myself or others
☐ encourage responsibility for myself
☐ are fluent and easily understood in my language

Other attributes you want from health care professionals:_____

_____

_____

_____

The following are quotes from study participants sharing their view of ideal health care professionals:

"I want health care professionals who are willing to try other medications if one doesn't work and who feel I should feel as well as possible with few side effects."

"I want someone who is current on drug treatment, compassionate, open-minded, and willing to defer to and work with others."

"I want a health care team with more emphasis on alternative/supplemental kinds of treatment (vitamins, exercise, etc.), creating options and education. Using the whole person approach is indicated because of the effects which appear in every aspect of the person's life. The limits of traditional psychiatry must be recognized."

"My health care professionals must acknowledge that what I am feeling is real."

"...[someone who] identifies the cyclical nature of mood swings, gives credit to internal struggles, looks for established warning signs, knows that medications are not the whole answer, and strives to allow me as much independence as possible."

"...[someone who] talks about your feelings before, during, and after they occur, helping you figure out what triggers them."

"...someone who would hear my thoughts and treat me as a peer who was currently having difficulties, and would not suggest fixing it all with just medications."

"I need someone with whom I can check in twice a week, have a regular session every two weeks, and talk about suicidal feelings without feeling threatened."

"The professional must be willing to make sure that the diagnosis is accurate."

"I am a woman and I feel I must work with females, as I have a fear of male superiority brought on by abuse in my family."

"I want people on my health care team who are receptive to the idea of self-help, are honest, encouraging, very knowledgeable medically, and caring."

"The team approach works best for me, as it encourages doctors to try new approaches. It keeps me more informed about the medications. They listen to me when I say I have a problem taking medications due to my allergies and responses to medications. I am part of the team, not a victim of treatment."

"My doctor is a brain researcher who truly believes that bipolar disorder is a brain dysfunction. [My doctor] treats me like any other person with any disease—no discrimination, stigmatization, condescension, or paternalism. I am a respected, integral part of the planning of my treatment and management of my symptoms."

"…must impart a sense of reasonable confidence in you—a realistic person who monitors your drug levels and who helps you when you deliberately go off your medications—who doesn't give you a hard time when you get into trouble and call for help…getting and giving you help and being matter of fact—not punishing—is very important."

"I prefer that before medications are given, more is found out about the individual. A couple of days of observation and rest should preface any drug therapy; the patient must be given some choices to regain control. This active participation helps raise self-esteem and gives the person a sense of regaining control over their problem."

"My psychiatrist is retiring, and it's time to look for a new one. I had a good friendship with this fellow and hope to find some of his qualities in my new choice. He (or she) must be seasoned (I can live with a little rust), aggressive with medication (high miles per gallon), take an interest in my life's interests (tinted windows), does not dabble in psychological therapy (skip the vinyl roof), considers patient education as part of the services (full instrument control panel), is comfortable in using electroshock treatment (heavy-duty shocks), and does not indulge in mind games (a lemon?). As you can see, finding a psychiatrist is like shopping for a car."

"By the grace of God, I found a wonderful psychiatrist who began working with me in a very intense manner. He allowed me to cry, to scream, to pound pillows, to, in a word, emote. I wrote poetry, I drew pictures, I acted out dramas, and I expressed my feelings in such a way that I was able to heal the deep wounds of my past. He is different from any other doctor I have been to, in that he is not afraid of feelings. He conducts his sessions in a room with mats on the floor and pillows everywhere. He is 100 percent ethical and pays 100 percent attention to his patients while they are there. I worked with him for a year and a half. I saw him every week for two hours each session. He believed in me and gave me the confidence in myself to ride out the manic periods and the depressions until I was through the tough times. His work includes Gestalt, Reichian, Jungian, and psychodramatic techniques. He is a genius at his work and he has freed me from a very heavy stigma: manic depressive illness. I have been completely off all drugs for almost two years and I have had no depressions or manic attacks for that period of time. I have complete confidence in my recovery and I believe that it is possible for other so-called manic depressives to recover. I say so-called because I have very strong doubts that the illness is totally biochemical and requires life long drug therapy. I believe there are physiological components to illnesses like manic depression, but there are heavy-duty psychological aspects, too, and when the psychogenics are dealt with, the biology rights itself. That's certainly been the case with me."

Below are some unwanted attributes of health care professionals cited by people in the study. Which ones relate to how you feel?

☐ relies only on drug treatment
☐ not available when needed
☐ has more patients than can be handled well
☐ condescending
☐ overcharges
☐ authoritarian
☐ patronizing

☐ overmedicates
☐ too busy to do a good job
☐ afraid to try new treatment methods
☐ judgmental
☐ egotistical
☐ rigid
☐ acts bored

What other qualities in health care professionals do you want to avoid? _____

_____

_____

_____

People who feel that the care they receive is not good or is inappropriate say:

"My psychiatrist doesn't have time for anything besides prescription writing."

"My doctor is good about explaining the effects of drugs but not good in relating to my situation."

"...does not understand enough about lab tests and is a poor counselor for me."

"I have to ask for information about the illness."

Describe your ideal treatment scenario: _____

_____

_____

_____

_____

Why is this the ideal treatment scenario for you? _____

_____

_____

_____

_____

11

Support Groups

Other people with mood disorders know and understand exactly what I am feeling and exactly what I have to go through each day to maintain myself, and how frustrating the illness is. Listening to the various experiences with therapy and drug treatments helps in the exchange of information. Support during swings and advice on how others handle various situations is a tremendous coping device, probably the best.

Why Belong to a Support Group?

Fifty-two people who took part in the study belong to support groups. Twenty-three people who are not in support groups said they would like to be.

Support groups are helpful to people in many ways. It is healing to be with people who have similar problems—people who understand. It helps you feel that you are not alone. Communication is easy among such people. A group can help you appreciate how fortunate you are, that things are not as bleak as they seem: that there is hope; that others with similar problems are doing well.

A support group can also provide information and education on mood disorders, and is a great place to get tips from others on how they handle problems associated with mood swings. In my own experience, I've found support groups to be wonderful places to meet new, understanding friends. Several of my closest friends are people who I met through such groups many years ago. People in the study reported the same thing: many formed lasting friendships and even lifetime partnerships out of relationships begun in a support group.

You need a place where you can go and not feel that you have to hide your problem. A group can provide role models for solving the very same problems you are confronting every day.

Finally, in that a support group provides a positive activity for you, it can help to counter social isolation.

Study participants offered the following comments about support groups:

> "We share our ups and downs at meetings and elsewhere. We get to know the "signs"—weight loss, talkativeness, spending sprees, no sleep; or if someone doesn't answer the phone, cancels appointments. We've exchanged house keys. We have a telephone lifeline system. When someone is manic it is also a great reminder to the rest of us."

> "I think the importance of getting involved in support groups for manic depressive persons has not been emphasized enough. It has helped me more than any other thing except for lithium. I have been in- volved as a member/leader from 1974 to 1989 in 'Breakthrough' (patient self-help), the state mental health association, and the local Depressive and Manic Depressive Association chapter. It has certainly helped me to help others with manic depression and share my experien- ces. Furthermore, I think it helps to remove the stigma."

What Happens at Support Group Meetings

People reported that the number of members in their support groups vary from 2 to 400 (I would assume that where there are this many they break up into smaller groups), with most having between 10 and 20 members.

Study participants described a wide variety of formats and activities for their sup- port groups, including

- Sharing of people's problems and experiences—mutual counseling, advice, and support

- Pertinent educational speakers and programs

- Referral to appropriate services and resources

- Sharing of activities, such as crafts, games, field trips, cooking, and watching videos

- Lobbying for services to benefit people with mood disorders

One group holds large informational meetings each month to discuss different topics related to mood disorders, and has smaller groups that get together more often to provide mutual support.

Some groups have a policy of not dwelling on "sad tales or negativity," and instead focus on how to cope. I do not encourage any limits on the topics that can be discussed; although I do recommend that lashing out at, or being judgmental of, someone else in the group be considered inappropriate behavior. People need a place where they can freely and safely discuss and express their feelings. The rest of the group is available to validate these feelings, even if they can't understand or accept them. This is one of the most healing aspects of a support group.

Some groups limit the amount of time that each person can spend talking to the group about what is on his or her mind: otherwise everyone in the group might not get an opportunity to share. It is possible to get a lot said in ten minutes; this is often the upward time limit for an individual contribution.

I have found the following rules to be helpful in allowing support groups to run smoothly:

1. There should be no criticism or judging of other people in the group.

2. Sharing is optional and should not be either encouraged or discouraged.

3. Group members can talk about anything they want to share (except criticizing or judging other people in the group).

4. Attendance is optional.

List other rules you think support groups should have: _____

_____

_____

_____

_____

_____

If you are in a support group, what do you get from it? _____

_____

_____

_____

_____

If there are changes you would like to see in your support group, what are they?_____

_____

_____

_____

_____

_____

How could you help make these changes happen? _____

_____

_____

_____

_____

If you are not in a support group and would like to be in one, describe what you would like the group to be like? _____

_____

_____

_____

_____

_____

What would you want to get out of going to this support group? _____

_____

_____

_____

_____

_____

How To Start or Locate a Support Group

Locating an Existing Support Group

☐ *I would like to be in a support group.*

There are two categories of support groups: open and closed. An open support group is one that anyone can attend. A closed support group is one that started as an open group and then, when it's attendance stabilized, stopped accepting new members.

Check out the following sources to help you locate those support groups that are both open and appropriate to your needs and circumstances:

- Call the local mental health help line (listed in the front of your phone book under "Guide to Services, Health and Mental Health," or under "Mental Health Services" in the yellow pages.)

- Contact your local or state Alliance for the Mentally Ill

- Contact other mental health organizations and services in your community

- Call local mental health facilities (inpatient hospital units will often have affiliated outpatient support groups)

- Check the community calendar listings of support groups in local daily and weekly newspapers

- Check the community calendar listings of support groups on the radio and local public television stations

- Ask your health care providers

- Ask other people who have mood disorders

Here are some questions to ask when considering different support groups:

- When does the group meet? Will this fit into my work, activity, and family schedule?

- Will transportation be a problem? If so, is the location convenient to public transportation?

- Would car pooling with other group members be a possibility?

- Is there someone in my family or in the group itself who would help with transportation?

If there are several groups that seem to be appropriate, attend different meetings to see which one feels most comfortable and best meets your needs. It's important to attend a group meeting several times before making your decision.

The first time you attend a group is not easy. It takes courage to go to a new group for the first time, especially if you are feeling low and your self-confidence is down. Remember that open groups are always glad to find new members. The other group members will understand your hesitation in coming the first time, and are bound to be welcoming. You don't have to share your feelings or experiences until you feel comfortable doing so.

Give yourself a big pat on the back for attending the first time, even if your participation was limited. Subsequent meetings will be much easier.

Group meetings vary from session to session. After you go to a meeting, answer the following questions:

I attended the _____ group _____ times.

How did you feel at the meetings? _____

_____

_____

_____

_____

What did you hope to get out of going to these meetings? _____

_____

_____

_____

_____

Did they meet your needs or expectations? (Explain.) _____

_____

_____

_____

_____

This group feels right for me because _____

_____

_____

_____

_____

This group seems wrong for me because _____

_____

_____

_____

_____

     Repeat this process until you find the group that is appropriate to your needs. If you can't find an existing group that feels right, you may have to start your own.

Starting a Support Group From Scratch

     Starting a support group is not as difficult as it might seem. However, you may want to enlist some help in getting the group started. Apply to friends who have mood disorders, members of your support system, health care providers, and members of mental health organizations for assistance.

I am going to ask the following people to help me get the group started: _____

_____

_____

     Begin by arranging a place and time for the first meeting. It could be held in a school, church, library, or other public meeting place. A phone call is usually all that is required to make such an arrangement. Choose a time that you think will be generally convenient.

     Place a simple notice in the community calendar of local daily and weekly newspapers, and on the radio and public television stations. (There should be no cost for these notices.) Include the *place*, *time*, and *purpose* of the group, and, if you want, your phone number for further information.

     Here's a sample text for an announcement for your local paper:

> A support group for people who experience depression or manic depression is being started this (*day of the week and date*) at _____ o'clock at (*location*). Meetings will be free of charge and are open to the public. For more information call (*your phone number*).

> Support groups effectively counter the feelings of isolation experienced by people with depression or manic depression. The meetings provide a safe place where people can share their experiences and learn about community resources in an atmosphere of understanding, support, and acceptance.

For a community calendar listing, send your newspaper a brief note as follows:

Mood Disorders Support Group for people who experience mood instability (manic depression or depression)

FREE   ALL WELCOME

(*Date*)

(*Time*)

(*Place*)

For more information call: (*Phone number*)

You can sometimes arrange for community calendar announcements to appear for several days before each meeting on an ongoing basis. Check with your local media.

This sample poster on the next page can be filled in and copied for posting in public places such as grocery stores, libraries, town offices, and health care facilities.

Mood Disorders Support Group

for people who experience mood instability, depression, and manic depression

FREE   ALL WELCOME

Education

Information

Understanding

Support

Date:

Time:

Place:

For more information, call:

Many people in the study who started support groups found it to be a very worthwhile and rewarding experience.

☐ *I am going to start a support group.*

This is how I am going to do it: _____

_____

_____

_____

_____

_____

At your first meeting, you'll be able to work with other group members in defining the group more precisely to meet everyone's needs. Some of the issues that the group may need to consider are raised below.

Finances.   Most groups are arranged so that they do not incur expenses or require dues. In some circumstances, a group may need to raise money to pay for a meeting place, educational resources, printing, promotion, and speakers. You can raise money by requiring dues, taking up a collection at meetings, securing donations from individuals and organizations, applying for grants, or holding raffles and food sales. A treasurer can be elected from the group to be responsible for any monies. If you are going to raise money, it is best to hold it in a bank account, with two signatures necessary for withdrawal (that of the treasurer and one other person).

Our group will need to raise $_____ to pay for _____

_____

_____

Our group is going to raise money by _____

_____

_____

Time and frequency of meetings.   Some groups meet several times a week; others meet weekly or every other week. Meetings can be held at any time of the day that works well for the participants. Most groups hold their meetings in the evening.

Our group has agreed to meet (how often) _____ *on (day)*_____ *at (time)*_____

Facilitation. You have several options for how your group is run. Members of the group can take turns facilitating meetings; one person who feels comfortable with this task can do all of the facilitating, or a health care professional can provide this service (usually for a fee). Most of the groups described by people in the study are facilitated internally.

Our group will be facilitated by: _____

Format. Many support groups restrict their activities to informal discussions allowing members to share their feelings, experiences, and progress. Another possible format is to have a sharing time for the first hour or so, and then have a more structured discussion. The topic for discussion can be planned in advance, or can be based on issues that came up during the sharing time. Speakers, workshops, and videos on various issues related to mood disorders can also be included in your program. Your group might want to try out a couple of different formats to see which works best for the individuals involved.

Here are some ideas for topics for structured meetings:

- Dietary considerations
- How to get the exercise you need
- Getting a good night's sleep
- Housing and transportation issues
- Employment
- Getting the support you need
- Public services
- Health care facilities and services
- Medications
- Relationships
- Family support
- Preventing suicide
- Cognitive therapy
- Early warning signs of mania or depression
- Warning signs charts
- Stress reduction
- Relaxation techniques

Other topics I'd like to see discussed at meetings: _____

_____

_____

_____

_____

_____

_____

Some groups include a social hour in their format, with refreshments before or after meetings. Other groups plan separate social gatherings which might include meals and activities.

Our group will use or try out the following formats for our meetings: _____

_____

_____

_____

_____

Depending on the size of your group, it may be helpful to choose a program director or a program committee to be responsible for setting up special events, speakers, and workshops.

What an Ideal Support Group Might Look Like

Study participants gave the following descriptions of what, for them, would be an ideal support group:

> "It should be run by depressives and manic depressives. Caring and sharing is the essence of the program, with reduction of stigma, along with education for the client, family, professionals, and the public at large. They all need to understand this illness."

> "Support group implies the concept of 'self-help.' Sponsorship is helpful, particularly financial sponsorship; but when others become involved, their own agenda tends to overtake the goals of the group itself and professionals seem to translate everything into therapy."

"Meetings at least monthly with consumer leadership, an educational topic, rap sessions."

"Regularly scheduled meetings that have guest speakers but also—and mostly—time for small group sharing."

"Conducive space and time; open, safe ambience; minimum structure; multiplicity of healing methods. Undertake anti-stigma and integration projects; support hospitalized and borderline members becoming important in the community."

"It should be caring, accepting, a place to go for haven from the storm."

Some people suggest using the Alcoholics Anonymous or 12-step approach. Others recommend the Recovery, Inc., model (see the resource List). A survey participant wrote the following about Recovery, Inc.:

"Recovery, Inc., has been around for over 40 years. Dr. Abraham Low founded Recovery, Inc., in the late 1950s. There are Recovery, Inc., groups in many cities and even other countries. Recovery does not advertise, but is in the phone book. Members are usually referred by doctors or hear of Recovery from friends already in the group. Dr. Low, as far as I know, is the pioneer of cognitive techniques to combat depression and nervous symptoms. He was shunned, and his method ridiculed, by the psychiatric hierarchy of his day (1930s and 1940s). He was convinced that Freudian psychotherapy was based on fundamentally flawed theories and had virtually no therapeutic value. He pointed out the inefficiency of treatment, which typically takes many years, resulting in extreme financial strain on the patient and significant doubt as to improvement in the patient's quality of life. I have watched with some disappointment as cognitive therapy and Rational Emotive Therapy (its forerunner) have become accepted and widely used by the psychological and psychiatric community without any mention, much less deserved recognition, of Dr. Low. The most significant difference between Recovery and regular group therapy is in the structure of the meetings, which prevents the time being wasted in what Dr. Low calls the 'Complaint Hobby.' Significant gains in mood and symptom reduction are often seen in as little as three or four meetings."

Describe what would be an ideal support group for you:_____

_____

_____

_____

_____

_____

How do you plan to make this happen for yourself?_____

_____

_____

_____

_____

_____

12

Family Support

My sister can get through to me when no one else can. She's not afraid to touch me if necessary. She also sees symptoms quicker than anyone else, sometimes including myself.

Negative Interactions With Family Members

People in the study reported that their mood swings have had a great deal of negative impact on their family life, often creating complete havoc. Following is a list of these negative impacts and resulting emotions. **Which ones apply to you and your family?**

- ☐ was or became a dysfunctional family
- ☐ they think it's all in my head
- ☐ disruption
- ☐ tension, stress
- ☐ estrangement
- ☐ anxiety
- ☐ denial
- ☐ lack of trust
- ☐ financially draining
- ☐ emotionally draining
- ☐ embarrassment

☐ confusion

☐ loss of hope

☐ patronizing attitudes

☐ lack of understanding

☐ everyone is affected by the stigma

☐ turmoil

☐ exclusion

☐ loss

☐ fear

☐ anger

☐ overprotection

☐ physically draining

☐ unpleasantness

☐ worry

☐ grief

☐ they're tired of me

☐ divorce

☐ they feel helpless

☐ I'm devalued by family members

☐ caused depression in other family members

☐ family members refuse to learn about manic depression or take part in my treatment

"My family says it is 'like walking on eggshells,' never knowing what mood I will be in or when it will change. My family told this to the doctor. They also said that when I come to the house they would all stop talking until they could tell what mood I was in."

"A distance developed between us early in childhood; because of lack of understanding and support, it caused a great distance between myself and the rest of my family. I feel that my family is disgusted with my mood swings, yet they mention their concerns over the amount of medication. They do not understand the medications and make generalized statements like 'all these medications and they still don't seem to be working.' They do not understand that the episodes can and do occur even while I'm on medications."

"They think controlling me is a way of supporting me. I would have to do everything just my parents' way to have their support."

"They felt that I was trying to disgrace them, that my acts were a reflection on them, undermining their prestige."

"Some of my children and some of their spouses are supportive. Others, I feel, don't admit to my condition being caused by a physical thing—rather it's something I choose not to control. I realize in writing this—in doing the parts of the study—how angry I am with these children. One daughter who semi-understands said, 'Mom, you don't know what normal is: you've been swinging from high to low all your life. We kids don't know you any other way.' She still thinks anything can be overcome."

Describe any negative affect your mood swings have had on your family, and ways in which they have not been supportive: _____

_____

_____

_____

_____

Positive Influence on Family Life

Some people said that their illness actually strengthened their family relationships. Through the illness, they developed more mutual understanding, became closer, and learned to communicate better. One person said that her family hasn't given up on her and that they use each bout as a learning experience with love.

Those people who said that their families are supportive of them listed the following ways in which that support is expressed. **Which of these apply to you and your relationship with your family?**

- ☐ communication
- ☐ encouragement
- ☐ concern
- ☐ availability
- ☐ family members educated themselves about the problem
- ☐ monitoring
- ☐ financial support
- ☐ calling, writing, visiting
- ☐ understanding
- ☐ listening
- ☐ love

- ☐ tolerance
- ☐ attention
- ☐ education, advice, and counsel
- ☐ protection
- ☐ living space
- ☐ activities

"Each episode is dealt with individually; mania is usually confronted while depression is watched to see how I will handle it."

"When I am very ill, they do a lot. As I get better, they withdraw to give me and them time to pull ourselves together."

"My 24-year-old daughter has an unashamed, unembarrassed feeling for me."

Describe the other positive aspects of your relationship with your family and ways in which they have been supportive of you during your mood swings: _____

_____

_____

_____

_____

_____

_____

Involvement of Family Members

Forty-five people in the study said that the amount of support they receive from their family has changed over the years. Most of this change has been positive. They report:

"It has gotten better."

"There is greater understanding."

"They are more understanding and more accepting."

"They give me more support than in the past because of family counseling."

"My wife has always loved me and as I get better, she is encouraging."

"They realize it is not their fault."

"When I am trying to help myself, they're appreciative and support me even more."

"As bad as it is now, it used to be much worse. A few [family] members show that they are interested in knowing more about the illness and its treatment, and how the medications work. Fighting that used to occur has let up and overall there is a more generalized understanding, but only with a few family members."

"I am more able to cooperate and am more aware of [my family's] efforts and caring."

Describe any improvements in your relationship with your family relative to this illness.

_____

_____

_____

_____

What do you feel is responsible for these improvements? _____

_____

_____

_____

Is there anything you need to do to ensure that these improvements are maintained? If so, what? _____

_____

_____

_____

Forty-two people in the study have family members who have attended family meetings to discuss their situation. These meetings often occur while the person who has the mood disorder is in the hospital, when the meeting takes place as part of the hospitalization process. The person with the mood disorder may or may not attend the meeting, depending on the situation and individual preferences.

Family meetings can include either one or both parents, a spouse or significant other, grandparents, children (either minor or adult), brothers, sisters, aunts, uncles, cousins, and even close friends. The doctor, therapist, and other health professionals may also participate.

If the meeting is held in the hospital, the hospital staff usually takes care of arrangements and facilitation. If held outside the hospital, the meeting may be arranged and facilitated by the person with the mood disorder, a family member, therapist, social worker, doctor, or other health care professional.

These are the issues often discussed at family meetings. Which of these issues would you like to have discussed at a family meeting that involved you?

- ☐ understanding mood disorders
- ☐ medical intervention
- ☐ medications
- ☐ family dynamics
- ☐ relationships
- ☐ general mental health
- ☐ feelings
- ☐ ways to protect you
- ☐ depression
- ☐ mutual concerns
- ☐ getting outside help
- ☐ acceptance
- ☐ building trust
- ☐ doing more things together
- ☐ housing
- ☐ childhood issues
- ☐ ways to get along better
- ☐ coping with stress
- ☐ mania
- ☐ communication
- ☐ support
- ☐ stigmatization
- ☐ forgiveness
- ☐ monitoring
- ☐ suicide
- ☐ financial issues

What other issues would you like to cover? _____

_____

_____

_____

_____

Out of the 42 people in the study who have tried family meetings, 31 found them to be helpful. They said:

> "It gave me the feeling they were working with me—just knowing they loved me was so important."

> "It helped me come to a better understanding with my family about my illness."

> "It helped me to feel not so alone and isolated."

> "It is very reassuring to know that people who truly love you do have a full understanding of what you are battling every day in your life."

> "It gave me insight into the other person's point of view."

Eleven people felt that family meetings were not worthwhile. The reasons they cited included:

> "Nothing was accomplished."

> "My family is still stubborn about accepting a constitutional problem."

> "My family felt blamed, intimidated, were defensive and uninterested."

> "Everyone only sees their side, not mine; they hate me for being this way."

Which of the following models of ideal family meetings suggested by study participants would you prefer?

☐ Family, patient, and doctor discuss the situation together.

☐ Meeting with a therapist, uninterrupted for 1 to 1-1/2 hours; the illness is explained and there is ample time for discussion and comments.

☐ Benevolently confrontational; people are free to say anything that they care to say without being hurtful; the other person is allowed to respond; the meeting is open and positive, with give and take.

☐ The people involved should be encouraged to talk to each other (and not just to the therapist).

☐ The patient and family discuss what happens, the symptoms, feelings, when not to intervene, and the risks involved.

☐ Everyone speaks their mind and gives their opinion.

☐ The family express their concerns and ask lots of questions; the doctor is supportive of me, and the family says, "What can we, as a family, do to ease your pain or help you?"

☐ I could freely tell them what a constant struggle I go through; they would *listen* and learn about mood disorders.

☐ Help and lift, not judge, condemn, or disown.

☐ Education: here's what to expect; here's how to help. Everyone has enough interest and courage to let the others speak openly and to speak openly themselves—the only way to really find out what is going on and resolve questions and misunderstandings.

Describe a possible meeting with your family. What issues would you like to discuss? Who would you like to be there? What kind of atmosphere would be most comfortable and helpful for you?_____

_____

_____

_____

_____

_____

_____

_____

Fifty-nine people in the study have other family members who experience extreme mood swings. Eighteen of these respondents have been able to work with other family members to find solutions to their problems.

Do you have family members with mood swings? If so, which of the following approaches or strategies that other people have used have worked successfully for you?

☐ discussion of problems
☐ encouraging each other
☐ mutual understanding and support
☐ monitoring
☐ unconditional love
☐ defusing situations by providing quiet, "alone" time
☐ advocating of appropriate treatment for each other
☐ mutual assistance in recognizing symptoms
☐ educating each other
☐ mutual counseling
☐ building each other up
☐ increased communication

What other ways, approaches, or strategies have worked for you and family members with mood swings?_____

_____

_____

_____

_____

_____

What are some things that you'd like to try with depressive or manic depressive family members? _____

_____

_____

_____

_____

Below is a wish list for family relationships compiled by people in the study. Which items describe how you would like your relationship with your family to be?

- ☐ as it is
- ☐ free and open
- ☐ accepting
- ☐ loving
- ☐ like any normal family
- ☐ closer
- ☐ trusting
- ☐ I'd like to be appreciated for who I am
- ☐ smooth
- ☐ happy
- ☐ humorous
- ☐ cooperative
- ☐ attentive
- ☐ less volatile
- ☐ understanding
- ☐ having good communication

- ☐ respectful
- ☐ supportive
- ☐ honest
- ☐ having everyone be knowledgeable
- ☐ patient
- ☐ caring
- ☐ calm
- ☐ less controlling
- ☐ having fun together
- ☐ helpfulness
- ☐ more time together

Another respondent wrote:

> "We have a very casual lifestyle that goes a long way toward keeping the stress levels down to an easily manageable level."

What other attributes would you add? _____

_____

_____

_____

_____

The support of my grown children, their partners, my partner, and my mother was, and continues to be, essential to my own level of wellness. They monitored my episodes without overreacting to normal highs and lows. They made decisions for me when I could not make them for myself. They took me to my appointments when I couldn't get myself there. They stayed with me, or found friends to stay with me, when they knew it wasn't safe for me to stay alone. When they realized that I wasn't cooking for myself or eating, they made sure that I had plenty of good food, often shopping for the food, coming to my house, preparing a meal, and eating it with me. When I needed a more appropriate living space, they all pitched in and helped in the search and the moving. Most important, I could always find one of them who would take the time to listen to my frustrations and my dreams. When I felt as if I would never be normal again, they comforted and reassured me. Their belief in me, and love for me, sustained me through my darkest hours.

PART III

Developing
a Lifestyle That
Enhances Wellness

13

Taking a Look at Your Lifestyle

I believe the first major depression I had at age 19 was linked to stress I experienced at college. It was the first year and first time away from home and I was 1,000+ miles from home. Poor coping skills, lack of friends, and certain negative aspects of the school contributed to my unhappiness.

Fifty-seven of the study participants believe their mood swings to have started as the result of a particular life circumstance, stress, or experience. They reported high stress or increased levels of stress in general as triggering or exacerbating mood swings.

My own personal journey to get my life back began when I realized that my life was in my control. While I was honest with myself in knowing that I might always have a problem with mood instability, I began to see that there were many positive steps I could take on my own behalf, that many facets of my life were under my control, and that anything I could do to enhance my life would be a positive step toward stability and wellness.

It was at this point that I began to read everything I could find that was related to mood disorders and/or wellness, to attend related workshops and seminars, and to talk with people about their coping strategies. This book is one outcome of that search for clues as to how people cope with depression and manic depression.

I have made many changes in my life over the past few years. I have been in counseling almost continually. Through this process, I have changed my perception of myself as a dependent, needy, sick, incompetent, and limited individual to understanding that I am, in fact, quite competent, can take care of myself, and am a skilled writer, teacher, and counselor.

I have left a very destructive and abusive marriage. My relationships with my adult children, a long-time companion, and my wide circle of friends continue to improve. I have established myself in a living space that is cozy, comfortable, easy to care for—warm in the winter and cool in the summer—with easy access to transportation and services. I have explored a wide variety of traditional and alternative health care practices, and continue to use those that have had a positive effect for me. I use cognitive and relaxation techniques to help me sleep and calm my spirit. I am healthier and happier than I have ever been.

Using available public services and resources, I am successfully developing a new career for myself which takes into account my interests and abilities, my need for a flexible schedule, and my need to take good care of myself.

One study participant wrote:

> "At age 24 I was so very depressed emotionally. I lost weight and stopped menstruating, although I was able to function in my work. This [depression came about] because I was rejected by a man. At age 28, I had a similar, less serious depression. At age 55, I had a very good position. The hospital where I worked closed, I saw nothing ahead, and became extremely depressed. My 36-year-old son's diagnosis as bipolar and schizophrenic is contributing to my present depression."

> "I believe my mood swings are a genetic predisposition affected greatly by environment and my cognitive and behavioral reactions to that environment. This is a complex, constantly changing interaction. It is impossible to distinguish the components with absolute certainty, at least in my case."

Take Stock of Your Life

This is a list of the stressful events that survey participants feel triggered or worsened their mood swings. **Do any of these circumstances apply to your present situation or personal history**?

- ☐ marital problems
- ☐ alcoholism in the family
- ☐ child abuse
- ☐ death of a loved one or loved ones
- ☐ job stress
- ☐ a workaholic attitude
- ☐ hormonal surges
- ☐ lack of emotional support from parents
- ☐ working with toxic chemicals
- ☐ midlife crisis
- ☐ menopause
- ☐ lack of assertiveness
- ☐ perfectionism
- ☐ problems relating to peers
- ☐ substance abuse
- ☐ loss of custody of child or children
- ☐ physical disfigurement
- ☐ lack of exercise
- ☐ eating disorders
- ☐ smoking
- ☐ health problems of family members
- ☐ co-dependency issues
- ☐ lack of a support network
- ☐ control issues
- ☐ poor career or lifestyle choices

- ☐ divorce
- ☐ sexual abuse
- ☐ separation from loved ones
- ☐ overwork
- ☐ job termination
- ☐ post partum depression
- ☐ recall of past emotional hurts
- ☐ low self-esteem
- ☐ severe exhaustion
- ☐ sexual anxiety
- ☐ trying to endure too much alone
- ☐ excessively high expectations
- ☐ poor social skills
- ☐ trying to meet the expectations of others
- ☐ neglect during childhood
- ☐ physical disability
- ☐ self-neglect
- ☐ poor diet
- ☐ obesity
- ☐ chronic health problems
- ☐ excess responsibility
- ☐ lack of self-confidence
- ☐ financial problems
- ☐ inappropriate living space

What have been other sources of tension, stress, and pressure in your life? _____

_____

_____

_____

_____

Review the events you have noted. Which ones do you think are causing you the most stress, or having the greatest impact on your life? The next exercise will give you the chance to examine these events and their repercussions in more detail.

As you read about the coping strategies in this section of the workbook, think about which ones might be relevant to the events or situations you've noted. For now, simply fill in the blanks under Problematic Situation with a brief description of the top six problems from your list. Put a paper clip on this page to make it easy for you to find your place again.

As you get ideas from your reading, jot down notes in the places provided. You'll review the effects of the situation on your life and feelings; you'll consider which coping strategies might help; you'll record plans for implementing these strategies; and, finally, after you've tried some of the strategies, you'll record how they worked. Don't expect to complete this exercise until you've finished reading the entire workbook.

Problematic Situation

_____

_____

The effect of this situation on your life and the way you feel: _____

_____

_____

_____

_____

Strategies that might help: _____

_____

_____

_____

_____

Plans for implementing these strategies: _____

_____

_____

_____

_____

How these strategies have worked: _____

_____

_____

_____

_____

Problematic Situation

_____

_____

The effect of this situation on your life and the way you feel: _____

_____

_____

_____

_____

Strategies that might help: _____

_____

_____

_____

_____

Plans for implementing these strategies:_____

_____

_____

_____

_____

How these strategies have worked:_____

_____

_____

_____

_____

Problematic Situation

_____

_____

The effect of this situation on your life and the way you feel: _____

_____

_____

_____

_____

Strategies that might help: _____

_____

_____

_____

_____

Plans for implementing these strategies:_____

_____

_____

_____

_____

How these strategies have worked:_____

_____

_____

_____

Problematic Situation

_____

_____

The effect of this situation on your life and the way you feel: _____

_____

_____

_____

_____

Strategies that might help: _____

_____

_____

_____

_____

Plans for implementing these strategies: _____

_____

_____

_____

_____

How these strategies have worked: _____

_____

_____

_____

_____

Problematic Situation

_____

_____

The effect of this situation on your life and the way you feel: _____

_____

_____

_____

_____

Strategies that might help: _____

_____

_____

_____

Plans for implementing these strategies:_____

_____

_____

_____

_____

How these strategies have worked:_____

_____

_____

_____

_____

Problematic Situation

_____

_____

The effect of this situation on your life and the way you feel: _____

_____

_____

_____

_____

Strategies that might help: _____

_____

_____

_____

_____

Plans for implementing these strategies:_____

_____

_____

_____

How these strategies have worked:_____

_____

_____

_____

_____

14

How About Counseling?

*In therapy we identified issues and worked to resolve them. It enhanced
my understanding of my mood and behaviors.*

Almost all of the 120 people in the survey have been involved in counseling for help in
dealing with their mood swings and in working through related issues. Here are some of
the reasons given by people in the study for going into counseling. **Which reasons apply
to you?**

☐ depression
☐ need to understand the diagnosis
☐ to prepare for hospitalization
☐ to enhance recovery
☐ paranoia
☐ guilt
☐ fear
☐ an acute situation following an episode
☐ family problems
☐ stress

☐ inability to work
☐ desire to understand how to deal with stress
☐ desire to learn how to get along with people
☐ mania
☐ need to become reconciled to diagnosis
☐ an interim period following hospitalization
☐ suicidal thoughts and/or attempts
☐ anxiety
☐ worry
☐ feeling like my life is out of control
☐ marital problems
☐ problems in another relationship
☐ job stress
☐ severe personal losses
☐ desire to work on achieving goals
☐ childhood issues
☐ sexual abuse
☐ alcoholic family members
☐ incest
☐ partner abuse
☐ co-dependancy
☐ desire to change negative thought patterns to positive ones
☐ desire to change inappropriate behavior patterns
☐ desire to pick up more quickly on signs of oncoming mood swings
☐ desire to avoid more invasive treatment modalities
☐ other treatment modalities not working

Other reasons you might have for going into therapy: _____

_____

_____

_____

_____

What are your goals for therapy, even if you're not in therapy now?_____

_____

_____

_____

The Therapist

These are some of the attributes people want in a therapist:

- Extensive knowledge of the illness

- Availability, with someone else on call as needed

- Willingness to try alternative therapies, including those that are minimally invasive

- Knowledge and judgment needed to prescribe drugs appropriately

- Skill at giving support, counsel, advice, and at understanding

- Skill in communicating an attitude of caring and interest

- Affordable rates and/or willingness to work with insurance plans and Medicaid

Several people in the study said that they prefer working with a counselor of the same gender as themselves and of at least the same age or older.

What would your ideal therapist be like? _____

_____

_____

_____

Study participants found appropriate therapists by

- Getting recommendations from other people who have mood swings

- Getting recommendations from mental health organizations

- Getting referrals from their physician or psychiatrist

Before making a plan with a counselor to begin a series of sessions, ask if you can visit free for one time to see if you both feel comfortable working together. (Many therapists find that they must charge, even for an initial consultation—make sure that you settle this beforehand.) You may have to visit with several counselors before you find the one who best meets your needs.

Kinds of Therapy

Look in any list of classified ads for counseling, and you will find as many varieties of therapists as there are fish in the sea. Perhaps you've already made a study of the many kinds of therapy available; if you haven't, the range can certainly seem bewildering. I'll make some basic distinctions here, based on my own experience and that of people in the study, to help you make the wisest possible choices when choosing what type of therapy you want to pursue.

Therapeutic approaches can be divided into three basic categories:

- Psychodynamic
- Humanistic
- Problem-Solving

Psychodynamic Therapies. Freudian analysis is the most famous among the psychodynamic therapeutic approaches; it is also fading enormously in popularity as clients and therapists turn to more immediate and practical problem-solving techniques. In psychodynamic therapy, the emphasis is on gaining insight into the roots of problems (rather than finding ways to solve them). These therapists are almost always geared to the long term—10 or 20 years is not uncommon! The analyst or psychiatrist will explain symptoms in terms of emotional damage sustained during your early stages of development. You'll spend a lot of time hashing and rehashing the past, and may analyse dreams in terms of their personal symbolism. The focus is on the unconscious. It's quite possible to go through years of this type of therapy without ever discussing solutions to present symptoms at all!

As you might guess, psychodynamic therapies have not been shown to be effective treatment for depression, mania, or the management of their symptoms.

Humanistic Therapies. Some of the therapeutic approaches that fall into this category are Gestalt, existential, client-centered, and interpersonal therapy. All of these focus on your emotional growth and expressiveness, and strive toward evolving healthy patterns of communication. Some people in the study extolled the cathartic value of these types of therapy; it's unclear whether they'll do much to diminish your mood swings or help you manage your symptoms.

Problem-Solving Therapies. My bias is going to be obvious here; but it's a bias shared by many thousands of others. Problem-solving therapeutic approaches—such as cognitive-behavioral therapy—offer the most effective nonmedical intervention for the management of depression and manic depression. Those therapies tend to be short-term and are always aimed at practical solutions to problems in the here-and-now. Your unconscious or subconscious motivations don't enter the picture at all, although gaining some insight into your thinking process is most important. The basic tenet of cognitive-behavioral psychology is that if you change the way you think, you can change the way you feel. And I can say from my own experience that it works! All the problem-solving chapters in this workbook take a cognitive-behavioral approach.

Therapy Is Just One Tool

Bear in mind that your patient-client relationship will be just one tool in your wellness kit. Light, diet, exercise, and very possibly medication will all play their parts as well. Many, if not most, people coping with bipolar disorder or experiencing severe depression will need the help of a psychiatrist—a physician with a specialty in mental, emotional, and behavioral disorders. Only a psychiatrist can help you assess your need for medication, order diagnostic tests, write prescriptions, and monitor your progress on a given medication or combination of drugs.

The unfortunate part of it is that most psychiatrists, at this point in time, practice psychodynamic therapy: so you are likely to need to look elsewhere for effective counseling. You can be frank with your prescribing psychiatrist about your own therapeutic bias, if you form one. You have the right to pursue exactly the kind of counseling that will give you the most help in managing your symptoms.

Unless you live in a very isolated community, it's a buyer's market out there. Be as savvy and aggressive as you would be shopping for a car. After all, in entering into a therapeutic relationship, you're entrusting your emotional life and, to some degree, your physical health to another person. You have a duty to yourself to be a proactive consumer and to choose carefully. Listen to your gut feelings: a therapeutic relationship has all the inherent complexities of any other relationship, and perhaps a few more. Find someone you can trust. Find someone who inspires you with hope.

People in the study reported varying degrees of success in therapy, ranging from good and very effective to completely worthless. Therapy was not looked upon by most respondents as a cure, but mainly as a way of improving their ability to cope with mood swings.

Here's a sampling of what people had to say about their experience with different kinds of therapy:

"It was excellent, but it couldn't motivate me during the lows."

"Therapy helps. It gives me someone I can turn to."

"It makes me feel better to have a professional consultant."

"My therapist gave me confidence and insight."

"I learned about my illness and how to cope. It gave me someone to talk to when I couldn't talk to my family."

"Therapy is good for surviving impossible situations."

"It helped me make dramatic changes in my ability to deal with the activities of living."

"I was in psychotherapy. The counselor was dogmatic and didn't understand or sympathize with the illness. He had preconceived notions about me which were false."

"The counselor did not validate me as a person. Many times I left the office feeling worse instead of better, like the whole thing was my fault."

"It was really a waste of time. Nothing changed for me as a result of the counseling. Finally, I just stopped going."

"The counselor was not a good one for me. She was not a person I could like or relate to. I felt that she was always judging me according to her standards."

"She talked at me the whole time. She kept telling me what to do, but never gave me a chance to say what I wanted to do, or how I was feeling. I left her office feeling frustrated and confused."

I have seen several different counselors since I was first treated for manic depression. The first was a male psychiatrist who talked with me and prescribed my medication. It was there that I first began to get some sense of myself as a real person with needs and abilities. Prior to that, my life had always been totally focused on others. A process of real growth began, painfully and slowly at first.

My next counselor was a young woman. She also had a profound effect on me. I was beginning to get some sense that there was a real person inside me, competent, warm, and worthy. What a revalation!

My next counselor was a psychoanalyst who was recommended to me by a close friend. This was a very confusing and frustrating experience for me. The analyst expected me to do all the talking and I wasn't used to that. Consequently not much happened. It got even worse when she attributed the motives to my actions, such as the time when I missed an 8:30 appointment because I had a bad head cold and overslept. She said I was avoiding her because I didn't want to face my problems and share with her things I had done in the past for which I felt ashamed. She said this another time when I tried to change an appointment because my mother was coming for a visit. After six months, I ended this counseling feeling angry and confused, as if I had wasted a lot of time and money: for a while, I didn't see anyone. This experience had a very negative effect on my level of trust.

Soon afterwards, I got into a really horrible second marriage. When I realized how bad it was, that the charming man I had married was actually a very abusive alcoholic, I took the advise of a friend and began seeing a highly recommended counselor. She was in her sixties, had been through a lot, and understood completely where I was coming from. She got me back on track, and during the next eight years increased my level of self-understanding, taught me stress reduction and relaxation techniques, involved me in group therapy with other women with similar self-esteem and relationship problems (some of these women became lifelong friends), and helped me get out of that very bad marriage. She is still available to me if I need her.

During my marriage, my husband and I saw a family therapist for a short period of time to see if we could work out our maritial diffulties. This therapist said that the reason I was being abused was because my husband was jealous, and that I should stop smiling so much. Obviously, this was a very bad piece of advice. I let that counselor know my opinion, and stopped seeing him.

For the past 18 months, I have been seeing a counselor who is working with me intensively on childhood issues, such as my mother's illness, sexual molestation, and the death of my friend, while supporting and advising me about current life situations. Our relationship is one of peers and is very interactive. It has given me the courage to go on when I have been discouraged and low.

What are your positive feelings about any counseling experiences you've had? _____

_____

_____

_____

_____

_____

Do you have any fears associated with going into therapy? Are there any other impediments that keep you out of therapy (such as cost)?_____

_____

_____

What can you do to overcome any fears or impediments that may be keeping you out of therapy?_____

_____

_____

_____

The Therapy Model

Some people prefer one-on-one counseling and others prefer group therapy. Among study participants, the length and frequency of therapy also varied. Repondents had a lot of ideas about ideal counseling scenarios:

"Initially, group therapy—so that the person can see they are not the only one with these problems and that other people have made good progress. [This also] provides a network."

"Daily counseling sessions with documentation and review. Informal counseling dealing with how to get out of bed and get motivated: to do the bare minimum if depressed and to calm mania."

"Focus on education, self-care, and social skills, with periodic follow-up visits as issues present themselves.... making use of community resources, supporting self-monitoring, working on building a solid support system."

"A wise, insightful, knowledgeable, loving, and caring therapist or program that encourages independence and teaches you how to work with others."

"Provides knowledge about biochemical facts and helps me accept [the disorder] as an illness so that I don't have to feel guilty for not controlling myself well enough.... showing the effects of the illness on friends and family."

"In a neutral environment with empathy. Someone who projects genuine concern and who can relate."

"Insight-oriented with supportive therapy. The more you learn about yourself, the easier it is to make adjustments when life is rough."

"Deals with the ramifications of the illness, plus supports the person. Help with problems of living. Deals with more than just symptoms."

Describe what, for you, would be the ideal counseling scenario:

Kind of therapy: _____

Frequency of appointments: _____

Length of each appointment: _____

Term: ongoing, as needed, long-term (more than one year), short-term (less than one year) _____

_____

Other Comments: _____

_____

_____

_____

_____

_____

_____

_____

What, if anything, is getting in the way of this kind of couseling scenario being available to you? _____

_____

_____

What can you do about it? _____

_____

_____

_____

Peer Counseling

I recommend that everyone try peer counseling (also known as co-counseling, or reevaluation counseling): it's free, it really helps, and both people involved get time and attention devoted to their issues. Peer counseling has the added benefit of focusing at least part of your attention on your peer counseling partner's issues, a process that in itself is therapeutic.

Here's how peer counseling works. Two people who know and trust each other—that trust is critical—set up a peer counseling arrangement. They decide how often they want to meet and for how long. I suggest meeting weekly and at the same time each week. It helps you get in the habit and is often frequent enough to stay current. Divide the time you are spending together in half: if it is one hour, which is a convenient length of time, you each get half an hour. During your time, you can talk about anything you want and express any emotion you wish to express, short of hostility or unfairness toward your counseling partner. Your partner stays focused on your issues, giving positive support and advice. Criticism or negating your partner's feelings is definitely not part of the process. For the second half of the session, you focus on your parner's issues as he or she talks.

I want to try peer counseling. It sounds good to me because _____

_____

_____

People I could approach about being a peer counseling parner (remember, it has to be someone you trust): _____

_____

_____

Fill out this next section later, as events warrant.

My first peer counseling session is set for (date)_____, (time)_____, (place)_____

After you've met with your peer counseling partner, record your feelings about your first meeting. (Use extra paper if necessary.) _____

_____

_____

_____

I plan to continue peer counseling because _____

_____

_____

_____

I do not plan to continue or pursue peer counseling because _____

_____

_____

_____

15

Building
Self-Esteem
and Self-Confidence

I credit myself for remarkably courageous behavior, work, and attitudes as a manic depressive. I chew off small pieces and do them well, organize well, and rest frequently.

Mood disorders can have a disasterous effect on self-esteem, severely aggravating depression and mania and diminishing the quality of your life. Study participants repeatedly pointed to problems with low self-esteem. Many reported that they had high self-esteem when manic and low self-esteem when depressed.

Describe your level of self-esteem and self-confidence (and whether these correspond to your mood swings): _____

_____

_____

_____

In what ways have mood disorders contributed to lowering your self-esteem?

- ☐ weakened credibility
- ☐ feeling negative about myself
- ☐ feeling different from others
- ☐ failing at most things
- ☐ adversely affecting performance
- ☐ fear of interacting with others
- ☐ inability to reach goals
- ☐ inability to complete anything
- ☐ continually finding fault with myself
- ☐ rages and fits that cause self-loathing
- ☐ guilt and shame arising from actions
- ☐ inability to trust my own perceptions
- ☐ stimatization
- ☐ inability to commit
- ☐ difficulty with self-care
- ☐ feeling as if people know there's something wrong with me, no matter what I do
- ☐ feeling like I'm not as good as others
- ☐ loss of confidence in ability to accomplish even the smallest tasks
- ☐ guilt over what family members and friends have to go through because of my mood swings

If your self-esteem is low, what do you consider to be other contributing factors? _____

_____

_____

_____

_____

These are some more comments from people in the study:

"Because of the mood swings, I suffer from the long-lasting impact of having been thrown out of a graduate program where I was doing what I love and I was competent. This was indescribably painful."

"I don't know how I will be for any occasion, so I can't plan. I'm anxious about upcoming events, can't operate under pressure anymore, can't remember or concentrate either. These are crippling for a professor and medical administrator."

"I'm terrified of demeaning myself on personal and/or professional levels due to my discrepancy in mood: I have in the past. This is not conducive to feeling self-confident and is very discouraging."

Raising your self-esteem is absolutely essential to alleviating or eliminating your depression and/or manic depression.

Consider the following ways used by study participants to raise their self-esteem. Which of these strategies have you tried? Think about which strategies might work for you in the future.

- [ ] changing my thought processes
- [ ] measuring and focusing on my past successes
- [ ] believing in myself
- [ ] giving myself credit for accomplishments
- [ ] doing things I find scary or hard
- [ ] determination to get more out of life
- [ ] self-affirmation
- [ ] self-acceptance
- [ ] doing my best at all times
- [ ] self-discipline
- [ ] lowering my perfectionist standards
- [ ] not getting upset over things
- [ ] focusing on the positive
- [ ] living one day at a time
- [ ] believing others who affirm my worth
- [ ] realizing that I have not quit—that I've worked through my problems
- [ ] partitioning myself off from the bad memories of the past
- [ ] knowing that the mood swings are not my fault
- [ ] knowing that the stigma of mental illness is no basis for shame
- [ ] knowing that I am the same as others
- [ ] accepting that it will take longer to accomplish my goals
- [ ] thinking of myself as a good and positive person
- [ ] affirming, "I think and act with self-confidence"

What are other attitudes or strategies you have developed to help raise your self-esteem and self-confidence?_____

_____

_____

_____

_____

List attitudes you do not now have but want to work on to improve your self-esteem:

_____

_____

_____

_____

Which of these actions do you want to take toward increasing your self-esteem?

- ☐ develop a strong support system
- ☐ be a good friend
- ☐ listen to others who affirm my worth
- ☐ take classes
- ☐ learn new skills
- ☐ work hard
- ☐ seek counseling
- ☐ listen to good music
- ☐ exercise
- ☐ garden
- ☐ take part in community activities
- ☐ work as a volunteer
- ☐ keep my house in order
- ☐ dress well
- ☐ use daily affirmations
- ☐ be supportive of others
- ☐ listen to friends, family
- ☐ continue my education
- ☐ learn more about self-help
- ☐ pursue my career
- ☐ do work that I feel good doing
- ☐ pursue hobbies and crafts
- ☐ write in a journal
- ☐ do medidation and relaxation exercises
- ☐ join special interest clubs
- ☐ participate in church activities
- ☐ take care of family, pets
- ☐ keep my life in order
- ☐ take good care of myself
- ☐ use creative expression (draw, paint, write, dance, etc.)
- ☐ just keep getting out there and trying for the brass ring

☐ be goal-oriented

☐ gain success in certain areas of my life

☐ practice consistently affirmitive self-talk

☐ learn all I can about mood swings

☐ educate others who have mood swings

☐ monitor and respond appropriately to my early warning signs

☐ look at why I am low or high and do something about it

☐ learn to relate to others more effectively and appropriately through self-help books, counseling, and work in my support group

☐ be around people I like and who like me—positive people who are sympathetic and uplifting

☐ avoid people who bring me down

☐ be willing to take more risks, giving myself credit when I succeed

☐ take small risks in a safe place, getting feedback from people who know me well

☐ keep cards, pictures of friends, and positive notes on bulletin boards where I will see them frequently

☐ have a special place to keep momentos and reminders of my achievements

☐ keep a list of achievements on the refrigerator door

☐ keep a list of achievements beside the bed and review them before I go to sleep at night or when I wake up in the morning

☐ before going to sleep at night, remind myself of what I have accomplished that day

☐ write down all the things that are good about myself and read them over and over

Other activities that have helped you raise your self-esteem and self-confidence:_____

_____

_____

_____

_____

Make a list of confidence-building activities that you want to try. Then commit yourself to a beginning date.

Activity	When I Will Begin

"Doing things I love helped me regain my interest in life and my self-confidence—singing, getting a professional degree and a job, and living by myself."

Author's Note. My own lack of self-esteem and self-confidence has been an inhibiting factor all my life. I have always been highly motivated, but everything I have undertaken has seemed like such a struggle. This low self-esteem started early on with messages I received from hypercritical family members. Those feelings were reinforced in traditional classroom situations, which focused my attention on the negative aspects of my performance, with little positive reinforcement. I feel as a child that I was always trying to please the adults in my life, and yet was never quite successful. In my two marriages, I was always the brunt of extensive criticism. Our society further perpetuates such criticism through the media, which set up unrealistic standards for what we should be like. Living in a patriarchal society, in which women are not as highly regarded as men, has further exaggerated these negative self-assessments.

Through years of extensive counseling, reading various self-help books, working on cognitive therapy techniques, attending lectures and workshops, as well as making it a point to share my life with people who are supportive and validating, I have come a long way toward gaining a high level of self-confidence and respect. It has been a difficult journey, but my life is now rich, full, and beautiful.

16

New Ways of Thinking

There are thoughts that plague me, that go around and around in my head. I feel like I have no control over them. They don't do me any good, and they make me feel terrible.

Negative Thinking

I used to tell myself over and over again how worthless I am, how bad I look, and that everything is hopeless. Irrational phobias about crowds and heights limited my experience. I was plagued with unrealistic fears for my own safety and well-being, as well as that of my family and, sometimes, the whole world.

People who experience depression or manic depression are often plagued by obsessive, largely irrational thoughts. The authors of *The Relaxation and Stress Reduction Workbook* note that this type of thinking is characterized by "repetitive and intrusive thoughts that are unrealistic, unproductive, and often anxiety producing."

Much of what you feel is caused by what you tell yourself, how you think, the ways in which you choose to interpret situations, and your personal point of view. Many people, when they're young, develop the habit of filling themselves with negative thoughts about themselves and the circumstances of their lives. In effect, people program themselves and their lives to be a particular way. Negative programming can be reinforced by one's family situations and by societal expectations.

Negative obsessive thoughts can take the form of self-doubt, generalized fears, and specific phobias. Participants in the study shared the negative thoughts that plague them in these three general categories Mark the thoughts that you identify with, then add your own thoughts to the list.

Self-Doubt

- ☐ I will never be able to get this job done.
- ☐ I don't look good enough for anyone to like me.
- ☐ I am not smart enough to figure this out.

List your own self-doubts: _____

_____

_____

_____

_____

_____

_____

_____

_____

_____

_____

_____

Fears

- ☐ The house will catch on fire.
- ☐ We will have a bad accident and all be killed.
- ☐ I think I have cancer.
- ☐ I will never be well.
- ☐ I will have another deep depression and land in the hospital.
- ☐ I will experience all the side effects of this drug.

List other fears you have: _____

_____
_____
_____
_____
_____
_____
_____
_____
_____
_____
_____

Phobias

☐ bugs		☐ spiders	
☐ snakes		☐ dogs	
☐ cats		☐ birds	
☐ horses		☐ guns	
☐ knives		☐ heights	
☐ flying		☐ deep water	
☐ darkness		☐ public bathrooms	
☐ stores		☐ crowds	
☐ small, enclosed places		☐ going out	
☐ going out alone		☐ medications	
☐ injections		☐ doctors	
☐ dentists		☐ driving	
☐ driving on freeways		☐ driving on dirt roads	

List other phobias you have: _____

_____
_____
_____
_____

_____

_____

_____

_____

Distorted Thinking Styles

On examination, negative thinking can very often be identified as distorted thinking. When you become aware of the distortions in your thinking, you will be able to actually change negative thoughts to positive ones, effectively eliminating the depression and anxiety that these thoughts create.

Distorted thoughts can be easily identified because they 1) cause painful emotions, such as worry, depression, or anxiety, and/or 2) cause you to have ongoing conflicts with other people. Fifteen distorted thinking styles are examined in *Thoughts and Feelings* by Matthew McKay, Martha Davis, and Patrick Fanning.

As you read through the definitions and examples that follow, think about how your own thinking has been distorted through the years. Answering the questions will help you come up with ways in which to combat your distorted perceptions. For each distorted perception, you'll be asked to come up with a rational comeback to knock it down. The examples show you how.

Filtering

Filtering entails looking at only one part of a situation to the exclusion of everything else.

Example. "Thanksgiving is going to be a disaster. I get along so horribly with my mother."

Distorted Perception. "My enjoyment of the Thanksgiving holiday depends exclusively on how I get along with my mother."

Rational Comeback. "Even though I often fight with my mother or feel hurt by her, I have a great relationship with my father and sister, brother-in-law, and nephew. They're going to be there, too, and there's a good chance that I'll have a decent time."

Think of an example when you filtered your thoughts: _____

_____

_____

Identify the distorted perception in your example: _____

_____

_____

_____

How did you feel when you filter your thoughts in this way? _____

_____

_____

_____

When you filter your thoughts does it ever cause conflict between yourself and others? Describe examples of this: _____

_____

_____

_____

Write a rational comeback to replace your distorted perception:_____

_____

_____

_____

Polarized Thinking

This distortion involves perceiving everything at the extremes, as either black or white, with nothing in between. You can understand how polarized thinking is a particular pitfall for people who have mood swings! Things are all great, or all horrible: there's no middle ground.

Example. "I had trouble scraping together the money for the rent this month. I'm a horrible spouse, and a failure as a provider."

Distorted Perception. "My financial performance this month defines my worth as a spouse and a provider."

Rational Comeback. "I had a bad month, without a lot of work. Sometimes I have much better months. My wife says that she loves me and that I'm a good husband, no matter what kind of month I've had. The economy's bad now, and we're both working hard to make ends meet."

Think of an example of when you've used polarized thinking: _____

_____

_____

_____

Identify the distorted perception in your example: _____

_____

_____

_____

How did you feel when your thoughts were polarized in this way? _____

_____

_____

_____

When you've used polarized thinking, has it ever caused conflict between yourself and others? (Describe) _____

_____

_____

_____

Write a rational comeback to replace your distorted perception:_____

_____

_____

_____

Overgeneralization

When you overgeneralize, you reach a broad, generalized conclusion based on just one piece of evidence.

Example. "My friend rejected me, therefore nobody will ever love me."

Distorted Perception. "This one rejection is the sole determinant of whether or not I'll be loved by other people in the future."

Rational Comeback. "Just because this one friend rejected me, it doesn't mean that no one will ever love me again. It just means that the one person rejected me. Many people do like me, and I continue to make new friends."

Give an example of when you've used overgeneralization in your thinking: _____

_____

_____

Identify the distorted perception in your example: _____

_____

_____

_____

How did you feel when you overgeneralized? _____

_____

_____

_____

When you've overgeneralized in the past, has it caused conflict between yourself and others? (Describe) _____

_____

_____

_____

Write a rational comeback to replace your distorted perception:_____

_____

_____

_____

Mind Reading

Mind reading is just what it sounds like: you base assumptions and conclusions on your "ability" to know other people's thoughts.

Example. "He looked at his watch while I was in the middle of my presentation. He was afraid that I was boring everyone."

Distorted Perception. "I know what he was thinking about when he looked at his watch."

Rational Comeback. "Only he knows what he was thinking about when he looked at his watch (if it was even a conscious gesture). It more than likely had no reference to me or my presentation. *I* was the one who was worried about boring people."

Can you think of a time when you've used the cognitive distortion of mind reading? __

_____

_____

_____

Identify the distorted perception in your example: _____

_____

_____

_____

How did it make you feel when you assumed that you could read other people's minds (and when you saw unflattering thoughts there)? _____

_____

_____

_____

When you've fallen prey to mind reading, has it caused conflict between yourself and others? (Describe) _____

_____

_____

_____

Write a rational comeback to replace your distorted perception: _____

_____

_____

_____

Catastrophizing

When you catastrophize, as the word suggests, you turn everything into a catastrophe, always expecting the worst-case scenario.

Example. "My son has a cold that's probably going to turn into pneumonia—my God, he's going to die!"

Distorted Perception. "Colds always lead to pneumonia and, ultimately, death."

Rational Comeback. "My son is strong and healthy, and uses good judgment. If his cold gets any worse, he'll see a doctor. He'll get antibiotics if he needs them. In this day and age, young healthy people just don't die from colds or pneumonia."

Can you think of an example of catastrophic thinking on your part? _____

_____

_____

Identify the distorted perception in your example: _____

_____

_____

_____

How did it make you feel to think this way?_____

_____

_____

_____

When you've used catastrophic thinking, has it caused conflict between yourself and others? (Describe) _____

_____

_____

_____

Write a rational comeback to replace your distorted perception:_____

_____

_____

_____

Personalization

When your thinking is distorted by personalization, you interpret everything around you in ways that reflect on you and, often, your self-worth. Personalization is a double-edged sword, in that sometimes it makes you feel great—as when everyone you deal with in the course of a day is kind and cheerful, and you take this as a sign of your winning personality and charm. But the grumpy person you encounter, who isn't won over by your brightest smile, can convince you that you've lost your looks, your personality has gone flat, and you've just been fooling yourself all these years.

Example. "If I'd done a better job as a mother, my daughter wouldn't be depressed."

Distorted Perception. "I should be able to control my daughter's happiness or unhappiness."

Rational Comeback. "No one—not even a parent—can determine whether another individual is happy or unhappy. My daughter's depression is determined by many factors, and unfortunately most of these are beyond my control."

Can you think of an example of when you have used personalization? _____

_____

_____

_____

Identify the distorted perception in your example: _____

_____

_____

_____

How did it make you feel when you've used personalization? _____

_____

_____

_____

When you've used personalization, has it caused conflict between yourself and others? (Describe) _____

_____

_____

_____

Write a rational comeback to replace your distorted perception: _____

_____

_____

_____

Control Fallacies

This distortion entails feeling either that the events in your life are totally controlled by a force outside of yourself or that you are responsible for everything.

Example 1. "What's the use of looking for work in my field? Everyone who's any good already has a job."

Distorted Perception. "No one who's competent ever has to look for a job; the work just magically appears."

Rational Comeback. "I've got to play an active role in getting work—even geniuses have to pound the pavement sometimes and knock on doors. People aren't necessarily thinking about me (and passing me over) when they hand out jobs to other freelancers. I've got to remind all my contacts in the field that I'm available."

Example 2. "How can I possibly take a vacation now? The whole office will fall apart if I leave."

Distorted Perception. "Even though lots of other people are employed at my office, I'm the one who's really doing all the work and holding things together."

Rational Comeback. "The staff has been structured so that every employee can take a vacation once a year—including me. My work is certainly important, but it's no more important than anyone else's; and it's important for me to take my vacation, too."

Can you think of an example of when you have used one or both of the control fallacies?

_____

_____

_____

_____

_____

Identify the distorted perception in your example: _____

_____

_____

_____

How have you felt when you've used this fallacy?_____

_____

_____

_____

When you've used control fallacies, has it caused conflict between yourself and others? (Describe) _____

_____

_____

_____

Write a rational comeback to replace your distorted perception:_____

_____

_____

_____

Fallacy of Fairness

When you use the fairness fallacy, you fall into the trap of judging people's actions by rules that you've concocted about what is and what isn't fair. The trouble is that in personal interactions at least, everyone has different ideas about fairness, so you're bound to wind up feeling hurt, slighted, or wronged.

Example. "If my husband really cared about my wellness, he'd take on more responsibility with the house and kids."

Distorted Perception. "How much my husband cares about my wellness is defined by the amount of housework he takes on."

Rational Comeback. "My husband does a lot of other things that show how much he cares about my wellness: he's very attentive and tender toward me, he reads to me in bed, he does all the yardwork, takes care of the dogs, and works very hard at his job (which pays my doctors' bills). I can talk to him about feeling overburdened by the housework and all the demands the kids make on me. If we work together, we might find some solutions."

Can you think of an example of when you used the fallacy of fairness? _____

_____

_____

_____

Identify the distorted perception in your example: _____

_____

_____

_____

How did you feel when you used the fallacy of fairness? _____

_____

_____

_____

When you've used this distortion, has it ever caused conflict between yourself and others? (Describe) _____

_____

_____

_____

Write a rational comeback to replace your distorted perception:_____

_____

_____

_____

Emotional Reasoning

This is the mistaken belief that everything you feel must be true.

Example. "I feel stupid, therefore I must be stupid."

Distorted Perception. "My subjective feelings always reflect reality."

Rational Comeback. "My opinions about myself change all the time, often depending on my mood. No one is *just* smart or *just* stupid. I probably make poor choices or use poor judgment sometimes, but that's just part of being human. Most people would probably say that I'm pretty intelligent."

Can you think of an example of when you have used emotional reasoning? _____

_____

_____

_____

Identify the distorted perception in your example: _____

_____

_____

_____

How did you feel when you used emotional reasoning? _____

_____

_____

_____

When you've used emotional reasoning, has it caused conflict between yourself and others? (Describe) _____

_____

_____

_____

Write a rational comeback to replace your distorted perception:_____

_____

_____

_____

Fallacy of Change

This is the assumption that other people will change to suit you if you pressure them enough. The illusion is that your happiness depends on bringing about these changes. Co-dependent behavior, which you may have read about in other contexts, relies heavily on this fallacy.

Example. "If my father would only start going to A.A. meetings, we could make another attempt at having a decent relationship."

Distorted Perception. "The quality of my relationship with my father depends on whether or not he goes to A.A. meetings."

Rational Comeback. "I have no control over whether or not Dad goes to A.A. meetings. The only part of our relationship that I *can* control has to do with my own thoughts and feelings and actions. To the extent that I can change these, I can change our relationship."

Can you think of an example of when you have used the fallacy of change? _____

_____

_____

Identify the distorted perception in your example: _____

_____

_____

_____

How did you feel when you used the fallacy of change? _____

_____

_____

_____

When you've used this distortion, did it ever cause conflict between yourself and others? (Describe) _____

_____

_____

_____

Write a rational comeback to replace your distorted perception: _____

_____

_____

_____

Global Labeling

This is making a broad judgment based on very little evidence.

Example. "One of the mangos I bought at that store turned out to be rotten, therefore the store has rotten produce and I'm never going back there."

Distorted Perception. "It's accurate to judge the quality of this store's merchandise on the basis of one piece of fruit."

Rational Comeback. "Just because I got one bad mango does not mean that the store as a whole is no good. It just means that they had some rotten mangos. (If I go back and tell them, maybe they'll give me a refund—or a better mango!)"

Can you think of an example of when you have used global labeling? _____

_____

_____

Identify the distorted perception in your example: _____

_____

_____

_____

How did you feel when you used global labeling? _____

_____

_____

_____

When you used global labeling, did it cause conflict between yourself and others? (Describe) _____

_____

_____

_____

Write a rational comeback to replace your distorted perception: _____

_____

_____

_____

Blaming

This is a very common distortion and is just what it sounds like: bad things that happen are someone's fault, either yours or someone else's.

Example. "*I'm depressed because my family of origin was completely dysfunctional.*"

Distorted Perception. "Dysfunctional families always cause people to suffer from depression when they grow up."

Rational Comeback. "It's true that I grew up in a dysfunctional family; but my depression has also involved a lot of other factors, including choices I've made and continue to make."

Can you think of an example of when you have used the logical distortion of blaming?

_____

_____

Identify the distorted perception in your example: _____

_____

_____

_____

How did you feel when you used blaming as an explanation? _____

_____

_____

_____

When you've used blaming, has it ever caused conflict between yourself and others? (Describe) _____

_____

_____

_____

Write a rational comeback to replace your distorted perception:_____

_____

_____

_____

Shoulds

This entails operating from a rigid set of indisputable rules about how everyone, including yourself, should act.

Example. "I should never feel jealous."

Distorted Perception. "My behavior should always conform to a rigid set of rules."

Rational Comeback. "I'm as subject to as wide a range of emotions as any other human being. Jealousy is one of these emotions."

What are some of your shoulds, the rigid rules that you invoke for yourself and others?

_____

_____

_____

_____

_____

_____

How do you feel when you think in terms of shoulds? _____

_____

_____

_____

When you use shoulds, does it ever cause conflict between yourself and others? (Describe) _____

_____

_____

_____

Write a rational comeback to each of the shoulds you listed above: _____

_____

_____

_____

_____

Being Right

This distortion involves continually needing to justify your point of view or way of behaving. The need to be right can make it impossible for you to really listen when someone offers a new perspective or a conflicting point of view. For an example, consider the following dialogue:

Example.

Daughter: I felt so sad after our visit. I felt like you were completely indifferent to me when I arrived and when I left, even though it had been six months since we'd seen each other.

Mother: I swear to God, no matter what I do, it's never right and it's never enough. All my friends think I'm just great—it's my kids who complain about me.

Daughter: I cried as I drove away. I kept saying to myself that I'm a good person and a lovable person, even though you don't seem to think so.

Mother: I don't know what you want from me, Susan. I've tried everything, and all I get is criticism. We used to have a great relationship before you were married. I don't know what happened.

Daughter: Mom, I've been married for 17 years!
Distorted Percep-
tion.   [*Mother*] "It's impossible that I'm at fault."

Can you think of an example of when you have used being right as a cognitive distortion?

_____

_____

_____

_____

Identify the distorted perception in your example: _____

_____

_____

_____

How did you feel when you used being right? _____

_____

_____

_____

Has this distortion ever caused conflict between yourself and others? (Describe) _____

_____

_____

_____

Write a rational comeback to replace your distorted perception:_____

_____

_____

_____

Heaven's Reward Fallacy

This could be called the martyr's fallacy. You believe that if you always do the right thing, you will eventually be rewarded (even if doing the right thing means ignoring your own needs).

Example. "My career comes second after my kids. Actually, I'm ready to postpone my career for 20 years, if need be, to give my children the attention they need. I may be messed up; but if it's the last thing I do, I'm going to make sure that my daughter has good self-esteem."

Distorted Perception. "My self-sacrifice will make my children into happy individuals, and I will be proved in the end to be a good mother."

Rational Comeback. "How can my daughter possibly end up with good self-esteem when she has me for a role model? I'm the family doormat! I love my kids, but it's a waste to put a successful career on hold for 20 years. I can work out a compromise between my needs and theirs—and we'll all be happier as a result!"

Can you think of an example of when you have used the heaven's reward fallacy? ____

_____

_____

_____

Identify the distorted perception in your example: _____

_____

_____

_____

How did you feel when you used the heaven's reward fallacy? _____

_____

_____

_____

Did this ever cause conflict between yourself and others? (Describe) _____

_____

_____

_____

Write a rational comeback to replace your distorted perception: _____

_____

_____

_____

A Four-Step Process for Eliminating Distorted Thoughts

There are several simple and very effective techniques for changing or eliminating stress-producing, distorted, and negative thought patterns to positive ones. By systematically examining thought patterns and applying behavioral techniques, you can change the way you think and feel about yourself and your life. This will have a profound effect on your moods, and will greatly enhance the quality of your life. The four steps in this process involve

- Identifying your emotion

- Describing the situation that gave rise to the emotion

- Identifying the distortion in your thought process

- Refuting the distortion

Read through the example below.

1. What emotion (or emotions) are you feeling now?
I am feeling angry, tense, and anxious.

2. Describe, *in detail*, the event or situation that gave rise to your emotion.
I went to my friend Peter's house at 4:00 p.m., as previously arranged, to go for a walk and have dinner together. He was not at home when I got there.

3. Describe your thoughts, and identify any distortions in your thinking.
Because Peter wasn't there, I decided he really didn't want to spend the time with me, that he really doesn't like me and doesn't respect my feelings. (This would fit in the category of mind-reading.)

4. Refute the distortions.
There was only one piece of evidence, his not being there when I arrived, that was the basis for my distortion. The truth is, Peter and I have been close friends for a long time. All evidence indicates that he likes me a lot. An emergency may have come up, he may have gone to do an errand that took longer than anticipated, he may have misunderstood the plan that we made or he may have forgotten that we made a plan (or I may have misunderstood)— any of which are acceptable reasons and do nothing to lend credence to my distorted thought. The best course of action for me would be to wait on his porch (doing relaxation exercises) until his return; or leave him a note asking him to call me when he gets in.

Practice using this four-step process to work on straightening out your distorted thoughts. For your first try, choose a situation in which the distortion in your thinking is fairly easy for you to identify. As the process becomes clearer, you can work on situations in which the distortion is more subtle (or in which there are several distortions operating at once). Use separate sheets of paper to analyze each situation.

1. What emotion (or emotions) are you feeling now? _____

_____

_____

_____

2. Describe in detail the event or situation that gave rise to your emotions: _____

_____

_____

_____

3. Describe your thoughts and identify any distortions in your thinking: (Refer to the descriptions of distorted thinking styles in this chapter.)_____

_____

_____

_____

4. Refute the distortions: _____

_____

_____

_____

As you grow more familiar with this process, it will come as second nature to you, so that you can straighten out your thought distortions before they have a negative effect on your mood.

Thought Stopping

Thought stopping is a simple way to bring thoughts to consciousness and eliminate them. By eliminating a negative thought, you can eliminate the emotions and feelings that go along with it.

Step 1. Identify a Negative Thought for Target Practice

Review the self-doubts, fears, and phobias that you listed earlier. Check off those that are currently most bothersome, cause you the most stress, and interfere the most with your life. Then choose one of these thoughts to practice on. It's best to begin with a thought whose logic is pretty easy to topple. As you grow more adept, you can tackle more and more formidable beliefs and notions.

Bothersome Thought: _____

_____

Ask yourself the following questions to determine whether this thought needs to be changed:

Is this thought realistic or unrealistic? _____

Is the thought productive or counterproductive? _____

Is this thought easy or hard to control? _____

How uncomfortable does this thought make me feel? _____

_____

How much does this thought interfere with my life? _____

_____

Sample Thought-Stopping Exercise

Bothersome Thought: *I'm afraid that I'll have another deep depression and need hospitalization.*

Is this thought realistic or unrealistic? *It is realistic, because I have had deep depressions before for which I needed to be hospitalized. However, the circumstances of my life have changed significantly since then. I understand depression. I have an excellent support system of health care workers, family members, and friends. I watch for early warning signs and get help early. Several related medical problems have been appropriately treated. I use relaxation techniques, exercise regularly, and carefully manage my diet. I have eliminated sugar and caffeine from my diet. There is limited stress in my life and I have learned to handle stress that is unavoidable.*

Is the thought productive or counterproductive? *Definitely counterproductive.*

Is this thought easy or hard to control? *At times this thought is very hard to control.*

How uncomfortable does this thought make me feel? *Very uncomfortable!*

How much does this thought interfere with my life? *It interferes a lot, because it makes me feel depressed and discouraged.*

Based on the answers to these questions, it is clear that I would benefit from eliminating this thought from my mental repertoire.

Step 2. Dwell on the Thought

Bring the thought to the level of consciousness and focus on it for several minutes. You might want to do this when you're very relaxed, or combined with a meditation.

Step 3. Interrupting the Thought

When first working with a persistent thought, it's important to stop it by means of a powerful response.

One way to do this is to set a timer for 3 minutes. Now think about the thought. When the timer goes off, shout "Stop!" You could also raise your hand, snap your fingers, or stand up quickly. Then empty your mind of the thought. Keep your mind blank or focused on a positive thought for at least 30 seconds. If the intrusive thought returns during that time, shout "Stop!" again.

Another way to do this is to tape record yourself shouting "Stop!" at timed intervals. Focus on the thought, then drive it from your mind each time you hear yourself shout "Stop!"

Some people wear a rubber band on their wrist to snap instead of saying "Stop!" when unwanted thoughts come up. Others pinch themselves or dig their nails into the palms of their hands. You will discover what works best for you.

Whenever you realize that you are thinking the unwanted thought, shout "Stop!" After you have done this successfully several times, you can progress to saying "Stop" in a normal tone of voice when unwanted thoughts come up. Eventually you can move on to a whisper, and finally to just saying "Stop" to yourself silently whenever negative thoughts resurface.

Step 4. Substitute a Positive or Assertive Thought for the Negative One

Whenever the negative thought comes up, immediately replace it with an alternative thought. For example, instead of thinking, "I will have a deep depression and need hospitalization," replace it with, "I am feeling fine."

Stopping a thought takes time and patience. But, gradually, you will notice that the thought recurs less and less frequently.

Exercise: Thought Stopping

Bothersome Thought:_____

_____

Is the thought realistic or unrealistic? _____

Is the thought productive or counterproductive? _____

Is the thought easy or hard to control? _____

How uncomfortable does this thought make me feel?_____

_____

_____

How much does this thought interfere with my life? _____

_____

_____

_____

Based on the answers to the above questions, do you still feel that this is an appropriate thought to stop? If your answer is no, choose another thought and begin the process again.

Bring the thought to consciousness and focus on it for several minutes. How did that feel? _____

_____

Working with either a timer or a recording, focus on the thought and then interrupt it by shouting "Stop!"

- ☐ *I am going to use a timer to alert me when to shout "Stop!"*
- ☐ *I'll use a recording of my own voice that says "Stop!"*
- ☐ *I'll raise my hand when I shout "Stop!"*
- ☐ *I'll snap my fingers when I shout "Stop!"*
- ☐ *I'll stand up when I shout "Stop!"*

You can use all or one of these strategies to reinforce your cognitive-behavioral change. Repeat this process until you feel ready to move on to the next step. Then interrupt the thought without using a timer or recording. Progress from shouting, to saying, to whispering, and, finally, thinking the word "Stop." **How did this work for you?** _____

_____

When you feel ready, substitute a positive or assertive thought for the intrusive one. *The positive or assertive thought I will substitute is:*_____

_____

_____

When you have become proficient at this technique, you can use it to eliminate other obsessive self-doubts, fears, and phobias. You can work on one or several thoughts at a time, whichever feels best to you. Remember to give yourself credit for your success.

Examples of Changing Negative Thoughts to Positive Ones

Many of us have gotten into the habit of thinking in ways that are inaccurate, irrational, and self-defeating. This negative "self-talk" causes unnecessary stress, anxiety, and depression. By examining these negative thoughts and changing them to positive ones, you can make great strides toward improving and stabilizing your moods and enhancing your overall well-being.

Below I've listed some commonly held belief patterns of people with mood disorders, followed by suggestions on how these patterns can be changed to have a positive effect on your feelings.

Negative Thought: *I will never be well. I will always have problems with depression and/or mania.*

The Truth: *There's no reason why I can't continue to stay well.*

My mother was in a hospital for 8 years with severe mood swings. In the past 35 years, she has had only one brief episode, which was quickly brought under control through psychotherapy and short-term drug therapy.

Of people in the study, 82 expressed a belief in finding solutions to their problem with mood swings; 50 people have had times when they felt that their mood swings were over for good (these periods lasted from 1 month to 25 years).

The ways in which people achieved these results include the use of medications, appropriate treatment of medical problems, and a variety of therapies, including stress reduction and relaxation work, exercise, diet, and lifestyle changes. They did it, and you can, too!

One study participant said, "At the present time, my mood has been stabilized for over a year. It would be unrealistic to think it will never happen again, but at the same time, I don't want the anticipation of another episode to stop me from living and functioning right now. I just live with the security that if and when it happens again, I will handle it—'just like before.' I have established a solid support system."

If "I will never be well" is part of your negative self-talk, write thoughts you can use to change that negative thought pattern to thoughts that are more positive: _____

_____

_____

_____

_____

Negative Thought: *I am not worth anything.*

Low self-esteem plagues those of use who have experienced mood disorders. Recurring bouts of debilitating depression, sometimes countered with manic extremes, including bizarre behavior, make it difficult for people with mood disorders to maintain a positive self-image.

The Truth: *I have a great deal of value.*

To really get this one refutation programmed into your brain, spend some time reading books on positive thinking (see the Resources List).

Write here some personal positive statement of your value: _____

_____

_____

_____

_____

Negative Thought: *I have never accomplished anything.*
The Truth: *I've already accomplished a great deal.*

Give yourself some credit! Take a few moments for some serious and honest thought about your achievements so far.

Make a list of your accomplishments. I'm providing plenty of space, as people with mood disorders tend to have high levels of achievement! You can use additional pages if you need to. Be sure to include all educational and personal achievements. Be true to yourself and give yourself a break. Don't minimize anything you have accomplished. _____

_____

_____

_____

_____

Make photocopies of the list of your accomplishments, and post it in prominent places. Let it be a reminder of your self-worth whenever you are feeling as if you have never accomplished anything.

Negative Thought: *I will never accomplish anything.*

The Truth: *I have the capacity to accomplish just about whatever I want to, with the exception of a few physical restrictions.*

What is it that you would like to accomplish in your life? What are your dreams and goals? Write them here. Use additional pages if you need to. _____

_____

_____

_____

_____

_____

_____

Read your list of dreams and goals over again and again. As you reread it, you will begin taking positive steps toward the achievement of these goals. (Fantasy is a powerful tool toward the fulfillment of your hopes and dreams!) If you have setbacks, just pick yourself up, dust yourself off, and get going again.

Negative Thought: *I cannot allow myself to make mistakes.*
The Truth: *Everyone makes mistakes.*

We don't like to make mistakes, but we all do. And it's not the end of the world. No one is perfect. It doesn't mean that you are stupid or worthless if you make a mistake. It just means that you made a mistake. Acknowledge your errors, then do whatever you can to learn from them.

Negative Thought: *In order for me to be happy, everyone must love and approve of me.*
The Truth: *It would be great if I could be loved and approved of by everyone, but it just isn't the way the world works.*

Just as you don't love or approve of everyone you meet, it's not possible for everyone to love and approve of you. It doesn't mean that you are bad or that anything is wrong with you. Tastes are so diverse that no one can please everyone. The important thing is to make sure that you love and approve of yourself.

Negative Thought: *I want to die.*

This thought is all too common among people when they are depressed. I know that I have said this over and over again in my mind, literally hundreds of times a day. That is what my mother repeated constantly when she was in a deep depression. I've learned to stop this negative thought before it even surfaces.

The Truth: *I want to live and be happy.*

Replace that old, worn-out "I want to die" with "I choose life."

Take it from me, this works! I really had to work at changing this debilitating negative thought, but I have succeeded in committing myself to living, no matter what comes up.

For yourself, your loved ones, and the world, for all you can achieve, give yourself the gift of life. I have and I'm glad. Even when the going is really rough, and I don't feel like I can get out of bed one more time, I choose life. In the next moment my daughter could poke her head around the corner, a good friend could call, the swallows could return, or a beautiful sunset could paint the sky. Take a chance on what's around the corner and choose life.

☐ *I choose life.*

Negative Thought: *There is no reason for me to go on living.*
The Truth: *There are many compelling reasons why I should live my life.* Your reasons might include your loving feelings for family members, friends, and pets; flowers, trees, the ocean, the mountains; your enjoyment of skiing, skating, walking, making love, eating wonderful food; the pleasure you get from movies, television shows, art, music, and travel; the satisfaction you get from artistic and productive work, from helping others, from communicating meaningfully with others, or communing with Nature or God.

Make a list of the reasons why you should live: _____

_____

_____

_____

_____

_____

_____

_____

_____

_____

_____

For Christmas, my three granddaughters gave me an enlargement of a wonderful picture of them all laughing, mounted on brightly colored poster board and surrounded by their hand prints. I have it displayed on a wall where I see it constantly. It gives me such a lift, I smile every time I see it. It reminds me of how much I want to go on living.

I'm going to fill my living space with the following reminders of why I should live: _____

_____

_____

_____

_____

This is my personal plan for how I'm going to spend more time with people I enjoy: _____

_____

_____

_____

_____

_____

This is how I plan to make more time in my life to do the things I like to do: _____

_____

_____

_____

_____

Further Positive Comebacks for Negative Thoughts

The following negative thoughts were expressed by people at a mood disorders support group I belong to. The group helped everyone develop positive thoughts to counter their negative ones. (I highly recommend this activity for support groups.)

Negative Thought: *I am lazy.*
Positive Thought: *I am a hard worker when I am feeling well.*

Negative Thought: *I don't have any goals.*
Positive Thought: *I am developing some goals for myself.*

Negative Thought: *I am unmotivated.*
Positive Thought: *I am a highly motivated person.*

Negative Thought: *I am an outsider.*
Positive Thought: *I am part of the group.*

Negative Thought: *I am unlovable.*
Positive Thought: *I am a lovable person.*

Negative Thought: *I am dysfunctional.*
Positive Thought: *I'm having a hard time right now, but I'm working hard at getting better.*

Negative Thought: *I don't have any social skills.*
Positive Thought: *I'm developing my social skills.*

Negative Thought: *I'm getting older and yet I'm not where I should be in life.*
Positive Thought: *Everyone is getting older, and everyone develops at a different rate. I'm just where I should be.*

Negative Thought: *I am all alone in the world.*
Positive Thought: *I know and love many people.*

Negative Thought: *I will always be alone.*
Positive Thought: *I might continue to be alone, but there are many people who are precious to me.*

Negative Thought: *I have wasted many years of my life.*
Positive Thought: *I have done many good things during my life.*

Negative Thought: *I am hurting my body by smoking and drinking.*
Positive Thought: *I'm working hard on giving up smoking and drinking, and I know that I will soon achieve my goal.*

Negative Thought: *I am getting older and I look like it.*
Positive Thought: *Everyone gets older—but happiness is the best cosmetic. The happier I feel, the better I'll look.*

Negative Thought: *I will never succeed, so why bother trying?*
Positive Thought: *I will succeed—that is why I am trying so hard.*

Negative Thought: *What's the use?*
Positive Thought: *Life is worthwhile.*

Negative Thought: *Even if I do succeed, I am going to die anyway.*
Positive Thought: *Of course, everyone dies; but I might as well try to make the best of my time while I'm alive.*

Negative Thought: *Nobody loves me.*
Positive Thought: *Many people love me.*

Negative Thought: *I have leaned on those who love me so much that they are sick to death of me.*
Positive Thought: *There is joy in giving as well as receiving. Those who help me do so because they want to. I'm going to give back as much as I can—but first I have to get well.*

Negative Thought: *I drag people down.*
Positive Thought: *I often make people feel better by being an understanding and sympathetic friend.*

Negative Thought: *I am a burden.*
Positive Thought: *I have lots to give.*

Negative Thought: *I am unable to love.*
Positive Thought: *I know that I can love.*

Negative Thought: *I will never be independent again.*
Positive Thought: *I've been independent before, and I'll be independent again.*

Negative Thought:	*I will always be like this. It will not end. It's hopeless.*
Positive Thought:	*People with the kinds of problems I have do get well, and they stay well for long periods of time.*
Negative Thought:	*What's the point?*
Positive Thought:	*I'm alive, so I have plenty of gifts. It's my responsibility to make the most of them.*
Negative Thought:	*I blew my college education by getting fired.*
Positive Thought:	*I only got fired. I did not blow my education. I'll get another job. Nothing short of amnesia can take away the things I learned in college.*
Negative Thought:	*I don't deserve to live.*
Positive Thought:	*I deserve to live.*
Negative Thought:	*Why bother? Whatever I do, it won't work.*
Positive Thought:	*Sometimes the things I do work out well.*
Negative Thought:	*How can I succeed at suicide?*
Positive Thought:	*How can I succeed at life?*
Negative Thought:	*I am not as well equipped as everyone else to function in the world.*
Positive Thought:	*I am just as well equipped as everyone else to function in the world. I have a good mind and a good heart.*
Negative Thought:	*I am weak-willed; I have a character defect.*
Positive Thought:	*I am basically a strong person. I am just having a hard time right now.*
Negative Thought:	*Why me? Why am I afflicted?*
Positive Thought:	*Everyone has problems. We just do the best we can with them.*
Negative Thought:	*It's my fault I'm depressed. If I tried harder, I wouldn't have mood swings.*
Positive Thought:	*Mood swings aren't anyone's fault, not any more than the flu or cancer. I'm doing the best I can to get well.*

Affirmations

Many people have made dramatic changes in their lives through the creation and repetition of positive affirmations. An affirmation is a statement that describes the way you would want your life (or you) to be at its very best. Although this notion may seem a bit simplistic, it really works: repeated over and over again, affirmations can have tremendous power to act as a very positive force in your life.

I have used affirmations successfully for many years, as have many people in the study. It has been interesting for me to review old affirmations from time to time to see how my life has changed. Some affirmations that were appropriate for me several years ago are not even necessary now, and I have replaced them with new ones. This is an ongoing process. I keep my affirmations in a journal by my bedside and review them daily, updating them as appropriate. I keep extra lists of them handy, one in my pocketbook to review when I am waiting for an appointment and another near my exercise bicycle for me to read while I'm pedaling.

Rules for Creating Affirmations

1. **When developing an affirmation, always use the present tense.** For example: *I am healthy, I am well, I have a good job,* as if the condition already existed.

2. **Use only positive words in your affirmations.** For example, *happy, peaceful, loving, enthusiastic, warm.* Avoid using negative terms such as *worried, frightened, upset, tired, bored,* even if you're negating them (don't say "I'm not upset"; say instead, "I feel calm").

3. **Use the first person:** *I, me,* or your own name.

4. **The affirmation should create a strong picture of you, successful in whatever way you desire, right now.**

5. **Keep your affirmation short and simple.**

6. **If you have a religious or spiritual faith, use your faith to enhance this process.** For example, "I trust the perfection and goodness of the universe."

Examples of Positive Affirmations

I think and act with confidence.
I am strong and powerful.
I fully accept myself as I am.
I have many accomplishments to my credit.
I am healthy and energetic.
I deserve the time and space to heal.
I have all the resources I need to do what I want to in my life.
I am loved by many people.
I am a very valuable person.
I am safe and protected.
I am effective and efficient in stressful situations.
I am peaceful and serene at all times.
My relationships are happy and fulfilling.
I am in charge of my life.
I look and feel wonderful.

I express myself easily and comfortably.
I choose life.

Developing Affirmations

Compose some affirmations of your own. You can use this opportunity to create an idealized picture of your life and circumstances, and the ways in which you respond. It's all right for your affirmations to stretch the truth, or even be complete fabrications, as long as they represent your image of the way you'd like things to be. Imagination is a powerful precursor to reality! _____

_____

_____

_____

_____

_____

_____

_____

_____

It's a good idea to keep a journal by your bedside with an updated list of the affirmations you find most helpful.

Practicing Your Affirmations

1. Once you have developed your affirmations, repeat them several times first thing in the morning and before going to sleep at night. Having your journal beside your bed will serve as a useful reminder.

2. Repeat your affirmations over and over again when you are relaxing or meditating.

3. Repeat your affirmations at any time during the day when you are not concentrating on something else (to yourself, or out loud when possible). For example, when you are doing the dishes, vacuuming, are stuck in traffic, waiting in line at the grocery store. The more you repeat your affirmations, the sooner they will reflect reality.

4. Reinforce your affirmations by writing them over and over again while repeating them silently or out loud.

5. It can help to repeat an affirmation in an overly loud tone of voice. Diminish the volume gradually until you are repeating the affirmation in a whisper and finally saying it silently inside your head. (This is a good exercise to do when you are traveling in your car.)

17

Using Relaxation To Stabilize Moods

Learning to release the tension in my body has been such a gift. I can use relaxation any time and it's free.

Relaxation and Mental Health

More and more people are using relaxation techniques—also referred to as meditation—to make themselves feel much, much better. The value of deep relaxation in achieving wellness is also being recognized increasingly by the medical community. Research shows that the benefits of practicing relaxation techniques increase dramatically over time. Many studies have found that regular relaxation can speed psychotherapy, lessen chemical addiction, and decrease anxiety.

People in the study noted that they use relaxation techniques to lift themselves out of depression and to alleviate mania (sometimes only temporarily—but any kind of break helps). Relaxation is particularly successful at decreasing the agitation that is often a warning signal of an impending mood swing.

To be able to use relaxation techniques during a crisis, it's essential to learn how to relax when you're stable (it's pretty much impossible to learn relaxation when you're either too high or too low). Relaxation techniques can be a valuable resource in helping you work through difficult times and in lowering your stress level on an ongoing basis.

The first step is to learn how to relax. In our fast-paced society, this is not as easy as it sounds.

Learning To Relax

Because relaxation is being recognized as such an important adjunct to good health, you have many resources available for learning the state of the art in relaxation techniques. Read and practice the relaxation techniques described later in this chapter. You may also want to utilize any or all of the following supplementary tools.

Take a relaxation or meditation course. Such courses are now available in most geographical areas and are often free. In my area, a relaxation class was recently sponsored by the local hospital. Learning with others, and under the guidance of an instructor, is an excellent way to learn how to relax or meditate. Look for courses in the community calendar section of your local newspaper. Also check with your local hospital or mental health hotline (see the Resource List at the end of this workbook).

Use an instructional video. In my area, one can borrow excellent videos from the hospice office and the library on how to relax. Relaxation and meditation tapes may also be available for rent at you local video store. Several excellent relaxation videos are for sale (see the Resource List).

Listen to audio relaxation tapes. See lists of audio tapes at the back of this book. Relaxation tapes are also sometimes available at health food stores. I recommend that you buy several of these tapes. They can really help you relax at those times when it is most difficult.

Make your own audio tapes. Use the exercises in this book, or develop your own versions. You may still want to get a commercially produced tape to use as a model.

Check out other resources. There are many excellent books on learning how to relax. These are also listed in the Resource List. Some of these are available at libraries.

I, _____(your name)_____, am committed to learning how to relax, and to practice daily, so that these skills will be available to me when I need them.

These are the resources I'm going to use to learn how to relax: _____

_____

_____

_____

For any method of relaxation or meditation to be effective, you must practice daily at a regular time. I practice relaxation techniques for 15 minutes before I get out of bed in the morning and for 15 minutes before I go to sleep (sometimes it *puts* me to sleep). I also try to practice for half an hour after lunch, but my schedule does not always allow for this.

You will figure out for yourself the times when your house or workplace is most quiet, and when you can take a 15-minute break without interruption. Ask your family or co-workers to respect this time by keeping quiet and not disturbing you.

Locate a space or several spaces that are cozy, comfortable, and quiet. This might be in a corner, in your living room, a window seat in your bedroom, or the lunchroom at work. It's also possible to relax out of doors, in a secluded place in the woods, near a meadow, stream, by the ocean, or on a mountaintop. Churches, which are often open and empty on weekdays, are wonderful, quiet places where you can practice relaxation techniques.

Some people like to make their relaxation space special by adorning it with comfortable cushions, pictures, flowers, and candles. The only hard-and-fast rules are to make sure that the space is quiet, that you are comfortable there, and that you will not be disturbed.

I will practice relaxation in the following place or places: _____

_____

_____

_____

Set up a two-week trial period to determine how regular periods of deep relaxation will affect your life.

For two weeks I will relax _____ *times daily at the following times:* _____

_____

How I felt before I began this relaxation program: _____

_____

_____

_____

How I felt after I completed the two-week relaxation program: _____

_____

_____

_____

Based on what I learned through the trial period, I am going to take the following action regarding structured periods of relaxation: _____

_____

_____

_____

_____

I am going to practice my relaxation techniques every day at the following times: _____

_____

If you miss a session now and again, don't fret. Just do the best you can. Practice relaxing until it becomes second nature, and until you can use the technique any time you begin to feel nervous, tense, or irritable.

When you notice danger signs that you are getting either manic or depressed, spend more time using your relaxation techniques and practice more often during the day. At these times, it can be salvational to use an audio or video tape that has a guided meditation exercise (you may be too subject to distraction to meditate or relax on your own).

Relaxation Techniques

Breathing

Proper breathing habits and simple breathing exercises relax the body and mind. People who practice these exercises daily, either by themselves or before beginning a meditation session with others, find that breathing properly can alleviate depression and mania, enhance the meditation experience, and create a greater sense of overall well-being. Read through the techniques described below and decide which might work best for you. You may want to try them all.

Breathing Awareness

Lie down on the floor with you legs flat or bent at the knees, your arms at your sides, your palms up, and your eyes closed. Breathe through your nose if you can. Focus on your breathing. Place your hand on the place that seems to rise and fall the most as you breathe. If this place is on your chest, you will need to practice breathing more deeply so your abdomen rises and falls most noticeably. (When we are nervous or anxious, we tend to breathe short, shallow breaths in the upper chest.) Now place both hands on your abdomen and notice how it rises and falls with each breath. Notice if your chest is moving in harmony with your abdomen. Continue to do this for several minutes. Get up slowly. This exercise is something you can do during a break at work. If you can't lie down, you can do it sitting in a chair.

How I felt before I did the breathing awareness exercise: _____

_____

_____

How I felt after doing the breathing awareness exercise: _____

_____

_____

_____

Practice deep breathing every day for two weeks, then assess how it's affecting your moods and state of mind.

How I felt after practicing the breathing awareness exercise once or twice a day for two weeks: ___

_____

_____

_____

Deep Breathing

This exercise can be practiced in a variety of body positions; however, it's most effective if you can do it lying down with your knees bent and your spine straight. After lying down, scan your body for tension. Place one hand on your abdomen and one hand on your chest. Inhale slowly and deeply through your nose into your abdomen to push up your hand as much as it feels comfortable. Your chest should only move a little in response to the movement in your abdomen. When you feel at ease with your breathing, inhale through your nose and exhale through your mouth, making a relaxing whooshing sound as you gently blow out. This will relax your mouth, tongue, and jaw. Continue taking long, slow, deep breaths that raise and lower your abdomen. As you become more and more relaxed, focus on the sound and feeling of your breathing. Continue this deep breathing for five to ten minutes at a time, once or twice a day. At the end of each session, scan your body for tension. As you become used to this exercise, you can practice it wherever you happen to be, in a standing, sitting or supine position. Use the exercise whenever you feel tense.

How I felt before I did the deep breathing exercise: _____

_____

_____

How I felt after doing the deep breathing exercise: _____

_____

_____

_____

Practice deep breathing awareness every day for two weeks, then assess how it's affecting your moods and state of mind.

How I felt after doing the deep breathing exercise once or twice a day for two weeks: _____

_____

_____

_____

The Relaxing Sigh

Do you notice yourself sighing or yawning during the day? This is usually a sign that you are not breathing deeply enough to get enough oxygen. The sigh or yawn helps to remedy the situation and also releases tension. When you feel the need to relax, sit or stand up straight. Sigh deeply, letting out a sound of deep relief as the air rushes out of your lungs. Then let the air return to your lungs slowly and naturally. Repeat eight to twelve times whenever you feel tense or anxious.

How I felt before I did the relaxing sigh exercise: _____

_____

_____

_____

How I felt after doing the relaxing sigh exercise: _____

_____

_____

_____

Practice the relaxing sigh every day for two weeks, then assess how it's affecting your moods and state of mind.

How I felt after doing the relaxing sigh exercise once or twice a day for two weeks: _____

_____

_____

Complete Natural Breathing

This way of breathing will become second nature as you practice it.

Sit or stand up straight. Breathe through your nose. While inhaling, fill the lower section of your lungs (your diaphragm will push your abdomen out to make more room for the air). Now fill the middle part of your lungs with air as your lower ribs and your chest move forward slightly. Then fill the upper part of your lungs with air as you raise your chest slightly and draw in your abdomen a little. With practice these steps can be performed in one continuous, smooth inhalation in a few seconds. Hold your breath for a few seconds. Exhale slowly, pulling your abdomen in slightly and lifting it up slowly as your lungs empty. When you have exhaled completely, relax your abdomen and chest. Repeat this sequence at least five times, raising your shoulders and collarbone occasionally after the inhalation to be sure that the very top of your lungs is filled with fresh air.

Purifying Breath

This exercise cleans your lungs while stimulating and toning your entire breathing process and refreshing your body. It can be used with the other breathing exercises.

Sit or stand up straight. Inhale a complete natural breath, as described in the previous exercise. Hold this breath for several seconds. Exhale a little of the air with force through a small opening in your lips. Stop exhaling for a moment, then blow out more air. Repeat this procedure until you have exhaled the air. Practice for several minutes.

Tap Away Tension

This is a good exercise to relax you quickly while making you feel more alert.

Stand up straight with your hands at your sides. As you inhale slowly, lightly tap your chest with your fingertips, moving your hand around so that your entire chest is tapped. When you have inhaled as much air as feels comfortable, hold your breath and pat your chest with your palms. Exhale using the purifying breath described in the previous exercise. Practice a few more purifying breaths and then repeat the tap-away-tension exercise as many times as it feels comfortable. After you have repeated this exercise several times, try tapping the areas of your back that you can reach with your hands.

How I felt before I tried complete natural breathing, the purifying breath exercise, and the tap-away-tension exercise: _____

_____

_____

How I felt after trying these exercises: _____

_____

_____

_____

Practice complete natural breathing, the purifying breath, and the tap-away-tension exercises every day for two weeks, then assess how it's affecting your moods and state of mind.

How I felt after practicing these exercises every day for two weeks: _____

_____

_____

_____

The Bracer

This is a good exercise when your energy is low. It will stimulate your breathing, circulation, and nervous system.

Stand up straight with your hands at your sides. Inhale and hold a complete natural breath as described above. Raise your arms straight out in front of you, using just enough energy to keep them up and relaxed. Gradually bring your hands to your shoulders while contracting your hands into fists, so that when they reach your shoulders they are clenched as tight as you can make them. Keep your fists clenched as you push your arms out straight very slowly. Pull your arms back to your shoulders and straighten them out, fists tense, as fast as you can several times. Release your fists and let your arms drop to your sides, exhaling forcefully through your mouth. Practice a few purifying breaths as described previously. Repeat this exercise several times until you feel its purifying effects.

The Windmill

This is a good exercise to revive you when you feel overworked and tense.

Stand up straight with your arms in front of you. Inhale and hold a complete natural breath as described previously. Swing your arms backward in a circle several times and then reverse directions. You may also try rotating them like a windmill. Exhale forcefully through your mouth. Practice several purifying breaths as described earlier. Repeat the exercise several times.

Bending

This is another exercise that will relieve tension when you have been working hard. It will also stretch your torso and make it more flexible.

Stand straight with your hands on your hips. Inhale and hold a complete natural breath as described before. Letting the lower part of your body remain stiff, bow forward as far as you possibly can while exhaling slowly through your mouth. Stand up straight again, inhale, and hold another complete natural breath. Bend backwards while slowly exhaling. Stand up straight again and hold another complete breath. Repeat this exercise, bending to the left and right. After each round of four bends, practice one purifying breath. Do four full rounds.

How I felt before I tried the bracer, the windmill, and the bending exercises: _____

_____

_____

_____

How I felt after trying these exercises: _____

_____

_____

_____

Practice the bracer, windmill, and bending exercises every day for two weeks, then assess how you feel.

How I felt after practicing these exercises every day for two weeks: _____

_____

_____

_____

Complete Natural Breathing and Imagination

Lying down, place your hands on your solar plexus (across your lower ribs) and practice complete natural breathing for several minutes. Imagine that with each incoming breath, energy is rushing into your lungs and being immediately stored in your solar plexus. As you exhale, imagine that this energy is flowing to all parts of your body. Practice daily for at least five to ten minutes. You can also use this exercise to imagine sending energy to a place in your body where there is pain, moving one hand from your solar plexus to the place on your body that hurts.

Alternate Breathing

This is an excellent relaxation exercise. Some people also find that it alleviates tension and sinus headaches.

Sit in a comfortable position with good posture. Rest the index and second finger of your right hand on your forehead. Close your right nostril with your thumb. Inhale slowly and soundlessly through your left nostril. Close your left nostril with your ring finger while opening your right nostril by removing your thumb. Exhale slowly, quietly, and as thoroughly as possible through your right nostril. Inhale through your left nostril. Close your right nostril with your thumb and uncover your left nostril. Exhale then inhale through your left nostril. Begin by doing five cycles of alternate breathing. Gradually increase the number of cycles to ten or twenty-five.

How I felt before I tried complete natural breathing and imagination, and alternate breathing exercises: _____

_____

_____

_____

How I felt after I did these exercises: _____

_____

_____

_____

Practice complete natural breathing and imagination, and the alternate breathing exercises every day for two weeks, then assess what effect they've had on your moods and your state of mind.

How I felt after practicing these exercises every day for two weeks: _____

_____

_____

_____

Many of these exercises are adapted from yogic breathing techniques, and can be practiced and perfected by taking a yoga class (yoga classes are available in most communities around the country).

Progressive Muscle Relaxation

The purpose of progressive muscle relaxation is to focus on body sensations and how relaxation feels by systematically tensing and then relaxing different muscle groups in your body. Make a tape recording of this exercise so that you can use it when you need to. Be sure you leave yourself time on the tape to tense and relax your muscles.

Find a quiet space where you will not be disturbed. You can do this exercise either lying on your back or sitting in a chair, as long as you are comfortable.

Close your eyes. Now clench your right fist as tightly as you can. Be aware of the tension as you do so. Keep your fist clenched for a moment. Now relax. Feel the looseness in your right hand and compare it to the tension you felt previously. Tense your right fist again, then relax it; notice the difference between tension and relaxation.

Now clench your left fist as tightly as you can. Be aware of the tension as you do so. Keep your fist clenched for a moment. Now relax. Feel the looseness in your left hand and compare it to the tension you felt previously. Tense your left fist again, relax it, and again notice the difference.

Bend your elbows and tense your biceps as hard as you can. Notice the feeling of tightness. Relax and straighten out your arms. Let the relaxation flow through your arms and compare it to the tightness you felt before. Tense and relax your biceps again.

Wrinkle your forehead as tightly as you can. Now relax it and let it smooth out. Feel your forehead and scalp becoming relaxed. Now frown and notice the tension spreading through your forehead again. Relax and allow your forehead to become smooth.

Close your eyes now and squint them very tightly. Feel the tension. Now relax your eyes. Tense and relax your eyes again. Now let them remain gently closed.

Now clench your jaw, bite hard, and feel the tension. Now relax your jaw. Your lips will be slightly parted. Notice the difference. Clench and relax again.

Press your tongue against the roof of your mouth. Now relax. Do this again.

Press and purse your lips together. Now relax them. Repeat this.

Feel the relaxation throughout your forehead, scalp, eyes, jaw, tongue, and lips.

Hold your head back as far as it can comfortably go and observe the tightness in your neck. Roll your head to the right and notice how the tension moves and changes. Roll your head to the left and notice how the tension moves and changes. Now straighten your head and bring it forward, pressing your chin against your chest. Notice the tension in your throat and the back of your neck. Now relax and allow your shoulders to return to a comfortable position. Allow yourself to feel more and more relaxed. Now shrug your shoulders and hunch your head down between them. Relax your shoulders. Allow them to drop back, and feel the relaxation moving through your neck, throat, and shoulders; feel the lovely, very deep relaxation.

Give your whole body a chance to relax. Feel how comfortable and heavy it is.

Breathe in and fill you lungs completely. Hold you breath and notice the tension. Let your breath out and let your chest become loose. Continue relaxing, breathing gently in and out. Repeat this breathing several times and notice the tension draining out of your body.

Tighten your stomach and hold the tightness. Feel the tension. Now relax your stomach. Place your hand on your stomach and breathe deeply into your stomach, pushing your hand up. Hold for a moment and then relax. Now arch your back without straining, keeping the rest of your body as relaxed as possible. Notice the tension in your lower back. Now relax deeper and deeper.

Tighten your buttocks and thighs. Flex your thighs by pressing your heels down as hard as you can. Relax and notice the difference. Do this again. Curl your toes down, making your calves tense. Notice the tension. Relax. Bend your toes toward your face, creating tension in your shins. Relax and notice the difference.

Feel the heaviness throughout your lower body as the relaxation gets deeper and deeper. Relax your feet, ankles, calves, shins, knees, thighs, and buttocks. Let the relaxation spread to your stomach, lower back, and chest. Let go more and more. Experience deeper and deeper relaxation in your shoulders, arms, and hands, deeper and deeper. Notice the feeling of looseness and relaxation in your neck, jaws, and all your facial muscles.

How I felt before I did the progressive relaxation exercise: _____

_____

_____

_____

How I felt afterwards: _____

_____

_____

_____

Practice progressive muscle relaxation every day for two weeks; then see whether it's made a difference in the way you feel.

How I felt after practicing progressive muscle relaxation once or twice a day for two weeks: _____

_____

_____

_____

Body Scan

This exercise will help you become more aware of how you are feeling right now. As you become aware of your body, mind, and emotions in a nonjudgmental way, you will begin to experience a new clarity and self-acceptance that will help you relax deeply. Do your very best not to judge yourself as you are doing this exercise. Just allow yourself to complete the body scan without worrying about the results.

Get into a comfortable position, either sitting up or lying down in a place where you won't be disturbed.

Gently close your eyes and focus your complete attention on your breathing. Notice the cool air as it is breathed in through your nose, and the warm air as it is breathed out. Focus your full attention on each breath, cool air being breathed in, warm air being breathed out. Just breathe naturally, noticing each breath. Let each breath flow into the next without trying to make anything happen. If your mind strays away from your breath with thoughts about something else, just bring your focus gently back to the breath.

Focus all your attention on your feet and toes. Simply notice how they are feeling.

Now, with all your attention on your toes and feet, allow these areas to relax, release, and then let go. Don't try to make anything happen—just allow it to happen.

Focus your attention on your legs—the lower legs, knees, and upper legs. Notice how they are feeling without making any judgment. Are there any sensations in your legs—tightness, tingling, itching, warmth, cold? Feel whatever it is you feel. Now allow your legs to fully and completely relax. Just let go and let them relax.

Focus your attention on your buttocks and lower abdomen. Notice how they feel. Comfortable, warm, relaxed, loose, whatever. Just notice how they feel. Are there any tight or tense areas? With your mind completely focused on these ares, allow them to fully and completely relax.

Focus your attention on your stomach, chest, and back. Notice any sensations in these areas. Is there any tightness or discomfort present? Feel whatever it is you feel in these areas. Then let go; simply and completely let go.

Now put your full attention on how your hands, arms, shoulders, and neck are feeling. Are there areas of discomfort here? Notice and feel whatever you feel. Then, simply and completely, let go.

Focus your attention on your mouth, nose, face, eyes and head. Are you experiencing any tightness or discomfort in these areas? Completely feel whatever you are feeling. Relax your mouth, nose, face, eyes, and head. Your jaw and eyelids may begin to droop with relaxation.

Notice how the relaxation is penetrating every organ, every muscle, and every cell of your body. Let your whole body and mind completely relax. Enjoy this feeling of deep relaxation throughout your body. Notice how good it feels. Appreciate yourself for allowing this to happen.

Focus your attention again on your breath, noticing the cool air come in as you inhale, and the warm air go out as you exhale. Stay focused on each breath as it goes in and out, breath by breath. Notice how relaxed, refreshed, and energetic you feel. This relaxation and feeling of renewed energy will stay with you as you get on with the things you do. Slowly get up and resume your activities. Remember that each time you do this exercise, you will relax more fully and deeply, continuing to enhance your wellness.

How I felt before I did the body scan exercise: _____

_____

_____

_____

How I felt after I did the body scan exercise: _____

_____

_____

Practice the body scan exercise every day for two weeks; then assess how this practice has affected your moods and state of mind.

How I felt after doing the body scan exercise once or twice a day for two weeks: _____

_____

_____

Meditation

Meditation is described in *The Relaxation and Stress Reduction Workbook* as "the practice of uncritically attempting to focus your attention on one thing at a time." You can choose to meditate on anything that appeals to you. Gazing at an object, such as the second hand on a wristwatch, a candle flame, a flower, or a favorite picture, will focus your attention. Or you may choose to repeat, either aloud or to yourself, a syllable, word, or group of words.

It can be helpful before meditating to bring yourself into a quieter frame of mind by reading an inspiring passage from a book that means a great deal to you. I sometimes use this quote from *The Power of Myth* by Joseph Campbell:

> One thing that comes out of myths is that at the bottom of the abyss comes the voice of salvation. The black moment is the moment when the real message of transformation is going to come. At the darkest moment comes the light.

Some people refer to Kahil Gibran's chapter "On Love" in *The Prophet*. You might spend a few moments studying a flower, plant, rock, piece of jewelry, or picture. Use your creativity and you will come up with plenty of inspirations to launch your meditation.

As you attempt to focus your mind, you will find that it wanders from one thought to another. When you realize this, notice the new thought, then bring your focus back.

How To Meditate

The following step-by-step instructions will show you how to begin.

Select a position that is comfortable for you:
- Sit in a chair with your feet flat on the floor, your knees relaxed, and your hands resting in your lap.

- Sit cross-legged, tailor fashion, on the floor, with a cushion under your bottom.

- Kneel on a cushion, with another cushion between your feet and the floor.

Your back should be comfortably straight with the weight of your head balanced on top of your spinal column (pull your chin in a bit) and an arch in the small of your back. Now rock from side to side and from front to back until your torso feels balanced on your hips. Close your mouth, breathe through your nose, and have your tongue in the roof of your mouth.

Now spend several minutes getting in touch with yourself. With your eyes closed, focus on the places where your body touches the chair, cushion, or floor. Notice what this feels like. Now notice those places where one body part touches another. Pay attention to the sensations at these places of contact. Notice how much space your body takes up. Feel the boundary between your body and the space around it.

Take several deep breaths and notice your breathing. Notice whether your breathing is fast or slow, deep or shallow, and where your breath goes in your body (high up in your chest, near your stomach, or down low in your abdomen). Now practice moving your breath from one place to another, breathing first into your chest, then down into your stomach area, then down into the lower parts of your torso. Notice your abdomen expanding and contracting. This deep breath is the most relaxing one to use when meditating. This may be hard at first, but it will become easier as you practice.

Maintain a passive attitude when meditating. Remember that you will have many intrusive thoughts when you first begin to meditate, but your moments of fixed attention will increase as your ability to let go of stray thoughts improves. Don't worry about whether you are doing things correctly or well enough. Realize that whatever happens is what is supposed to happen.

You may want to spend some time practicing the process of letting go of intrusive thoughts. I often do this when I am having a hard time quieting down enough to sleep. Take several deep breaths. As you have a thought or perception, imagine that you are enclosing that thought or perception in a bubble. Then just watch the bubble float away. You may think of other images that are easier for you to use, such as puffs of smoke or leaves floating down a stream.

For some meditations in which you are not gazing at a particular object, you may close your eyes, or keep them focused on a particular spot on the floor or wall. Maintain the meditation for as long as feels comfortable to you. You can start out with just a five-minute meditation. As you become more accustomed to meditating, you will want to spend more time—up to 20 or 30 minutes, twice a day, at regularly scheduled times. You may want to find a group to meditate with on a regular basis.

Different Styles of Meditation

There are many different ways to meditate—but all ways lead to the same result. Chose the style or styles you think you will most likely be able to practice on a regular basis. I use all of the meditations described below, and find them to be very helpful in stabilizing my moods. I have found that I can use these techniques to relax myself in many different situations, not just when I am in a quiet place and in the right position—such as before surgery or other medical treatments, when stuck in traffic, or when I'm feeling anxious about someone or something.

Mantra Meditation

Select a syllable, word, or group of words that you enjoy saying: this is your mantra. Many people use the neutral sound *om*. Say your mantra over and over again to yourself or out loud, whichever feels better to you. Let your mantra find its own rhythm as you repeat it. Try to stay aware of the mantra with each repetition. Notice any sensations in your body. If your mind wanders, acknowledge this, then bring your attention back to your mantra.

How I felt before trying mantra meditation: _____

_____

_____

How I felt after trying mantra meditation: _____

_____

_____

Practice the mantra meditation twice a day for two weeks; then think about whether it has affected your mood or state of mind.

How I felt after practicing the mantra meditation twice a day for two weeks: _____

_____

_____

Breath-Counting Meditation

Take several deep breaths, focusing your attention on each part of the process (inhale, the point at which you stop inhaling and begin exhaling, exhaling, and before breathing again). Pay attention to the pause and use that time to notice any sensations in your body. Now count your breaths, counting one for the inhale and two for the exhale. If you lose count, simply start over again. Note any thoughts that intrude, but just let them float away. Always bring your focus back to your breathing.

How I felt before trying the breath-counting meditation: _____

_____

_____

How I felt after doing the breath-counting meditation: _____

_____

_____

_____

Practice the breath-counting meditation twice a day for two weeks; then think about whether you feel any different as a result.

How I felt after doing the breath-counting meditation once or twice a day for two weeks: _____

_____

_____

_____

Gazing

Set the object of your choice on a surface that is at eye level and about a foot or two away from you. Choose something simple: a flower, a candle, a stone—something without a lot of emotional associations for you. Now gaze at the object while keeping your eyes relaxed. Notice everything about it: texture, size, color, shape. Trace the edge of the object with your eyes; see all the minute details that you wouldn't usually take the time to notice. If you become distracted, simply return your gaze to the object.

How I felt before trying the gazing meditation: _____

_____

_____

_____

How I felt after trying the gazing meditation: _____

_____

_____

_____

Practice the gazing meditation twice a day every day for two weeks; then think about whether it has affected your mood or state of mind.

How I felt after practicing the gazing meditation for two weeks: _____

_____

_____

_____

Other Styles of Meditation

Below are ten additional meditations you can try. With each one, repeat the pattern of two weeks of practice, then make an assessment of how you feel. Testing in this way will allow you to find the styles of meditation that work best for you. All of these meditations can be used as a mix-and-match resource, depending on your mood.

Almost any activity that doesn't consciously engage your brain can become a meditation. All you need to do is concentrate on every action and every sensation. You can meditate as you eat, walk, garden, wash the dishes, make a bed, dust the furniture, wash your car, and so on.

The Moving Band Meditation

Imagine that a three-inch-wide band is around the top of your head. Focus all your attention on that part of your head. Notice the sensations. If there is any tension, try to release it. Now mentally lower the band three inches and again focus your attention on the area encompassed by the band. What does it feel like? Again, try to relax any tension in this area. Continue to "move" the band slowly down your body in this way. Have it circle each leg or arm individually. Sometimes you may want to move this imaginary band very slowly. At other times it will feel more relaxing to move it more quickly.

The Inner Exploration

Pick one part of your body on which to focus all your attention. Explore that part of your body in detail with your mind. What are the sensations in this part of your body? How does it move? What does it do? Is it tense? If it is tense, practice relaxing this part of your body in isolation. You may want to choose parts of your body that tend to be tense, such as the neck, shoulders, jaw, forehead, or lower back. Or you may choose internal areas that tend to be tense, such as the stomach or chest. Another idea is to focus on body parts that you rarely think about, such as your toes, your elbows, or behind your knees.

Softening

We all tend to respond to pain, irritation, and discomfort by tensing all or part of our body, even though this automatic reaction tends to increase the pain or level of discomfort. The more it hurts, the more we respond with tension. This is a good meditation to do when you're tense or in pain. Get relaxed, then focus on the feeling of pain, irritation, or discomfort. Reassure yourself that everything is all right. Now consciously focus on relaxing (softening) the muscles you had been tensing.

Don't Move

Make an agreement with yourself that you will not move for a predetermined period of time—this can range from one to ten minutes. As you meditate, you will notice that some part of your body is moving without your realizing it. Just notice this movement and keep meditating. As you proceed you will begin to anticipate your need to move. Is it in response to an itch? Sore muscles? Identify the uncomfortable sensation and, rather than move, consciously soften around the sensation. Soften any muscle groups that feel tense. Be sure that you are breathing deeply. When your time is up, allow your body to move to whatever position is comfortable. Focus on what that feels like. Is the relief immediate or gradual? Release any tension in you body before resuming your activities.

Lifted Arm

Place your left hand on your lap, bend your right arm at the elbow (as in signaling for a right-hand turn), and lift that arm so the tips of your fingers are level with the top of your head. As the right arm begins to tire, focus your attention on the sensation of tiredness. See if you can find a way to relax the muscles in your arm without dropping it. Check out the rest of your body for tension. Relax any areas that feel tense. If you notice that you are beginning to feel anxious, take several deep breaths and remind yourself to relax. When you have finished meditating, lower your arm very slowly. Focus on what your arm feels like. How does the discomfort or tiredness change as you lower your arm? Relax any tension you feel in other part of your body before you resume your activities.

Warming Up and Cooling Down

Meditate in an area that is slightly warmer or cooler than you would normally prefer. As the extra warmth or coolness becomes noticeable, focus on your body's reaction to it. Is your body tensing? Are you starting to sweat or shiver? See if you can find a way to relax your body's reaction to the temperature. Does focusing on your object of meditation help? When you have finished meditating, spend a few minutes in an area that has a comfortable temperature and notice how your body adjusts to this change.

Responding to Irritation

Use any irritating sound or sensation as the focus of your meditation. It could be a barking dog, a printer, the noise of traffic, or an itch. Notice what your body does in reaction. Then relax any tension that your body has formed in response to the irritant. (This is a good meditation to use when you're in a place where it would normally be difficult to meditate because of noise or other distractions.)

Being Present in the Moment

Most of the stress in our lives comes from thinking about the past or worrying about the future. When all your attention is focused in the present moment, it is difficult to feel either stress or worry. Get relaxed, then focus all your attention on what you are doing right now. When other thoughts intrude, just turn your awareness back to the present moment of meditation. It is not necessary to be alone in a special place to do this meditation. Try it when you are feeling irritated waiting in a line, stopped at a street light, stuck in traffic, or feeling overwhelmed or worried. Notice how focusing on the present moment makes you feel.

Eating Meditation

Sit down in front of your food. Take several deep breaths. Notice the color, shape, and texture of the food. Notice how looking at the food makes you feel. Reach slowly for your food. Now begin eating very slowly. Stay aware of how you are feeling and what you are tasting all the time you are eating. Eat as if you were eating in slow motion, being very conscious of each bit of food and each motion involved in eating it. How do your teeth and tongue feel? What does it feel like to swallow? Can you feel the food moving down your esophagus and into your stomach? When other thoughts intrude, notice them and return your attention to eating.

Walking Meditation

Stand up and relax your body all over. Take several deep, focused breaths. Now begin walking. Be aware of every process involved in moving. Try to match you breathing rhythm to your walking in a way that is comfortable to you. Pay attention to all the sensations of walking. Notice your muscles contracting and relaxing as you move. How do the various part of your body feel as you walk? After you've scanned the feelings in you body, become aware of everything you can see as you walk. Then become aware of everything you can hear and everything you can smell. As thoughts intrude, let them go and notice everything about the experience of walking instead.

Reactions of People in the Study

Nineteen people in the study have effectively used meditation. The benefits they noted are listed below. **Which of these would you like to achieve?**

☐ relaxation
☐ sense of control
☐ lifting of symptoms
☐ grounding
☐ clearer thinking
☐ enhanced sense of life
☐ feeling of safety
☐ relief from depression
☐ enhanced ability to sleep

☐ calmness
☐ inner peace
☐ balance
☐ ability to keep mania within bounds
☐ refreshment of the mind
☐ feeling free
☐ relief from manic episodes
☐ increased ability to deal with symptoms
☐ diminished tension

One of the great advantages of meditation is that it doesn't depend on the presence of anyone or anything; it's a therapeutic tool that is *always* available to you.

Other benefits you'd like to achieve from meditation: _____

_____

_____

_____

_____

Three Calming Exercises

Guided Imagery Meditation

Guided imagery focuses your imagination on relaxing and healing images. A detailed example is given below, but you can make up your own healing and peaceful scenarios. The important thing is to include as much sensory detail as possible. Try to include all five senses: touch, taste, smell, hearing, and sight. Try the following guided imagery meditation.

Get in a very comfortable sitting or lying position. Make sure that you are warm enough but not too warm, and that you will not be interrupted by the phone, doorbell, or the needs of others. You might want to make a tape recording of these instructions.

Stare at a spot above your head on the ceiling (if you're lying down) or stare straight ahead. Take a deep breath to a count of eight, hold it for a count of four, let it out for a count of eight.

Again—in to a count of eight; hold for a count of four; exhale for a count of eight.

Again—in to a count of eight; hold for a count of four; exhale for a count of eight.

Now close your eyes, but keep them in the same position they were in when you were staring at a spot on the ceiling or in front of you.

Breathe in to a count of eight; hold for a count of four; exhale for a count of eight.

Now focus on your toes. Let them completely relax. Now move the feeling of relaxation slowly up your legs, through your heels and calves to your knees. Now let the warm feeling of relaxation move up your thighs. Feel your whole body relaxing. Let the relaxation move very slowly through your buttocks, lower abdomen, and lower back. Now feel it moving, very slowly, up your spine and through your abdomen. Now feel the warm relaxation flowing into your chest and upper back.

Let this relaxation flow from your shoulders, down your arms, through your elbows and wrists, out through your hands and fingers. Now let the relaxation go slowly through your throat and up your neck, letting it all soften and relax. Let the feeling move up into your face. Feel the relaxation fill your jaw and cheek muscles, and surround your eyes. Relax your eyes. Let the feeling of relaxation move up into your forehead. Now let your whole scalp relax and feel warm and comfortable. Your body is now completely relaxed, with the feeling of relaxation filling every muscle and cell of your body.

Picture yourself walking on the beach on a sunny day. As you stroll along, you feel the warmth of the sun on your back. You lie down on a soft towel in the sand. The sand molds to your body and you feel warm and comfortable. The sun warms your skin, the salt air smells fresh. You can still taste the fresh-squeezed juice you just drank, the juice that a friend made for you because she knows how much you like it. You hear the waves breaking against the shore in a steady rhythm. The sound of seagulls calling overhead completes your feeling of blissful contentment.

As you lie here you realize that you are perfectly and completely relaxed. You feel safe and at peace with the world. You know you have the power to relax yourself completely at any time you need to. By completely relaxing, you are giving the body the opportunity to stabilize itself, and that when you wake up you will feel calm, relaxed, and able to get on with your tasks for the day.

Now slowly wiggle your fingers and toes. Gradually open your eyes and resume your activities.

Focusing on Detail

For a quick relaxer when your day gets hectic, focus on detail. If you are at home, keep several picture postcards or greeting cards with lots of attractive detail handy. I recommend the book *Animalia* by Graeme Base. It is filled with detailed pictures which are very interesting to study. When you start to feel rushed or agitated, sit down in a quiet, comfortable spot, and focus on the detail in your chosen picture for ten minutes. Notice if you feel calmer afterwards.

You can do this exercise anywhere by just focusing on your surroundings. It can keep you from getting irritated when you're waiting in line or stuck in traffic. If you are waiting in a doctor's office, focus on the detail in a picture in a magazine.

Checking In

Every so often throughout the day, take a brief break, take several deep breaths, and get back in touch with how you feel. Check yourself out all over. And then imagine the tightness flowing out of the tense places in your body. Let your mind take a brief but complete break.

18

Diet

When I stick to a diet that is high in grains and vegetables, I feel better and my moods are more stable. Junk foods that are high in fat, sugar, and salt deepen my depressions and make me more hyper when I'm manic.

What You Eat Affects the Way You Feel

My own personal experience has shown me clearly that what I eat affects the way I feel. It is very important for me to avoid sugar. It makes me feel lethargic, foggy, bloated, and uncomfortable. Caffeine speeds me up, so I avoid it if I'm already going faster than is comfortable and am working to slow myself down. I have learned that I cannot digest dairy foods; so I avoid all except yogurt.

Thirty-eight of the people in the survey said they had particular eating habits that affect their moods. I know that number would be even higher if people were paying more attention to what they eat and how they feel after they eat it. Many of the study participants say that food allergies worsen their mood swings.

Avoid eating any one food excessively or exclusively. You need a varied diet to get all the nutrients necessary to keep you healthy. People with mood swings need to be particularly cautious, because they are so easily thrown out of balance. Especially if an undetected food allergy is in the picture, a varied and healthy diet can go a long way toward minimizing symptoms.

If you're like so many others, you often crave particular foods in excess. People in the study most frequently mentioned craving foods that are high in sugar, (especially chocolate), carbohydrates, such as bread or pasta, beverages that contain caffeine, and salty foods. Often the foods we crave are the ones we should avoid (a craving can indicate a food allergy!). With a healthy diet, these cravings diminish.

I recommend *The Self-Healing Cookbook* by Kristina Turner (see Resource List) for making the transition to a good diet. It contains information on how foods affect moods and gives a variety of simple recipes that you can alter to suit your tastes and lifestyle. It's a lot of work to get into the mode of eating well, but it's a change that is definitely worthwhile.

You don't have to be super strict. Allow yourself to splurge occasionally and have a treat. Note how you feel afterward. Any negative symptoms you feel may keep you from splurging too often. Eventually you will get used to the foods in your new, healthy diet, and some of them will seem like treats.

Keep on hand healthy foods that are easy to fix or ready to eat—and that you enjoy eating—so you don't stop eating when you are feeling too low to cook.

Weight Control

Half the people in the study reported that they are significantly overweight. They often blamed this on the drugs they are taking and/or the bingeing or lethargy that can accompany mood swings.

Food is sometimes the only thing you can find that alleviates the low feeling, at least while the food is still in your mouth.

Besides being unhealthy, excess weight makes people feel self-conscious and unattractive, lowering their self-esteem and further complicating their depression.

I myself have been significantly overweight. At one time I weighed 30 pounds more than the weight suggested for a woman of my age and build. This was at a time when I was experiencing a lengthy depressive episode and was in an abusive marital situation. I found that I craved sweets and salty foods. As I needed to buy bigger and bigger clothes, I felt worse and worse about myself and my appearance, further aggravating my depression. When I realized that I was using food to numb my pain, I started to take better care of myself, avoiding sweets and fast foods, and treating myself to a good, healthy diet along with a regular program of exercise. I lost most of the weight, but find that it's a constant battle to keep it off. While I realize that it's best for my health if I control my weight, I am also learning to like my body and the way I look, no matter how much I weigh.

Many of the people in the study reported talking to their doctor about the relationship between weight gain and the drug or drugs they're taking. Based on the doctor's recommendation, and using all the resources available to them, they made a decision about the best and safest course of action relative to continuing or changing their drug treatment program.

Some have gone on a weight reduction diet and exercise program based on the best available information. If you have health problems or take medications, it's imperative that you get your doctor's advice before making any changes in your eating or exercise routine. Many study respondents said that they go to weight control support groups such as Overeater's Anonymous or Weight Watchers.

Because feelings about food often have strong emotional connections, many of the people who have successfully lost weight and kept it off have worked closely with a therapist and read resource books about problems with food addiction. Geneen Roth has written a self-help workbook, *Why Weight? A Guide to Ending Compulsive Eating*, which may be helpful to you.

Several people in the study said that they have made the decision to live with their extra weight. They're determined not to let it get in the way of living a full and satisfying life. One woman said: "The effect of my excess weight is diminishing to nothing. About three years ago, I decided I was going to stop feeling inferior, stop talking about it, wear attractive clothes, and go swimming in a $60 lovely suit."

Another respondent said that her weight directly correlates with her self-image and level of self-esteem. She has recently lost weight, is still losing, and feels great about it.

Another person, who lost 130 pounds, found that it was scary going from heavier to so much lighter; but the weight loss helped alleviate a back injury, as well as her mania and depression.

Hypothyroidism, or low thyroid function, can cause weight gain and make it difficult to lose unwanted pounds. If you are overweight, make sure you have a complete battery of thyroid tests (see the chapter entitled "Possible Causes of Mood Disorders").

If you've decided that your weight is a problem that needs to be addressed for reasons of health or to enhance your self-esteem, what is your weight goal? _____ pounds

How many pounds less is this than your present weight?_____

How long are you going to give yourself to lose these pounds?_____

Be easy on yourself. Remember—it is never healthy to lose more than two pounds a week. And weight loss does not usually progress evenly, no matter what you do. Don't be discouraged if you hit a plateau that lasts for a while. Be patient. Your weight will eventually continue to drop if you still have more to lose.

If you give in to temptation, don't give up. You haven't done anything serious. Just get back on the diet and stick to it as best as you can. And be sure to give yourself a pat on the back for every good day. When I am dieting, I like to put a star beside the date in my engagement calendar for every day I stick to the diet.

Weight Loss Plan

Recommendations of doctor or health professionals:_____

_____

_____

Results of a complete battery of thyroid tests showed that:
☐ my thyroid is fine
☐ I need further testing
☐ I need treatment for a thyroid disorder

*Based on these findings, I am going to take the following action:*_____

_____

_____

*I plan to attend a weight loss support group (when)*_____ *(where)*_____.
(Local newspapers usually list these groups.)

Resources I plan to use (books, videos, classes, etc.): _____

_____

_____

Sugar

The number one food culprit for many people is sugar. One study participant described it as "a mood-altering substance that should be avoided by all people with mood disorders, as it can be very dangerous." Other descriptions of the effects of sugar include mood elevation, hyperactivity, fatigue, increased pulse rate, mood instability, depression, loss of control, headaches, irritability, agitation, distorted and exaggerated anxiety, exaggerated moods, and worsened depression.

Many people in the study said that they avoid sugar in any form. It's useful to bear in mind that 100 years ago sugar was a rare and occasional treat. Now it is a standard ingredient used to enhance flavor in most of the prepared foods we buy. Our bodies seem to be having trouble adapting to this increased sugar load.

Dr. Wayne London in his book, *Back to Basics*, advises avoiding or severely limiting your intake of simple carbohydrates (sugar, corn sweeteners, honey, maple syrup, and so on). "If you eat sugar, the yeast in your body ferments the sugar into alcohol and alcohol-like substances. Your body is acting as a brewery." His patients have told him that they experience a "hangover" after eating sugar.

Sugar Blues by William Dufty describes in detail the effects of sugar on the body. *The Yeast Connection Cookbook* by William C. Crook looks at the role of sugar in medical problems involving the yeast *Candida albicans*, and gives dietary solutions. Medical doctors are becoming more aware that excess yeast in the system can cause or worsen mood instability, depression, inability to concentrate, and mental fogginess.

As an experiment, eliminate all sugar from your diet for two weeks. You'll really have to read labels! Closely monitor how you feel—keeping a daily journal will make this easier.

Did eliminating sugar from your diet affect the way you feel? Note whether the symptoms below were aggravated, alleviated, or remained unchanged.

Symptoms	Aggravated	Alleviated	Unchanged
Depression			
Mania			
Food cravings			
Bloating			
Heartburn			
Constipation			
Diarrhea			
Headaches			
Sinus problems			
(Other)			

If you noticed significant positive changes as a result of two weeks without sugar, you may want to continue on a low- or no-sugar diet. I eat very little sugar. When I am tempted and give in, I only have to eat a small amount of sugar before I begin to notice symptoms. The first symptom I notice is an intense feeling of fatigue.

Because of what I have learned about the effects of sugar on my body, I have decided to take the following action regarding the use of sugar in my diet: _____

_____

_____

Caffeine

Many people in the study noted that limiting the caffeine in their diet lessens the intensity of their mood swings. Caffeine can cause mood elevation, nervousness, hyperactivity, jitteriness, irritability, insomnia, anxiety, shakiness, restlessness, pounding heart, sluggishness, headaches, and overstimulation.

Before you ingest foods containing caffeine, look at it as a drug and give it the same level of consideration. Remember, caffeine is not only in coffee. It is found in tea, various soft drinks, cocoa, and chocolate products. The caffeine content of various foods, taken from the *Wellness Encyclopedia*, is listed below. Of course, these figures can vary according to product and method of preparation.

per 5-ounce serving:

Coffee, drip	110-150 mg.
Coffee, perk	60-125 mg.
Coffee, instant	40-105 mg.
Coffee, decaffeinated	2-5 mg.
Tea, steeped for 5 minutes	40-100 mg.
Tea, steeped for 3 minutes	20-50 mg.
Hot cocoa	2-10 mg.

per 12-ounce serving:

Cola drinks	45 mg.

per 1-ounce serving:

Milk chocolate	1-15 mg.
Bittersweet chocolate	5-35 mg.

per slice:

chocolate cake	20-30 mg.

There are many decaffeinated products on the market that can be used as substitutes but, as you can see, even decaf coffee contains some caffeine!

Check labels to determine the caffeine content of foods and drinks. Being aware of the possible effects of caffeine allows you to make appropriate decisions about when and in what amounts to use it.

It can be very difficult to give up caffeine. People who withdraw abruptly from using all caffeine often experience unpleasant reactions, such as a mild but persistent headache, a general feeling of tiredness, an inability to focus mentally, and a constant temptation to "have another cup of coffee." These symptoms decrease over time, but may last up to two weeks. Cutting out caffeine may not be something you can do when you are trying to make many other changes in your life. Gradual withdrawal is an answer for some people.

After I drink caffeine I feel _____

_____

_____

I intend to make the following changes with regard to the use of caffeine in my diet: _____

_____

_____

Dairy Products

People respond to dairy products in different ways. Some people say they help, some people say they hinder in the alleviation of mood swings. Positive effects cited by people in the study include soothing, leveling, inducing sleep, and a feeling of well-being. Negative effects include fatigue, irritability, acne, racing pulse, thick mucous, sinus congestion, and intensification of premenstrual syndrome. I find that I can no longer digest dairy products at all. I suffer severe digestive symptoms when I give in to the temptation of these delicious foods. Yogurt, mercifully, is an exception, and satisfies my desire for dairy products.

It's a good idea to test your reaction to dairy products by eliminating them from your diet for two weeks, just as you did with sugar. (Don't try both experiments at the same time, as you won't be able to tell which food type has been causing what set of symptoms.)

Which of these symptoms do you associate with your intake of dairy products?

- ☐ fatigue
- ☐ gas
- ☐ irritability
- ☐ bloating
- ☐ acne
- ☐ heartburn
- ☐ racing pulse
- ☐ constipation
- ☐ sinus congestion
- ☐ diarrhea
- ☐ worsened PMS
- ☐ (other)_____

Go through the list again after you've eliminated dairy products from your diet for two weeks. **Was there a difference?**_____

Eliminating dairy products from my diet for two weeks made the following changes in how I feel: _

_____

_____

_____

I have decided to take the following action regarding my use of dairy products: _____

_____

_____

_____

Other Foods That Might Be Causing Problems

People in the study reported on other kinds of food that seem to aggravate their mood swings. Foods mentioned include wheat products, fermented foods, eggs, meat, and tomatoes. You can use the two-week experiment with any that you feel might be aggravating your mood swings or compromising your health. Each experiment will require careful reading of product labels and conscientious monitoring of your reactions in a daily journal. The advantage of this method is that you can eliminate offending foods from your diet one at a time, rather than going on an oppressively restrictive diet with the vague idea that some foods might be bad for you.

Complex Carbohydrates

A diet that is high in complex carbohydrates can increase your level of serotonin, a neurotransmitter that has an antidepressant action. (*Prozac* is an antidepressant that increases the level of serotonin in the brain.) Foods that are high in complex carbohydrates include whole grain breads, pasta, grains (such as rice, millet, and quinoa), potatoes, and vegetables, especially those in the cabbage family. Another way to raise your level of serotonin is to eat a diet that is high in complex carbohydrates, such as the one described in Turner's *The Self-Healing Cookbook*. I find—and my findings are corroborated by people in the study and people who have attended my workshop—that my cravings decrease when I am on a high complex carbohydrate diet, and I feel better.

I am going to make the following adjustments to my diet so that it includes more complex carbohydrates: _____

_____

_____

Follow a healthy diet that emphasizes complex carbohydrates for two weeks. You will have to read labels. Closely monitor how you feel.

Did following a diet high in complex carbohydrates affect the way you feel? Note whether the symptoms below were aggravated, alleviated, or remained unchanged.

Symptoms	Aggravated	Alleviated	Unchanged
Depression			
Mania			
Food cravings			
Bloating			
Heartburn			
Constipation			
Diarrhea			
Headaches			
Sinus problems			
(Other)			

If you noticed positive changes as a result of two weeks on a diet high in complex carbohydrates, you may want to continue with it. It's important to make any significant dietary change in consultation with your physician or a nutrition specialist, especially if you are in poor physical health.

*Because of what I have learned about the effects of complex carbohydrates in my diet, I've decided to make the following changes in my eating habits:*_____

_____

_____

Vitamins

There is anecdotal evidence that vitamin supplements can make you feel better. However, there is no exact clinical data to corroborate this. A diet that is high in complex carbohydrates and low in fats is the best insurance that your body is getting the nourishment it needs to function optimally. If you are considering using vitamin supplements, check with your doctor and a competent nutritionist.

Changing Your Diet

Let me emphasize that making dietary changes is not easy. Your new diet may require more cooking. It may require separate meals for yourself and other people you live with. It certainly requires changes in habits that have developed over a lifetime. Your new diet may even seem costlier at first, as you stock up on new staples and find out where to buy everything you need.

Again, be gentle with yourself. Give yourself a pat on the back for a job well done, and don't be too hard on yourself for a little backsliding. Change is always difficult. But, believe me, it's worth the effort.

19

Exercise: Do It

Exercise lifts my moods and makes me feel, overall, more confident and secure.

There was universal agreement among study participants that exercise makes them feel better. If they are depressed, exercise improves their mood. If they are manic, gentle exercise, such as a leisurely walk, helps calm them down.

Caution: Some people in the study noted that strenuous or very active exercise, such as heavy labor or fast running, exacerbates mania. Choose mild forms of exercise when you're feeling manic.

"I do hard-work toning consisting of water aerobics and low-impact dance aerobics. It gets the heart rate up, increases my sense of well-being, and the body benefits, too. This is most effective if in a class where one has rapport with other class members. The classes are also good for structure. Exercise is a necessity for me. I benefit by having small, medium, and large depressions lifted right out of my mind."

According to *The Anxiety and Phobia Workbook* (see Resource List), the physiological benefits of regular exercise include:

- Reduced skeletal muscle tension

- Increased metabolism of excess adrenalin and thyroxin in the bloodstream (excess adrenalin and thyroxin tend to keep you in an uncomfortable state of arousal and vigilance)

- Discharge of pent-up frustration

- Enhanced oxygenation of the blood and the brain, increasing alertness and concentration

- Stimulated production of endorphins, which increase your sense of well-being

- Increased energy level through increased acidity of the blood

- Improved circulation

- Improved digestion

- Improved elimination from the skin, lungs, and bowels

- Decreased cholesterol levels

- Decreased blood pressure

- Suppressed appetite and consequent weight loss

- Improved regulation of blood sugar

In addition to these physiological benefits, people who exercise notice the following psychological benefits:

- Increased feeling of well-being

- Reduced dependence on alcohol and drugs

- Reduced insomnia

- Improved concentration and memory

- Alleviation of depression symptoms

- Greater control over feelings of anxiety

- Increased self-esteem

These factors are ample reason for anyone to begin exercising regularly. However, most people find it very difficult to exercise when they're depressed. Typically, during depression your energy level and motivation are low. The chronic physical aches and pains that often accompany depression can make the prospect of a workout even less appealing. The tendency to isolate yourself can also be an inhibiting factor if your exercise of choice involves classes or appearing in public.

I find it easier to exercise when I am depressed if exercise is already an established part of my daily wellness routine, like brushing my teeth and eating breakfast. Every day, over the lunch hour, I take a 20-minute walk or bicycle ride. You may prefer to walk in the morning or evening (the season may make a difference in the time of day you exercise if you exercise outdoors). If I'm low, I make my exercise session as easy for myself as possible. I choose places to go where I am not likely to meet many people, and where the trails are flat and unchallenging. I have a stationary bicycle that I ride indoors if the weather is bad. I often ride it while watching something pleasant on TV or reading to break the monotony. Aerobic exercise records, tapes, and television programs are another good way I have found to get in the exercise I need indoors at home.

Varying the kind of exercise you do from day to day may make the regimen more interesting for you. On the other hand, when you're depressed, the same thing over and over, every day, can feel easier and more comfortable. Whatever works best for you is what you need to do.

Some people find it easier to exercise in a group. Your local newspaper or recreation department is a good resource for locating exercise groups or classes. When you're really depressed, you may not feel comfortable in a group—so make whatever arrangements necessary to make exercise palatable. Exercising with a friend can also enhance your motivation and make the experience more pleasurable.

I always found it hard to exercise the first day or two after making some change in my drug treatment program. I found myself tiring quickly, and feeling short of breath. Pay attention to what your body is saying, and act accordingly. Don't force yourself to exercise when you feel ill or overstressed, or when you are experiencing some unexplained physical symptoms. (This is a good time to try relaxation techniques.)

Again, it helps to have a regularly scheduled time to exercise. If you exercise consistently, you'll reap enormous benefits. Try to exercise for at least fifteen minutes, three times a week. More frequent sessions will be even more beneficial.

If you miss a day or two, don't give yourself a hard time about it. Just do the best you can. Be sure to give yourself a pat on the back when you *do* exercise. I always reward myself with a short rest and sometimes with a piece of fruit when I finish exercising.

Remember, it is always a good idea to get your doctor's approval before increasing your activity level, especially if you have a medical condition requiring treatment.

If you have a hard time exercising when you are depressed, why do you think it is a problem for you?_____

_____

_____

_____

_____

What could you do for yourself that would make it easier to exercise when you are depressed? _____

_____

_____

_____

_____

I find that even very slow exercise, such as neck rolls, leg lifts, and yoga, can help lift depression. Physical therapists, and people who do therapeutic body work or massage (sometimes known as body workers or body counselors), have good advice to offer on gentle exercise that can help lift depression. These are the kinds of exercise most enjoyed by study participants. Check those which you participate in already, and those which you would like to try.

Exercise	Do It Now	Plan To Try
Walking		
Jogging		
Swimming		
Hiking		
Gardening		
Yoga		
Ice skating		
Outdoor physical work (such as mowing the lawn)		
Speed walking		
Biking		
Skiing		
Working out at a gym		
Dancing		
Aerobics classes or *Jazzercise*		
Roller skating		

Other forms of exercise I plan to try: _____

_____

It helps to have a regularly scheduled time to exercise. Walking for half an hour at lunchtime works for some people. Others prefer to exercise early in the morning or in the late afternoon. If you exercise consistently at a particular time, the regime becomes a habit. Even if you miss a day or two a week, you'll still reap enormous benefits.

Many people find it easier to exercise in a group. Your local newspaper or recreation department is a good resource for locating exercise groups or classes.

Remember: It is always a good idea to get your doctor's approval before increasing your activity level, especially if you have a medical condition requiring treatment.

How would you rate your current fitness level?

☐ *I feel that I already get all the exercise I need.*
☐ *I feel that I need to increase the amount of exercise I get. I will do it*
(how long)_____ (days per week)_____
☐ *I am going to join an exercise group or class*
(where)_____ (when)_____

You can determine if you are really out of shape and need more exercise by considering the following symptoms. Check the ones that apply to you.

☐ Out of breath after walking up a flight of stairs or climbing a hill
☐ Takes a long time to recover after walking up a flight of stairs or climbing a hill
☐ Feeling exhausted after short periods of exertion
☐ Chronic muscle tension
☐ Poor muscle tone
☐ Obesity
☐ Muscles are cramped and ache for days after participating in a sport
☐ Generally tired, lethargic, and bored

Other symptoms you have which might be due to lack of exercise:_____

_____

_____

_____

_____

If you feel that you're out of shape, I suggest that you commit yourself to a regular program of exercise, at least four times a week, for two weeks. Check in with your doctor to determine the kind and duration of exercise that would be best for you, especially if you have not been exercising for some time.

☐ *I feel that I am already in good shape, and plan to stick to the exercise program I have.*

☐ *I commit myself to a regular program of exercise, four times a week, for two weeks.*

☐ *I am going to join an exercise group* (when)_____
(where)_____

Exercise at the same time each day. Choose the time of day that fits into your schedule—early in the morning, during your lunch break, or early in the evening. Your work schedule and family responsibilities may need to be considered. Avoid exercising within 90 minutes of a meal, or just before going to bed.

I am going to exercise at (time)_____ *on the following days*:

_____

_____

_____

_____

Enjoy yourself while exercising. Don't consider your exercise session as something you *have* to do or a chore, but rather as something you *want to do. Cons*ider this as special time that you are giving to yourself and your body.

If you have not been exercising regularly, start slowly and increase your time and exertion gradually. At first you may be able to exercise for only five minutes. Age and physical shape make a difference. Try adding five more minutes of exercise each week if you feel comfortable doing so.

When you first begin to exercise, you will notice some aches and pains that you didn't have before. These will go away in several days. A warm bath after exercising always helps.

Use the chart at the end of this chapter to monitor your exercise program and help you answer the following questions:

How I felt before I began a program of regular exercise: _____

_____

_____

_____

_____

_____

How I felt after exercising regularly for two weeks: _____

_____

_____

_____

_____

_____

After exercising when depressed I felt: _____

_____

_____

_____

_____

After exercising when manic I felt: _____

_____

_____

_____

_____

My long-term exercise goals are: _____

_____

_____

_____

_____

Use this daily chart to keep track of your exercise program (copy it for future use).

Date	How long I exercised	Type of exercise	How I felt before	How I felt afterwards

Daily Exercise Record

Week of:_____

20

Light, Electromagnetic Radiation, and the Biological Clock

I started getting outside for a few minutes every day, just sitting on the porch because it was so hard for me to move or be seen and, like a miracle, my deep depression started to lift.

The Importance of Full-Spectrum Light

Overwhelming scientific evidence shows that exposure to light on the skin or through the eyes affects mental as well as physical health. It turns out that people need full-spectrum light—that is, light that contains all the wavelengths of sunlight. Not getting enough full-spectrum light, or prolonged exposure to distorted spectrum light from fluorescent bulbs, seems to have a profound affect on mental outlook, moods, and health in general. This has been borne out by generations of bleak suicide statistics and high rates of alcoholism in Northern countries whose inhabitants are deprived of sunlight for months at a time.

Recently dubbed "seasonal affective disorder" (SAD), these winter doldrums have been shown to be highly responsive to supplemental doses of full-spectrum light.

Research has shown that students in classrooms illuminated with full-spectrum light have one-third fewer sick days than students in classrooms lit with distorted spectrum lights. The full range of health benefits from full-spectrum lights continues to be revealed.

Dr. Wayne London was one of the first to discuss these matters for a nonscientific audience in his book, *Back to Basics*.

Full-spectrum light has two distinguishing characteristics: it contains 1) the same rainbow colors and 2) the same amount of near-ultraviolet light as sunlight. There are two sources for full-spectrum light: sunlight and specially designed full-spectrum light bulbs. Full-spectrum light bulbs—*Vita-Lite* bulbs (the same lights used as "grow" lights for indoor gardening) can be purchased in hardware stores, some specialized nurseries and, sometimes, in health food stores. These bulbs can be used to replace the distorted spectrum light bulbs that are usually found in fluorescent light fixtures. If your hardware store does not have the size bulbs you need, have them special ordered. *Vita-Lite* is a trade name; these bulbs are currently the only ones of their kind on the market. To date, no type of incandescent light bulb produces full-spectrum light.

Studies have shown that full-spectrum light, in order to be effective, must be absorbed through the eyes. You do not need to look directly at the source, however (in the case of the sun, this is certainly to be avoided). Exposure on the skin is not effective; and, as is well known, prolonged exposure to the sun may be harmful. Although it is not yet known precisely how light works to affect moods, it seems clear that it has a physiological effect on the nervous, immune, and endocrine systems.

More and more people are reporting success using light—either sunlight or supplemental full-spectrum light from specially made bulbs or in light boxes.

Light: A Natural Mood Elevator

In the last hundred years, our lifestyles have changed rapidly and significantly. Exposure to full-spectrum light has been drastically reduced because

- People spend much more time indoors, working and playing. Some people work the night shift and sleep during the day.

- Changes in our modes of transportation—from walking and riding in a buggy to traveling by car, train, and plane—have further reduced the time we spend out of doors.

- Office buildings and factories often have only a few small windows or none at all. Indoor lighting, which is almost always distorted spectrum light (because it is the least expensive), has replaced windows as a light source.

- People wear glasses, sunglasses, and contact lenses, which block part or, in the case of hard contact lenses, all of the near UV light.

- Sulphur dioxide and ozone in the air block near UV light.

These factors make it necessary to pay particular attention to the amount and kinds of light you are exposed to. Some people seem to need more light than others. The amount of full-spectrum light received through the eyes is reduced on cloudy days and by window glass (up to 50 percent).

I first became aware of the usefulness of supplemental light when I attended a workshop given by Dr. Wayne London in Brattleboro, Vermont. I was suffering from a deep episode of major depression at the time, and it was all I could do just to get out to this one-hour workshop. I decided that I didn't have anything to lose from trying this simple, inexpensive, and noninvasive treatment.

Based on what I learned from Dr. London, I purchased a shop light: a simple, hanging-type light fixture that is usually used in garages, basements, and indoor nurseries, requiring two four-foot fluorescent bulbs. The cost for this was $12 at the hardware store. I replaced the distorted spectrum bulbs the fixture contained with two full-spectrum fluorescent light bulbs ($15 each). Then I set the fixture on the table in the room where I spent most of my time, and used it as my light source. After several days, I noticed a significant improvement in my depression. It isn't necessary to sit right in front of the fixture: just use it as your light source.

Because this initial experiment was so successful, I had my son build me a light box. He made a bank of lights by mounting three shop light fixtures on a piece of plywood, again replacing the distorted spectrum bulbs with full spectrum bulbs. I set this up in the room where I spend the most time, and noticed that I was feeling better and better. This alternative is much less expensive than purchasing a commercially built full-spectrum light box and, although cumbersome, is perfectly acceptable.

Commercial full-spectrum light boxes cost between $200 and $600. I use one of these in my office. I like it because it is smaller than my homemade version (reflectors are used to increase the amount of available light), more attractive, and I can take it with me when I travel. The intensity of the light from these fixtures is low, not nearly enough to get a suntan.

I am now much more aware of my needs for full-spectrum light, especially on cloudy days and through the dark days of late fall and early winter in New England.

See the Resource List for more information on purchasing full-spectrum light bulbs and light boxes.

Ways To Get the Light You Need

Glasses, especially tinted glasses, block some wavelengths from the sun. If you can, exercise out of doors without glasses. If you can't see well enough to do this safely, then simply sit outside with your glasses off for half an hour every day.

Avoid tinted glasses (but consult with your eye doctor to make sure that you get adequate protection from ultraviolet rays, which can promote the formation of cataracts). Hard contact lenses block all the full-spectrum light; soft contacts block 50 to 90 percent of it. If you wear contact lenses, spend some time outdoors every day without them.

Spend at least a half hour a day outside, even on cloudy days. Avoid the hours between 10 a.m. and 2 p.m. in the middle of summer, as the sun's rays are too intense then and can cause skin cancer, especially if you are fair. Never look directly at the sun.

This is the cheapest and usually the most convenient way to get the light you need. Being near windows helps, but 50 percent of the full-spectrum rays are blocked by window glass, and you won't get the same benefit as from being out of doors.

Supplement your sources of artificial light with full-spectrum fixtures.

- Replace the bulbs in your fluorescent fixtures with Vita-Lite bulbs. Ask to have the fluorescent bulbs in your office replaced with full-spectrum bulbs. Point out to your employer the health benefits of such a change. If your boss won't spring for the expense, you could replace the distorted spectrum bulbs at your own cost, and then take the bulbs with you if you change jobs.

- Purchase one or more shop-light fixtures, replace the fluorescent bulbs with Vita-Lite bulbs, and use these to light your work and living space.

- Buy a full-spectrum light box. Avoid using the light box when you are feeling hyperactive or manic.

Try the cheapest and simplest method first: get outside for at least half an hour every day. If this has a noticeable affect on your mood, make the investment and try the full-spectrum bulbs. Depending on the results, you may want to purchase a light box. They are portable, attractive, and provide a lot of light. Some outlets are noted in the Resource List at the back of this book.

Assessing Your Own Reactions to Light

Read through the statements below, then spend as much time as you need to determine whether or not they're true for you. You might want to consult old journals and calendars in thinking about your answers.

    I notice that I have more problems with depression in the late fall and early winter.

☐ *I notice that my mood is lower on cloudy days and worsens when there is a series of cloudy days.*

☐ *I notice that I feel better on bright sunny days and when I get some light during the day.*

☐ *I plan to be outside for at least half an hour every day (I can get both the exercise and light I need during a half-hour walk).*

My plan for increasing the amount of my exposure to full-spectrum light: _____

_____

_____

After two weeks of increased exposure to full-spectrum light, I've noticed the following changes: __

_____

_____

_____

After two months of increased exposure to full-spectrum light, I've noticed the following changes:

_____

_____

_____

I intend to make the following changes in my daily routine based on my observations of how I felt after two months of increased exposure to full-spectrum light: _____

_____

_____

_____

_____

The Dangers of Electromagnetic Radiation

I have become aware that some of the scientific advances we take for granted and we trust can really be very harmful.

Nobody really knows what the scoop is on electromagnetic radiation. But new and more compelling evidence surfaces daily that exposure to electromagnetic fields poses significant health risks.

This is really startling in light of our universal exposure to electromagnetic fields, from the transformers that flank our houses to the electrical appliances we use every day. Some researchers believe that electromagnetic radiation can be held responsible for the tremendous increases we're seeing in cancer; other equally distinguished scientists believe the whole thing to be a lot of hooey. What is certain, though, is that the safety of electromagnetic radiation is becoming a critical health issue for the 1990s. It is thought that the production of melatonin in the body decreases with exposure to electromagnetic radiation. Melatonin regulates the biological body rhythms, enhances the immune system, and inhibits tumor growth-enhancing hormones.

Depression and/or agitation are included in the list of effects of overexposure, or, in some cases, any exposure, to this type of radiation. Some people in the survey noted an increase in their level of agitation and a general uneasiness with overexposure to low-frequency (ELF) electromagnetic radiation. I noticed a marked decrease in these symptoms when I stopped using an electric blanket in 1989. I had always felt an uneasiness about electric blankets that I should have paid attention to before science confirmed my intuition. It is interesting to note that the sale of electric blankets has been plummeting ever since information was made public on the hazards of their use.

There are three factors that affect the health risk of your exposure to electromagnetic fields:

1. The strength of the electromagnetic field
2. How close you are to the source of the field
3. Length of exposure

Here are some general guidelines to follow:

Avoid using electric blankets. Even when an electric blanket is switched off, surges of power can course through its wires. You can use your electric blanket to warm up the bed before you get in; then unplug it, or switch it off at a power bar surge protector (these are available at hardware and electronics stores). If the blanket is kept on when you are in bed, you are exposed for a long time to a strong electromagnetic field close to the source of emission. Use a warm, cuddly comforter instead.

Avoid electrically heated waterbeds. If you must use a waterbed, heat it up before you get into it, then turn the heater off. A power bar surge protector is also a good way to turn off the heater, as well as protect you from power surges.

When using a video display terminal, be sure that you are at least an arm's length away from it. Radiation diminishes rapidly as you distance yourself from its source. I use an antiradiation screen on my computer.

Minimize your exposure and keep a safe distance from computer terminals, copying machines, and video display terminals, even if they are on the other side of a wall. Stay 28 inches from the front and 3 to 4 feet from the back and sides. If you work at a video display terminal, move the keyboard as far away from the screen as practical, and spend at least 10 minutes of every hour away from your work station. This may require some negotiation if you work for someone else.

Avoid wearing battery-operated watches. Although such watches have a relatively weak field, your exposure to them is prolonged. Consider also your length of exposure to beepers and personal stereos. Do not keep a digital or electric clock by the head of your bed. Use a battery-operated clock instead, and keep it two to three feet from the bed.

Avoid sitting closer that six to eight feet from the front or sides of your TV or VCR. Most TVs have an instant-on feature and VCRs have a digital clock, so that even when they're off, they're giving off a magnetic field. These features can be bypassed by unplugging the sets or having them plugged into a power bar, which turns these appliances off when not in use (however, you will lose the programming on your VCR if you unplug it).

Stay three feet away from fluorescent lights and one to three feet away from electrical appliances, if possible, when they are on. Turn off electrical devices when they are not in use. This limits your exposure and also helps alleviate depression by lowering your electric bill!

Make sure that no one in your household sleeps or spends a great deal of time where low-voltage power lines from the street come into your house.

If electricity in your house is grounded to water or plumbing pipes, they will generate an electromagnetic field; they should be grounded into the earth. Have this checked by an electrician.

Watch newspapers and magazines for the most current findings on the health effects of electromagnetic radiation. There are some excellent studies on electromagnetic radiation in the Resource List. The medical library at your local hospital is also a good source of information.

Milligauss is a measure of the frequency and wavelength of electromagnetic fields. It is not yet clear how much exposure is unsafe, but some people try to avoid prolonged exposure to fields stronger than two to three milligauss, which is the level that has been linked in some studies to an increased risk of childhood cancer.

Here are the electromagnetic "doses" associated with some common household appliances, measured in milligauss:

Blender	5.2 at 1 ft.
Electric can opener	30 at 225 ft.
Clothes dryer	1 at 24 ft.
Dishwasher	1 at 15 ft.
Freezer	1 at 3 ft.
Garbage disposal	1 at 5 ft.
Iron	1 at 3 ft.
Microwave oven	3 at 40 ft.
Mixer	5-100 at 1 ft.
Electric oven	1 at 8 ft.
Refrigerator	1 at 8 ft.
Electric stove or range	1 at 8 ft.

Toaster	0.6 at 1 ft.
Vacuum cleaner	1.2 at 18 ft.
Computer	1 at 25 ft.
Ceiling fan	1 at 11 ft.
Fluorescent desk lamp	6-20 at 1 ft.
Sewing machine	1 at 23 ft.
Typewriter	1 at 23 ft.
Electric clock	5 at 10 ft.
Electric blanket	3 at 50 ft.
Waterbed heater	1 at 9 ft.
Electric shavers	50 at 300 ft.
Fluorescent light fixture	2 at 32 ft.
Hair dryer	1 at 75 ft.
Baseboard heater	3 at 2 ft. for a 4-foot-long heater
Portable heater	2.5 at less than 3 ft.
Television	1.5 or less at 3 ft.
Electric drill	56 at 194 ft.

(Source: *Associated Press/Valley News*)

The Biological Clock

In the hypothalamus of the brain there is a "biological clock" that controls your body's daily rhythms. For example, your temperature is lowest in the morning and highest in the evening. Another rhythm is the natural tendency to sleep at night and be awake in the daytime. Several hormones that are associated with depression and mood stability, such as cortisol, melatonin, and thyroid-stimulating hormone, have similar biological rhythms.

Apparently, the body's biological clock is set for a 25- instead of a 24-hour day. You are constantly resetting this "clock" through sleep and exposure to light: going to bed at the same time each day, getting up at the same time, and getting exposure to full-spectrum light.

When this clock does not get reset properly—for instance, if you sleep late on a weekend morning, have a job that keeps you up all night, or are indoors all day and don't get any full-spectrum light—you may notice an increase in depression and mood instability, accompanied by a loss of your sense of well-being.

You need to think about resetting your biological clock if you have trouble getting to sleep at night and trouble getting up in the morning.

I have trouble falling asleep at night.	☐ Yes	☐ No
I have trouble getting up in the morning.	☐ Yes	☐ No

If you answered yes to either of these questions, you should think about making the following suggested adjustments in your schedule and routine to allow for resetting your biological clock.

Early to bed and early to rise. Go to bed at the same time each day, by 10:00 or 11:00, and get up at the same time each day, by 7:00 a.m.

Occasionally get up an hour or two earlier than usual to raise your mood.

Get plenty of bright, full-spectrum light, particularly before noon.

Exercise daily. For some reason, this seems to help keep the biological clock in good order.

Avoid prolonged exposure to electromagnetic fields. Again, not all the data has come in—but such exposure seems to throw your body's clock off schedule.

Make adjustments in your schedule to compensate for changes to daylight savings or standard time. To anticipate the spring change, go to bed and get up a half-hour earlier during the week before the time changes. The change is not as noticeable in the fall, but it would help to reverse that process, going to bed and getting up half an hour later the week before the time changes.

Late-afternoon naps are good for you. Many people find it very easy to fall asleep between 2:00 and 4:00; during these hours, efficiency is normally lower, and more accidents occur. The tendency to want to take a siesta is more than just a Latin tradition: the impulse is internally generated by the human brain. Consider taking a half-hour nap in the afternoon between 2:00 and 4:00 PM. If this is not possible because of your work schedule, plan your day so that the time you need to be most alert and creative is in the morning. (I feel much better in the evening if I get a short nap in the afternoon.)

I am going to make the following adjustments to my schedule to allow for "resetting my biological clock" for two weeks: _____

_____

_____

_____

_____

How I felt before I made these adjustments to my schedule and routine: _____

_____

_____

_____

_____

_____

How I felt afterwards: _____

_____

_____

_____

_____

I intend to make the following changes in my daily routine based on what I learned from my two-week experiment: _____

_____

_____

_____

_____

_____

I plan to take the following action with regard to my exposure to low frequency electromagnetic radiation: _____

_____

_____

_____

PART IV

Looking at Suicide

21

Suicide: The Tragedy of Mood Instability

The reality is that depression does end. It does not go on forever. There is light at the end of the tunnel. Life is rewarding and worthwhile. I have experienced many depressive episodes, they have ended, and I am glad I am alive.

The tragedy of depression and manic depression is that so many people who suffer from these illnesses end their lives through suicide.

Of the 120 people who took part in the survey, 77, or just over 64 percent, have thought seriously about or made plans to commit suicide. Fifty-five respondents (46 percent) have made serious attempts to end their life. Sixteen percent of people who are diagnosed as having some type of mood disorder eventually commit suicide. These figures are far too high to ignore.

Twenty-one survey participants have a close family member who has committed suicide. This points to the strong family pattern in these disorders. One person said of her suicide attempt, "I was scared because I realized that my grandmother had done the same thing."

The fear of eventually committing suicide weighs heavily on the minds of those who have experienced manic depression or depression. Of the 45 percent of survey participants who attempted to take their own lives, over half were grateful that they had not succeeded.

One respondent said that the only reason she attempted suicide was because she was in a panic: she just wanted help, and could not arrange to get into the hospital on time. Others said they had attempted suicide so that someone would pay attention to their pain. As people moved toward wellness, the great majority were grateful to still be alive.

I myself tried to commit suicide several times. Suicidal ideation and planning was my constant companion through numerous deep depressions and agitated depressive states. It truly seemed like the only way out of the hopelessness and pain. Now, after many years of stability, I am leading a happy and productive life. I'm glad to be here. Take it from me—choose life.

I asked study participants to describe what it is that triggers suicidal thoughts. Their responses fit into 12 categories:

hopelessness	depression
desperation	low self-esteem
loneliness	guilt
bad memories	seasonal triggers
psychosis	fatigue
chemical imbalance	exposure to chemical vapors

Hopelessness

Many people cited hopelessness as a trigger for their suicide attempt. **Have you ever had these feelings**?

- ☐ no hope for the future
- ☐ no hope that things will ever change
- ☐ no hope that I will ever be well and/or stable
- ☐ no hope that I will ever be able to meet my goals in life
- ☐ no hope I will ever be able to have a successful relationship or career
- ☐ no hope that I will ever be able to accomplish anything
- ☐ no point in being alive
- ☐ no control over my life

The truth is, even though in this state of profound depression a person can rarely see reality clearly, there is hope. After many years of suffering from this illness, I am quite well and have been happy for a long time. My mother was diagnosed as a manic depressive and spent 8 years in a psychiatric ward for the incurably insane. That was 33 years ago. She is now involved in numerous volunteer activities and enjoying her 28 grandchildren. She has become a respected member of the community.

Fifty people in the survey had extended periods of time (up to 25 years) with no mood swing problems. Nineteen others felt that their problem with mood swings is gone for good.

The educational levels of survey participants, their areas of expertise, and the significant achievements in their lives would be exemplary even if they had no emotional problems. All of these people have spent long periods of time completely incapacitated, periods when their lives were in constant turmoil. And yet they got well, or got things under control. There is no such thing as a "hopeless case" of depression or manic depression. By taking charge of your life, you can and will accomplish your goals.

Have you ever felt hopeless? _____ **Describe this feeling:** _____

_____

_____

_____

_____

What is the positive reality of your situation and your life? (For instance, do you have a pleasant place to live, a good job, a nice family a good education, friends, a loving partner, good physical health, a pet, a talent, a hobby?) _____

_____

_____

_____

_____

Depression

Many people feel that suicide is the only way to end the deep, horrible, overwhelming despair of depression, agitated depression, or agitated mania. The pain and blackness inside are so overwhelming that suicide is seen as a relief. The need to stop this excruciating pain becomes overwhelming.

The reality is that depression does end; it does not go on forever. There truly is light at the end of the tunnel.

How long have your episodes of depression lasted? _____

Do you remember feeling as if the depression would never end? _____

Repeat these affirmations over and over to yourself whenever you need to: *Depression Ends. Life is worth living.* Write them on 3 by 5 cards to carry with you and post in prominent places around your home or where you work. Use them as a mantra as you fall asleep at night.

Desperation

People with suicidal thoughts often feel totally overwhelmed, that they have too many problems all at once, that others are expecting more from them than they can possibly accomplish (this may be the result of promises made during a manic phase). Sometimes suicide appears to be the only way out. You may have the feeling that you are trapped and that there is no other alternative.

The reality is that there is always a way out other than death, no matter how dreadful or complicated the situation. You may have to tell people you are sick and can't do what you said, that you need to take some time off to get well, that you need to reduce your stress level to control your illness—whatever it takes. Enlist the help of people in your support system to work out compromises and solutions. Get whatever help you need to work out your problems. Sometimes the thorniest problem only requires a fresh perspective.

Describe times in your life when you have felt desperate: _____

_____

_____

_____

_____

How did you work yourself out of these desperate situations? _____

_____

_____

Now remember: you have done it before; you can do it again.

Low Self-Esteem

The low self-esteem that accompanies depression and manic depression is a key contributory factor to suicide. Despite any rise in self-esteem during manic episodes, mood swings themselves rob people of their sense of self-worth.

Some people in the study expressed the opinion that the world would be a better place without them. Self-accusation and guilt go hand in hand with such perceptions. We feel that we are complete failures in every sense of the word and that there is no point in being alive. We become obsessed with memories of past failures and feelings of inadequacy.

Wait a minute. Take a good and honest look at yourself. Make a list of all your accomplishments, all the people you've ever befriended or helped, all your acts of compassion and kindness. Don't forget that you achieved these things in spite of obstacles greater than most people face. You deserve a pat on the back.

Dedicate yourself to raising your self-esteem (see "Building Self-Esteem and Self-Confidence"). Make a habit of noticing the good things about yourself. There are many excellent books that can help you in this very important learning process; some of these are noted in the Resource List.

Loneliness

An overwhelming feeling of loneliness and isolation is also a contributing factor in suicides. People who experience depression and manic depression feel that no one cares for them, and sometimes have the mistaken notion that their family and friends wish they were dead. One person in the study felt that suicide was a way of "getting back" at her family for not wanting her. Everyone experiences these feelings at times, but in clinical depressions, the feelings are greatly exaggerated.

Depression is often accompanied by a deep fear of desertion by friends, family, and other support system members. A number of suicide attempts alluded to in the study coincided with the ending of a close relationship, either by death, separation, or abandonment. Difficulty sustaining close, lasting relationships plagues and discourages people who experience mood disorders.

Most likely, your family and friends really do care about you. And if for some reason they aren't there to support you, get involved in your local mental health support or advocacy group, a manic depressive support group, a church or special interest group; or volunteer for a worthy cause. Your circle of friends will widen. You will find that you are not alone.

Who are the people in your life about whom you really care and who care about you?

_____

_____

_____

_____

_____

If you can't put five people on this list, refer to "Building a Strong Support System" and start working on setting up a support system for yourself.

*I do not yet have five people in my support system. Therefore I am going to begin developing my support system in the following ways:*_____

_____

_____

_____

_____

Guilt

When people come down from mania and realize what they have done, suicide often seems like the only way to escape the embarrassment, guilt, financial havoc, and other repercussions.

How do you cope when you realize that you've cheated on a beloved mate, run naked through the streets, spent large sums of money frivolously, created huge credit card debts, or announced to the public that you've found the cure to a dread disease?

One study participant wrote: "You won't be hearing from me again. This is just too much for me and my family. I have been picked up again for shoplifting while manic." Luckily, she did not carry through with her threat.

The reality is that the guilt is hard to deal with, but you can pick up the pieces, make amends where you have to, and go on. The world is much more forgiving than you would expect. Believe me, I know. I've done these things, too. And so have the many other survey participants who have learned to let go of guilt and embarrassment and get on with their lives.

*I feel guilty and embarrassed because I:*_____

_____

_____

_____

*What I need to do to pick up the pieces or make amends for my out-of-control behavior:*_____

_____

_____

_____

Get help from your mental health professionals and other members of your support system to let go of the guilt and embarrassment and to move on. With their help and through your own efforts, you will go far toward preventing further manic episodes.

Bad Memories

Depression combined with feeling overwhelmed by bad memories, particularly those associated with childhood abuse, can act as a trigger to suicide.

The following techniques can help you let go of bad memories:

Counseling. Short- or long-term therapy with a competent counselor is a very effective way to release the hold that bad memories can have on your life. (See the chapter called "How About Counseling.")

Alternative health care workers. There are many skilled people who do various types of massage and physical release work that can be part of your effort to overcome bad memories. Get good references from people you trust about the competency of these practitioners in your area.

Journal writing. Writing can be cathartic. Use a notebook to write down all your thoughts and feelings associated with a particular memory, recalling as much detail as you feel comfortable including. This process helps put the memory into perspective, and also helps you let go. As an alternative to the journal, you can write about each memory on separate sheets of paper and then throw them away or burn them as a way of symbolically ridding yourself of burdensome feelings. Remember, you don't have to write neatly, spell accurately, or worry about grammar: these notes are for your use only (unless you choose to share them with your therapist).

Talking it out. Scrutinize bad memories with a trusted friend, family member, therapist, or health care worker (but make sure that you choose someone who can listen without feeling uncomfortable). Peer counseling, group therapy, and support groups can all provide an appropriate forum. Whatever avenue you choose, you should be able to talk about the memory as much as you need to without fear of judgment, criticism, trivialization of its importance, or correction of details by your listeners. You may need to talk about the same memory over and over again until you get it out of your system. If you are using peer counseling or talking to a group, be sure to give the other participants time to share their experiences, too.

Creative arts. You don't have to be an artist to be able to use visual images as a way to unlock old memories. Many people in the study found it useful to work with crayons, magic markers, water colors, acrylics, and clay. In my town, they hold an art show called "Heartworks" of art created by people who are healing from the pain of sexual abuse. Look for art therapy clinics in your area, or sign up for an art or ceramics class at your local community college—whatever it takes to give color, shape, and texture to your feelings.

Confrontation. People who were harmed by adults when they were children may find that confronting the perpetuator of the abuse can be a healing experience. **It is absolutely essential to plan any such confrontation carefully to protect yourself, and to be working closely with a competent counselor, and have a strong support network before undertaking such a meeting.**

Self-help resources. Use the Resource List in this book for help in locating appropriate self-help books, tapes, and organizations.

Your doctor, counselor, support group, or some of the great self-help literature in your library or bookstore can help you let go of these memories and have them become a part of the past that doesn't affect the present.

Bad memories I need to let go of: _____

_____

_____

_____

_____

_____

How I plan to work at letting go of bad memories so they no longer diminish the quality of my life:

_____

_____

_____

Seasonal Triggers

The holiday season, when it seems as if everyone else is having such a great time and experiencing the joys of togetherness, can be the worst time of year for you if you're depressed. Couple this with the reduced daylight hours during the winter season and you have a recipe for suicidal ideation. As anyone who has ever worked on a suicide hotline will tell you, the Christmas holidays are the time when the greatest number of suicide attempts are made in this country.

Despite the difficulties, there are things you can do to make the holiday season less stressful. Don't overplan, overextend yourself, or spend more money than you can reasonably afford. Plan pleasant times with people you enjoy—eating simple foods and sharing simple pleasures. Call on members of your support system. If your family upsets you, explain as diplomatically as you can, and then plan to spend the holidays with people who make you feel good.

Things that have made the holidays hardest for me in the past: _____

_____

_____

My plan for the holiday season this year: _____

_____

_____

_____

The darkness of the season may have a lot to do with feeling rotten during the Christmas season. Full-spectrum lighting, described in the chapter on light, is now being used extensively to overcome winter doldrums. If you can't afford full-spectrum lighting, be sure that you get outside every day for at least 20 minutes without your contact lenses or glasses. If your vision is sufficiently keen, combining this with a walk is a great idea.

I plan to increase the light in my life by: _____

_____

_____

Psychosis

Severe psychosis, particularly when accompanied by hearing voices, was another precipitator of suicide attempts cited by people in the study. Suicide can seem like the only way to get rid of the voices telling you how bad you are, or to do dangerous things. It may also seem like the only way of getting rid of "things" swirling around in your head, the things you see that aren't there, the experiences you have that aren't real, and the other delusions that accompany severe episodes of psychosis.

Psychosis is very dangerous for you and others—get help immediately from health care professionals. At the earliest onset of even the most mild psychotic symptoms, ask someone in your support system to stay with you, or arrange for other people to stay with you, until you receive treatment and all your symptoms are gone. You should never be alone when you are psychotic.

For myself, I have arranged to be hospitalized in these circumstances. Although I hope I won't ever need it, this arrangement makes me feel more secure, as more aggressive treatment is possible in a hospital setting, and the symptoms can be brought under control more quickly. I have given my adult children the legal authority to make this decision for me in the event that I cannot make it for myself.

Psychosis can be experienced by people with either depression or mania and depression in either the manic or depressive phase. The key for people in either of these categories is to monitor their symptoms, get treatment at the earliest onset of symptoms, and formulate a plan in a time of wellness for how your psychosis will be handled when and if it occurs.

It's essential in these situations to get help immediately from your health care professionals. Condition yourself when you're feeling well to check yourself into the hospital at the first signs of psychosis, before things get worse.

Psychosis can be effectively treated. It's a terrible thing to experience, but you can get through it with support and, in some cases, medication. If you can't get help for yourself, tell trusted members of your support system to be alert to your symptoms and to get help for you if necessary.

If I become psychotic, my plan for getting the help that I need is: _____

_____

_____

_____

I will ask the following members of my support system for assistance if I become psychotic: _____

_____

_____

_____

In the event that these people become aware that I am psychotic, I give them permission and expect them to take the following action in my behalf: _____

_____

_____

_____

Fatigue

Many people in the study noted a correlation between being very tired and suicidal ideation. If your fatigue is due to a depressive episode, let someone in your support system know how you feel, especially if you are thinking about suicide. Have him or her arrange for someone to be with you at all times until your suicidal feelings pass.

Get appropriate treatment for depression. Eat foods that are high in complex carbohydrates; get plenty of full-spectrum light—just sitting outside, even on a porch will help. Get some exercise if you can.

Instead of thinking about suicide when you are overtired, take a break. Make sure that your lifestyle and career allow you to take good care of yourself. Even if you can't take a vacation, take some sick time and get rested up. Check in with your medical doctor to see if a physical problem might be contributing to your fatigue. Check in with yourself, your support system, and your mental health professionals to see if you are overdoing it. If you are, take action. Get more rest if you're overworking; schedule activities for yourself if you're simply tired all the time without a reason. Full-spectrum light can have a tonic effect on fatigue; some people have also reported success with acupuncture. The important thing is to strike the right balance for yourself between rest and activity, work time and play time, responsibility and relaxation. When you notice that you're tired all the time, do something about it! Fatigue can be dangerous.

*When I notice that I am feeling very fatigued, I will take the following action:*_____

_____

_____

_____

_____

Chemical Imbalances

Suicidal feelings and ideation can result from chemical imbalances in the body. Seventy-seven of the study participants (64 percent) believe that extreme moods are caused by a chemical imbalance. Scientists would agree.

In the introductory chapter of this workbook, Dr. Matthew McKay describes the various kinds of chemical imbalances that can cause manic depressive and depressive illnesses. With appropriate testing, you can determine if your mood instability or depression is cause by a chemical imbalance. Your doctor should be able to advise you about possible treatment strategies, including medications, and simple, inexpensive changes in the way you live.

Chemical imbalances and genes may indeed cause mood problems. Learn all you can about mood disorders, so you can insist on the right tests, ask the right questions, and get the most useful answers. Find out about what drugs, if any, might work for you; then look into alternatives to drugs. The question has still not been satisfactorily answered about whether bipolar illness is caused by a chemical imbalance or chemical imbalances are actually triggered by the disorder itself. What is certain is that treatment for these disorders is in a state of evolution. Read as much as you can, and work with health care professionals who care about staying current with the latest discoveries in psychiatry and alternative medicine.

*I plan to take the following actions to identify and treat chemical imbalances:*_____

_____

_____

_____

_____

_____

Exposure to Chemical Vapors

I recall vividly a harrowing experience one afternoon in winter when, with all the windows closed, my landlady was varnishing the stairs of my apartment. Feeling suddenly very strange, I decided to leave and walk to a friend's house. When I got there, I very calmly went in the bathroom and looked for something sharp to use to cut my wrists. Prior to exposure to the chemical vapors my mood had been stable. These vapors plummeted me to a deep suicidal level within half an hour.

Other study and workshop participants have related similar experiences with exposure to noxious vapors. It may be that those of us who are prone to mood swings are hypersensitive to the effects of these kinds of chemicals. I don't know; but why take any chances?

Steer clear of noxious vapors. When things start to smell bad, hit the road! If you have to work with toxic paints or chemicals, work outside, open as many windows as possible or wear a respirator.

☐ *I plan to be observant of the effects of noxious vapors on my moods and to remove myself from situations that might be causing or increasing my mania, anxiety, or depression.*

Treatment After a Suicide Attempt

Most people have trouble knowing how to act and what to say following the suicide attempt of a close friend or family member. Perhaps you might have been victimized by this ignorance and bewilderment in the past. People in the study noted that others treated them in the following ways following a suicide attempt. **Which descriptions match your own experience?**

☐ with deep understanding
☐ with helpfulness
☐ I was avoided
☐ with indifference
☐ others became detached and cool
☐ with disgust
☐ like I was a freak
☐ with a lack of understanding

- ☐ with compassion
- ☐ with sympathy
- ☐ with irritation
- ☐ people were afraid of me
- ☐ others were rejecting
- ☐ like I was stupid
- ☐ with resentment
- ☐ others seemed puzzled and confused
- ☐ with denial
- ☐ with caution
- ☐ others were shocked
- ☐ others were angry
- ☐ people were overprotective of me
- ☐ they acted guilty
- ☐ others were judgmental
- ☐ others were unable to believe or understand my wish to die
- ☐ others knew that I was ill and that this phenomenon is part of the illness
- ☐ I was treated no differently than before the suicide attempt
- ☐ members of my support system were angry

In what other ways have you been treated after a suicide attempt? _____

_____

_____

_____

One person in the study commented:

> "My support group ignored the attempt, saying, 'There really isn't a problem with you, you just need some rest.' But even worse than others discounting it were those I trusted and believed were friends becoming a menagerie of silent acquaintances, instantly acting as though I was never there.... Over the last ten years I have had only two friends who have come back when I've started getting better, and they were in two different hospitals for long periods of time. But even these people became distant when I really began the struggle again."

People in the study expressed their preferences for the behavior of family and friends following a suicide attempt.

- ☐ to be treated with understanding
- ☐ to be treated with love

☐ to be treated with compassion

☐ to be treated in a positive manner

☐ others to give me encouragement to live while recognizing the depth and validity of my despair

☐ acknowledge most of what has happened without dwelling on it

☐ to have opportunities to talk with someone I'm very close to and trust about my feelings, someone who can be objective and helpful

☐ that special help that comes from people who don't want me to make another attempt on my life and are committed to seeing that I don't

☐ to be treated normally—I'd prefer that the suicide attempt weren't mentioned, as if it hadn't happened

☐ to be left alone

Describe how you would like to be treated by others after a suicide attempt: _____

_____

_____

_____

_____

_____

_____

_____

_____

_____

_____

Another person from the study commented:

"After being in a four-day coma from a suicide attempt, I had incredible support from my church (70 cards) and so many visitors I would send them away because I was tired out. This greatly influenced my present stability."

22

Preventing Suicide

*Suicide can best be prevented if taken seriously, if I can talk to someone
I can trust, and they care: if they'll listen, be there, try to help, or get the
help I need. If I ask for a call and I don't answer, or don't answer the door,
something needs to be done. People need to believe, not just ignore me.*

Caution: Anyone who is talking about, contemplating, or making unusual arrangements that might precede a suicide attempt needs help immediately. This should be treated as an emergency situation.

When I was depressed, I was often overwhelmingly obsessed with thoughts of suicide.

In the early stages of suicidal ideation, I was still able to talk with others in my support system and would listen as they tried to convince me not to take my life.

At some point I crossed a threshold—very quickly—where I decided that I was definitely going to take my life. I'm not sure what convinced me of this; I think it was an imagined slight or rejection from someone I really cared about, or a feeling of being extremely isolated or in severe psychic or physical pain. It was as if I went into a different mode. My suicide plans became much more detailed. I decided how, where, and when I would end my life. I figured out who I wanted (the police) and who I didn't want (my family and support people) to find me. I stopped talking to anyone about my suicide intentions. I acted as if there were nothing wrong.

When others asked me how I was feeling, I tried to convince them that I was feeling "very well and stable." I became devoid of emotion. I usually gave myself away at these times by totally rejecting the person I imagined had slighted me (this was always someone who was very close). This person, or another member of my support system, ended up intervening by confronting me and forcing me to get help, thus thwarting my plan. Perhaps I set this dynamic up intentionally; I'm not sure.

Having been very suicidal many times, having made several attempts to take my life, and looking back from a vantage point of three years of stability, I urge anyone who has a tendency toward mood swings and/or suicide to set up the following system when they are stable. Learn relaxation techniques, set up a suicide support system, and take precautionary measures concerning medications, firearms, and your car. These things are described in greater detail below.

Learn Relaxation Techniques

There are many breathing and relaxation techniques that take one into a deep meditative state. Refer to the chapter on relaxation in this book. Study these techniques until they are second nature. I also recommend taking a course in relaxation techniques or meditation. Some people have found it difficult to learn relaxation techniques on their own, but very easy with the guidance of a good teacher.

*My plan to learn relaxation techniques:*_____

_____

_____

_____

Practice every day, at least once a day, but several times if you can. Ten or fifteen minutes at a stretch is long enough. Have several set times for relaxation. Do it at other times or more frequently if you begin to feel frantic, if you want to, or if you are having trouble sleeping. You will notice that when you are in a relaxed state you are not depressed. The more you practice, the better it works. Practice regularly; but if you miss one of your set times, don't panic or give up on relaxation. Just do it the next time you have scheduled.

☐ I plan to relax daily at _____, _____, _____(times of day).

☐ I will use relaxation when I notice early warning signs of mania or depression, when I feel frenetic, or when I am having trouble sleeping.

You can use this wonderful time in a relaxed state to review your past accomplishments, think pleasant thoughts, focus on inspirational readings or works of art, meditate on your affirmations (see "New Ways of Thinking"), or whatever makes you feel best. Relaxation really takes the pressure off.

When I am in a relaxed state I will think of:

Past accomplishments: _____

_____

Pleasant thoughts: _____

_____

Inspirational readings, works of art, etc.: _____

_____

Affirmations: _____

_____

_____

You may have heard people recommend that you make one sound or say one thing over and over when you're relaxing. If you're troubled with suicidal ideation, you might want to repeat the affirmation, "I choose life." This replaces "I want to die" (the thought that used to keep repeating itself over and over in my head during depressive episodes). If you really stick to it, *I choose life* becomes so firmly implanted in your brain that you can't say, "I want to die." The strategy is simple, cheap, safe, and noninvasive.

☐   *When I am in a relaxed state, I will repeat over and over the affirmation, "I choose life."*

Give yourself a "Live!" message. Obviously, you can't be relaxing all the time. But you can constantly reaffirm your decision to live. Make the decision that you don't want to die, and then don't allow yourself to consider dying as a possibility. Just forbid it. Take control of your life. Contemplating suicide is a habit. Change the habit, just as you have changed other bad habits like biting your nails, sucking your thumb, or smoking. You can replace the habit of suicidal thoughts with a good habit, such as looking at pictures of your children or grandchildren or playing with your dog.

Instead of contemplating suicide, I will: _____

_____

_____

_____

_____

Set Up a Suicide Support System

Make a list of the people you like and trust the most, with whom you're most comfortable, and by whom you're best understood. These people ought to be very familiar with mood disorders (you can teach them, if necessary). People in your support group are often good choices because they understand what you are experiencing. However, when they are having mood instability problems themselves, call on other people. Ideally, your support system should include stable and understanding family members, your health care professionals (doctor, counselors, etc.), and the staff at the local mental health or emergency phone line. Choose at least five people who are most accessible as potential members of your suicide support team.

Ask the people whom you've chosen whether they would be willing to be on your support team. If they are, spend some time with them individually, educating them about the problem, sharing your individual experience, explaining what possible scenarios might arise when their assistance and support would be needed, and the kinds of action you would like them to take on your behalf. If they are willing to take on this responsibility, share with them as much information as you possibly can about your illness and your feelings. Arrange for these designated people to visit with your doctor or other health care professionals if you think this would be useful.

It is also very helpful to get everyone in your support system together for a group meeting so that they know each other and feel comfortable being in contact and working cooperatively when the need arises. Arrange this as a simple gathering at your home or even in a cafe when you are feeling well, in anticipation of the time when you may not be doing well and support will be needed. An informal discussion of what you would like the group to do is all that is required.

You need at least five people to ensure that one is available in case of a crisis. You should never expect any one person to be available to you at all times.

Ideally, people in your suicide support system will know you so well that they may be able to spot your mood swings even before you do, and will promptly assist you in taking evasive action.

The five people in my suicide support system are:

Name _____ phone number _____

Name _____ phone number _____

Name _____ phone number _____

Name _____ phone number _____

Name _____ phone number _____

My plan for how I will educate members of my suicide support team and facilitate their support: _

Make a pact with these people that you will contact them when you are feeling suicidal. Have them arrange for someone to stay with you until you start to feel better, and to get you help. Give them permission ahead of time to do whatever they have to do to keep you safe. Remember, these are people you trust and who really care about you. In exchange for their promise to be part of your suicide support system, you promise them that you will call one of them without fail at times when you feel suicidal.

☐ *I promise to contact someone on my suicide support team if I am feeling suicidal or having suicidal ideation.*

☐ *I give members of my suicide support team permission to take the following actions on my behalf to protect me and prevent me from committing suicide.*

Regulate the Medications You Have on Hand

Many people with mood disorders keep old prescription medications hidden away in case they want to commit suicide at some later time. Medications are all too easy to accumulate. When the doctor changes prescriptions—which for some of us is often—patients often keep the leftovers from the old prescription.

In most cases, there is no system in place for tracking what happens to leftover medications. Neither the druggist nor the doctor may remember to monitor excess pills. People with mood swings need to do this for themselves.

Clean all the old drugs out of your house (even those in your bottom drawer you keep just in case). Flush them down the toilet. Get rid of them all. And tell the members of your support team what you have done.

☐ *I have flushed all my old medications down the toilet. I only keep on hand small quantities of the medications I use regularly.*

Talk honestly to your doctor about any suicidal tendencies you may feel. For your own protection, request that prescriptions be filled in small quantities. Although even a week's worth of a prescription could prove lethal under certain circumstances, depending on what the medication is, it may be hard, costly, and inconvenient to get less than that amount. It is therefore essential that other suicide prevention mechanisms be in place. When

I was suicidal, members of my support system confiscated my medications, gave me only the appropriate dose at the right time, and watched me take it.

☐ *I will discuss suicidal thoughts and ideation with my doctor and request prescriptions be filled in small quantities.*

Talk the situation over with your pharmacist, too. (Be sure that you have a good pharmacist who understands, knows you, and is truly interested in your welfare.) Drugstores keep records (often on computer) of just what drugs they have sold to you and when. If they sold you a month's supply of one drug, and two weeks later the doctor changes your prescription (as so often happens), have the pharmacists require you to return the amount you should have left over from the previous prescription before you can pick up the new one.

My pharmacist told me that, if requested, they can place a special marker by a person's name in their records to cue the computer program if it appears that the person has too much of any medication on hand. The pharmacist can then take some action (such as requiring that the old medication to be turned in) before the new medication is dispensed. My pharmacist expressed the opinion that any druggist would be glad to provide a similar service.

☐ *I will talk with my pharmacist about working together to prevent me from having a potentially dangerous amount of medications on hand.*

Members of your support system should know what medications you are taking, their expected side effects, and where you keep them in the house. There should be no secrets between you on this score. The issue is too serious. (If you need further incentive, it is unsafe to have these old medications around, because a child or another member of the family might take them either by mistake or on purpose.)

☐ *I will educate all members of my support system about the medications I'm taking, where I keep them, and possible side effects.*

Get Rid of All Firearms

No firearm should be kept in a home where there is anyone who has a tendency to be suicidal. They are a quick, easy-to-use, drastic, and horrible resolution to a temporary surge of emotion. Find an alternative if you have rationalized keeping a gun for purposes of self-defense (get a dog, carry a can of mace, take a course in martial arts, move to a safer neighborhood).

☐ *I will dispose of all firearms in my home or give them to a member of my support team for safekeeping.*

If people you live with collect firearms or use firearms in sports activities, ask them to store the firearms somewhere outside the home, where they are locked away and inaccessible to you.

☐ *I will ask anyone I live with to store firearms outside our home and to keep them locked away.*

Be Cautious About Driving

When you have early warning signs of depression or are starting to feel suicidal, give your car keys to a member of your support team. If you must get to work, ask someone on your support team to take you. You could also take public transportation or carpool with other workers. This is not a safe time for you to be driving. Give members of your support team permission to take your car keys away if you seem depressed or suicidal.

☐ *I will give my car keys to a member of my support team if I have early warning signs of depression or feel suicidal. I will ask others to take me to work , will take public transportation, or will join a carpool.*

☐ *I give members of my support team permission to take my car keys away if I seem depressed or suicidal.* (Remember, these are people whose judgment you trust.)

Express Your Emotions

Talk to a member of your support team. Let all your feelings out. Cry, scream, kick, carry on, hit pillows—whatever it takes to get rid of that black tension (short of hurting yourself, someone else, or some thing). Do this as often as possible. Members of your support team will want to take turns, as the experience of witnessing so much emotional release can be draining and exhausting. But keep at it, for at least an hour a day. (See the chapter "How About Counseling?")

☐ *When I get depressed, I will spend at least one hour a day expressing my emotions to a member of my support team.*

Get Support

Don't allow yourself to be alone when you're having suicidal thoughts, even though you may really want to be alone. Have someone with you around the clock, no exceptions. It's a pain, but it's critical. You may wish that everyone would just go away; but don't let them. Your life at these times depends on the presence of others. You will have to educate members of your support team that you are not to be left alone when you are feeling suicidal.

☐   *I will not allow myself to be alone when I am feeling suicidal. I will tell members of my support team to arrange for someone always to be with me at these times.*

Remind Yourself How Good You Are, and How Good It Is To Be Alive

Hang pictures of your favorite people (children, grandchildren, parents, friend, partner) and places all around the house. Post special letters, awards, diplomas, and all other honors where you can easily see them. Keep a list of your accomplishments on your refrigerator door, and another next to your bed. Keep mementos of special times in obvious places. When you feel like committing suicide, just look around at all these reminders of why you should live.

I have a bureau in my hallway—a place that I pass many times every day—which is decorated with favorite family pictures, special cards that I received, and mementos of special times and events. This display has helped me through many rough times.

What I will do to keep reminding myself how good I am, and how good it is to be alive: _____

_____

_____

_____

Recommendations From Study Participants

Suicide Prevention: Choices You Have To Make

Stay on prescribed medications. People don't like taking medications. They often make you feel lousy and have miserable side effects. However, many of the survey participants rely on medication, as I did for a long time, to protect themselves. It's to be hoped that, at some time in the future, better solutions to these problems will come along. But, for now, medications are the only thing that works. Be sure that you and members of your support team educate yourselves fully about any medication that a doctor recommends for your treatment.

Call the doctor at the first sign of depression. Letting the depression get out of hand is not a good policy. Don't wait until you are really low. Make that phone call right away, while you still can.

Schedule regular appointments with your health care professionals. Keep your appointments no matter how good or awful you are feeling. Remember that these appointments are just as much a matter of prevention as they are of cure.

Get together with your trusted therapist and talk, talk, talk. Get together with trusted friends and family and talk, talk, talk. It works. Just being with others and enjoying a meaningful exchange can lift your spirits and help you feel less alone.

Writing often helps people work through suicidal episodes. Write anything you want, anything you feel. No one is grading your work. No one is looking over your shoulder or judging you. You don't have to worry about correct spelling or grammar. Just remain open and honest emotionally (even if you're writing fiction or poetry). Drawing or painting can work in the same way to ease painful emotions.

Pray. Lots of people do it. And lots of people feel that it works.

Many people attend 12-step programs and find them to be helpful and supportive. Attendance at such a group may be a lot to expect of yourself when you feel like committing suicide; but if you can possibly get out, do it. (Have someone else drive you.)

Some participants advise checking into the hospital as soon as suicidal ideation starts. This is an issue that you should discuss and resolve with your health care team and members of your support group.

You might want to make a "suicide contract" with your health care professionals and members of you support group. This means that you promise to call them before you attempt to take your life.

Overall Life Changes To Prevent You From Becoming Suicidal

Learn everything you can about mood disorders. Scour the library and bookstores. (See the Resource List at the end of this book.)

Set up a lifestyle for yourself that causes you as little stress as possible. This is hard to do in this day and age, but it can be done. There are many helpful hints throughout this workbook.

Love yourself. (See "Building Self-Esteem and Confidence.")

Make provisions when you are feeling well so that you will be safe when you are suicidal. Take all the precautions you need to regarding medications, firearms, car keys, etc.

Ask for help when you need it.

Exercise, eat right, get plenty of rest and light. In essence, take good care of yourself in every way. Don't let up. Those of us who have mood disorders need to be very disciplined about this. (See chapters on exercise, diet, and light)

Keep your faith, whatever it is. Many participants feel that a strong spiritual support system is essential to their well-being.

Change your attitude. Think positively. Appreciate what you can do, and don't give yourself a hard time about what you can't do. (See "New Ways of Thinking.")

294 *The Depression Workbook*

Work on improving your interpersonal relationships. Get help on this from your health care professionals or members of your support group. It feels good to get along with others, and it makes life worth living.

Regularly attend a support group that is appropriate for you. Play an active role in the group when you can. (See the chapter on support groups.)

Additional thoughts about suicide from study participants:

> "I keep my medications in balance and am very aware of particular external things which precipitate depression. I continue learning about my illness and educate those close to me so they will recognize my shifts before I do."

> "I do everything I can—diet, socialize, take medications, see doctors, whatever—to feel I am in mastery of my illness and my fate."

> "[When I feel suicidal] I stay at home, doors shut. I would never do it at home—what a mess for those who find me! I also hint to my family that they are not responsible for me if I commit suicide."

> "I don't know if I was actually attempting to end my life. I remember just wanting to go to sleep, to get away from the bad feelings. I had constant feelings that I was causing everyone too many problems and we would all be better off if I were dead. I even had a master plan, but it wasn't an overdose. I really believe I was just trying to temporarily escape at the time I took the overdose. The more I took, the more out of touch I became, and it just got out of control. I just wanted to stop the pain. Afterwards, when I realized what I had done, I felt even worse. I felt very guilty for putting my close friends and family through that. It took a long time to get over it and establish trust from everyone."

Resource List

Anger

Lerner, H. (1985) *The Dance of Anger.* New York: Harper & Row.

McKay, M., P. Rogers, and J McKay (1989) *When Anger Hurts.* Oakland, CA: New Harbinger Publications, Inc..

Rubin, T. (1989) *The Angry Book.* New York: Macmillan

Anxiety

Bourne, E. (1990) *The Anxiety & Phobia Workbook.* Oakland, CA: New Harbinger Publications, Inc.

Desberg, P., and G Marsh (1988) *Controlling Stagefright: With Audiences From One to One Thousand.* Oakland, CA: New Harbinger Publications, Inc.

Handly, R. (19885) *Anxiety and Panic Attack: Their Cause and Cure.* New York: Rawson Associates.

Wolpe, J. (1988) *Life Without Fear: Anxiety and Its Cure.* Oakland, CA: New Harbinger Publications, Inc.

Anxiety Audio Tapes

Acquiring Courage. Oakland, CA: New Harbinger Publications, Inc.

Biological Clock

Coleman, R.M. (1986) *Wide Awake at 3:00 AM, By Choice or Chance.* New York: W.H. Freeman.

Czeisler, C.A. et al. (1990) "Exposure to bright light and darkness to treat psyiologic maladaption to night work." *New England Journal of Medicine* 322:1253-9.

Goleman, D. (1989) "Feeling sleepy? An urge to nap is built-in." *New York Times*, September 12, Science Section, p. 1.

Van Cauter, E., and F. W. Turek (1990) "Strategies for resetting the human biological clock." *New England Journal of Medicine* 322: 1306-7.

Career Planning

Bolles, R. (1983) *What Color Is Your Parachute?* Berkeley, CA: Ten Speed Press.

Irish, R.K. (1987) *Go Hire Yourself an Employer.* New York: Doubleday.

Lathrop, R. (1977) *Who's Hiring Who?* Berkeley, CA: Ten Speed Press.

Cognitive Therapy

Beck, A., J. Rush, B. Shaw, and G. Emery (1979) *The Cognitive Therapy of Depression.* New York: Guilford Press.

Burns, D. (1980) *Feeling Good.* New York: W. Morrow.

Burns, D. (1989) *The Feeling Good Handbook*. New York: W. Morrow.

McKay, M., M. Davis, and P. Fanning (1981) *Thoughts and Feelings: The Art of Cognitive Stress Intervention*. Oakland, CA: New Harbinger Publications, Inc.

McKay, M., and P. Fanning (1991) *Prisoners of Belief: Exposing and Changing Beliefs That Control Your Life*. Oakland, CA: New Harbinger Publications, Inc.

Cognitive Therapy Audio Tapes

Covert Modeling and Covert Reinforcement. Oakland, CA: New Harbinger Publications, Inc.

Combatting Distorted Thinking. Oakland, CA: New Harbinger Publications, Inc.

Systematic Desensitization and Visualizing Goals. Oakland, CA: New Harbinger Publications, Inc.

Thought Stopping. Oakland, CA: New Harbinger Publications, Inc.

Depression

Cammer, L. (1969) *Up From Depression*. New York: Simon & Schuster.

DePaulo, J., and K. Ablow (1989) *How To Cope With Depression*. New York: McGraw-Hill.

Flach, F. (1986) *The Secret Strength of Depression*. New York: Bantam Books.

Greist, J., and J. Jefferson (1984) *Depression and Its Treatment: Help for the Nation's #1 Mental Problem*. Washington DC: American Psychiatric Press, Inc.

Kline, N. (1974) *From Sad To Glad*. New York: Putnam.

Nairne, K., and G. Smith (1984) *Dealing With Depression*. London, England: The Woman's Press Handbook Series.

Papolos, J., and D. Papolos (1988) *Overcoming Depression*. New York: Harper & Row.

Rowe, D. (1984) *The Way Out of Your Prison*. New York: Routledge, Chapman & Hall.

Slagle, P. (1988) *The Way Up From Down*. New York: St. Martin's Press.

Winokur, G. (1981) *Depression: The Facts*. New York: Oxford University Press.

Depression Videos

Wellness Workshops: Depression (1991) Co-produced by William Hood and Mary Ellen Copeland. Brattleboro, VT.

Diet

Abramson, E. (1971) *Mind, Body and Sugar*. New York: Pyramid Books.

Appleton, N. (1985) *Like the Sugar Habit*. Santa Monica, CA: Choice Publishing.

Berger, S.M. (1986) *How To Be Your Own Nutritionist: The Immune Power Diet*. New York: Signet Books.

Crook, W.G., and M.H. Jones (1989) *The Yeast Connection Cookbook*. Jackson, TN: Professional Books.

Dufty, W. (1975) *Sugar Blues*. New York: Warner Books.

Fanning, P. (1990) *Lifetime Weight Control: Seven Steps To Achieving and Maintaining a Healthy Weight*. Oakland, CA: New Harbinger Publications, Inc.

Nearing, H. (1980) *Simple Food for the Good Life*. Walpole, NH: Stillpoint Press.

Roth, G. (1989) *Why Weight? A Guide to Ending Compulsive Eating*. New York: NAL/Dutton.

Sandbek, T.J. (1986) *The Deadly Diet: Recovering From Anorexia and Bulimia*. Oakland, CA: New Harbinger Publications, Inc.

Turner, K. (1987) *The Self-Healing Cookbook*. Grass Valley, CA: Earthtones Press.

Electromagnetic Radiation

Becker R.O. (1990) *Cross Currents*. Los Angeles: J.P. Tarcher.

Becker R.O., and G. Selden (1985) *The Body Electric*. New York: W. Morrow.

Brodeur, P. (1989) *Currents of Death*. New York: Simon & Schuster.

Brodeur, P. "Annals of radiation: Calamity on meadow street. *The New Yorker*, July 9, 1990, pp. 38-72.

Morgan, G. *Electric and Magnetic Fields for 60-Hertz Electric Power: What Do We Know About the Possible Health Risks?* Department of Engineering and Public Policy, Carnegie Mellon University, Pittsburgh, PA 15213. (This Brochure is available from many electric utility companies.)

Family and Friends

Bernheim, K., R. Lewine, and C. Beal (1982) *The Caring Family: Living With Chronic Mental Illness.* New York: Random House.

Bombeck, E. (1988) *Family Ties That Bind and Gag.* New York: Fawcett.

Committee on Psychiatry and the Community (1984) *A Family Affair: Helping Families Cope With Mental Illness.* New York:Bruner/Mazel.

Johnson, J.T. (1988) *Hidden Victims.* New York: Doubleday.

Morrison, J.R. (1981) *Your Brother's Keeper: A Guide for Families of the Mentally Ill.* Chicago: Nelson-Hall.

General Information

American Psychiatric Association, Janet B.W. Williams, D.S.W. Ed. (1987) *Diagnostic and Statistical Manual of Mental Disorders (DSM-IIIR).* Washington, D.C.: American Psychiatric Association.

Andersen, N. (1984) *The Broken Brain.* New York: Harper & Row.

Chamberlain, J. (1978) *On Our Own.* New York: McGraw-Hill.

Klein, D.F., et al. (1980) *Diagnosis and Drug Treatment of Psychiatric Disorders: Adults and Children, 2nd ed.* Baltimore: Williams & Wilkins.

Fieve, R. (1975) *Mood Swings.* New York: W. Morrow.

Garson, S. (1986) *Out of Our Minds.* Buffalo: Prometheus.

Glanze, W.D. (1986) *Mosby's Medical and Nursing Dictionary.* St. Louis: The C. V. Mosby Co.

Goodwin, F., and K. R. Jamison (1990) *Manic-Depressive Illness.* New York: Oxford University Press.

Jefferson, J., and J. Marshall (1981) *Neuropsychiatric Features of Medical Disorders.* New York: Plenum Press.

Jon, F. (1987) *Molecules of the Mind.* New York: Atheneum.

Klein, D. (1988) *Do You Have a Depressive Illness?* New York: NAL Penguin.

Millet, K. (1990) *The Looney Bin Trip.* New York: Simon & Schuster.

Park. C., and L. Shapiro (1979) *You Are Not Alone: Understanding and Dealing With Mental Illness.* Boston: Little, Brown.

Tsuang, M., and R. Vandermey (1980) *Genes and the Mind: Inheritance of Mental Illness.* New York: Oxford University Press.

Weis, B.L. (1988) *Many Lives, Many Masters.* New York: Simon & Schuster.

Light

Hyman, J. (1990) *The Light Book.* Los Angeles: J.B. Tarcher.

London, W. (1991) *Back to Basics.* Brattleboro, VT: London Research.

Ott, J.N. (1973) *Health and Light.* New York: Simon & Schuster.

Rosenthal, N. (1989) *Seasons of the Mind.* New York: Bantam Books.

Whybrow, P., and R. Bahr (1989) *The Hibernation Response: Why You Feel Fat, Miserable and Depressed From October to March and What You Can Do About It.* New York: Avon.

For information on where to get full-spectrum lightbulbs, call 1-800-937-0900, Ext 7041.

To Purchase a light box, contact: Wyman Way Lite Box, 331 Main St., Keene, NH 03431 (603) 357-4400; or Vermont Light Box Co., 20 Western Ave., Brattleboro, VT 05301 (802) 254-4310.

Mania

Belmaker, R., and H. Van Praag (1980) *Mania: An Evolving Concept.* New York: Spectrum.

Shopsin, B. (1979) *Manic Illness.* New York: Ravin Press.

Medications and Treatments

Abrams, R., and W. Essman (1982) *Electroconvulsive Therapy: Biological Foundations and Clinical Applications.* New York: SP Medical and Scientific Books.

American Society of Hospital Pharmacists. (1982) *Consumer Drug Digest.* New York: Facts on File.

Barnhart, E.R., ed. (1990) *Physicians' Desk Reference: PDR.* Montvale, NJ: Medical Economics Company.

Baudhuin, M., and Lithium Information Center Staff (1981-1982) *Lithium and Manic Depression: A Guide.* Madison, WI: Lithium Information Center.

Greist, J., and T. Greist (1979) *Antidepressant Treatment: The Essentials.* Baltimore: Williams and Wilkins.

Griest, J.,: J. Jefferson, and R. Spitzer (1981) *Treatment of Mental Disorders.* New York: Plenum Press.

Jefferson, J., J. Greist, and D. Ackerman (1983) *Lithium Encyclopedia for Clinical Practice.* Washington, D.C.: American Psyciatric Press.

Kaufman, J. (1983) *Over-the-Counter Pills That Don't Work.* New York: Pantheon Books.

Lewinsohn, P., R. Munoz, M. Younger, and A. Suiss (1989) *Control Your Depression.* Englewood Cliffs, NJ: Prentice-Hall.

Long, J. (1985) *Essential Guide to Prescription Drugs.* New York: Harper & Row.

Powell, A. (1981) *Layman's Guide to Mental Health Problems and Treatments.* Springfield, IL: Charles C. Thomas.

Schou, M. (1983) *Lithium Treatment of Manic Depressive Illness: A Practical Guide.* New York: Karger.

Simon, G., and H. Silverman (1990) *The Pill Book.* New York: Bantam Books.

Task Force 14 (1978) *Electroconvulsive Therapy.* Washington, D.C. American Psychiatric Association.

Wolfe, S. (1981) *Pills That Don't Work.* New York: Farrar, Straus, Giroux.

Mental Health and Wellness

Borysenko, J. (1990) *Guilt Is the Teacher, Love Is the Lesson.* New York: Warner Books.

Borysenko, J. (1987) *Minding the Body, Mending the Mind.* Redding, MA: Addison-Wesley.

Burns, D. (1985) *Intimate Connections.* New York: W. Morrow.

Buscaglia, L. (1982) *Living, Loving, and Learning.* New York: Ballantine.

Campbell, J. (1988) *The Power of Myth.* New York: Doubleday.

Crook, W. (1983) *The Yeast Connection.* Jackson, TN: Professional Books.

Cousins, N. (1983) *Anatomy of an Illness.* New York: Bantam Books.

Cousins, N. (1983) *The Healing Heart.* New York: W. Norton.

Cousins, N. (1981) *Human Options.* New York: W. Norton.

Davidson, J. (1988) *The Agony of It All.* Los Angeles: J.B. Tarcher.

Dobson, J. (1984) *Emotions: Can You Trust Them?* New York: Bantam Books.

Dyer. W. (1986) *Happy Holidays.* New York: W. Morrow.

Dyer. W. (1979) *Pulling Your Own Strings.* New York: Avon.

Eargle, J. (1981) *Healing Where You Hurt.* Knoxville, TN: John Eargle Ministries.

Ellis, A., and R. Harper (1975) *A New Guide to Rational Living.* Englewood Cliffs, NJ: Prentice-Hall.

Estroff, S.E. (1981) *Making It Crazy.* Berkeley, CA: University of California Press.

Friedman, M., and D. Ulmer (1984) *Treating Type-A Behavior.* New York: Knopf.

Gil, E. (1988) *Outgrowing the Pain.* New York: Dell.

Hay, L. (1988) *Heal Your Life and Body.* Santa Monica, CA: Hay House.

Hazelton, L. (1984) *The Right To Feel Bad.* New York: Ballantine.

Hyatt, C. and L. Gottlieb (1988) *When Smart People Fail: Rebuilding Yourself for Success.* New York: Penguin.

Jampolsky, G. (1985) *Goodbye to Guilt.* New York: Bantam Books.

Kushner, H. (1987) *When All You've Ever Wanted Isn't Enough.* Boston: G.K. Hall.

Kushner, H. (1982) *When Bad Things Happen to Good People.* Boston: G.K. Hall.

Low, A. (1984) *Mental Health Through Will Training*. Glencoe, IL: Willett Publishing Co.

Marks, I. (1979) *Living With Fear*. New York: McGraw-Hill.

Peale, N.V. (1978) *The Power of Positive Thinking*. New York: Foundation For Christian Living.

Peck, S. (1985) *The Road Less Traveled*. New York: Walker.

Pelletier, K. (1977) *Mind as Healer, Mind as Slayer: a Holistic Approach To Preventing Stress Disorders*. New York: Delacorte Press.

Ponder, C. (1985) *Healing Secrets of the Ages*. Marina del Ray, CA: DeVorss.

Powell, J. (1989) *Fully Human, Fully Alive*. Allen, TX: Tabor Publishers.

Schwartz, D. (1990) *The Magic of Thinking Big*. Englewood Cliffs, NJ: Prentice-Hall.

Seigel, B. (1990) *Love, Medicine, and Miracles*. New York: Harper & Row.

Seigel, B. (1989) *Peace, Love, and Healing*. New York: Harper & Row.

Sheehy, G. (1987) *Spirit of Survival*. New York: Bantam Books.

Sheldon, M., ed. (1991) *The Wellness Encyclopedia*. Berkeley, CA: University of California Press.

Veninga, R. (1986) *A Gift of Hope: How We Survive Our Tragedies*. New York: Ballantine.

Viscott, D. (1977) *The Language of Feelings*. New York: Pocket Books.

Waterman, R. (1988) *The Renewal Factor*. New York: Bantam Books.

Wegscheider-Cruise, S. (1985) *Choice Making*. Pompano Beach, FL: Health Communications, Inc.

Wender, P.H., and D. Klein (1981) *Mind, Mood, and Medicine*. New York: Farrar, Strauss, Giroux.

Whitfield, C. (1990) *A Gift To Myself*. Deerfield Beach, FL: Health Communications, Inc.

Whitfield, C. (1987) *Healing the Child Within*. Deerfield Beach, FL: Health Communications, Inc.

Wigoder, D. (1987) *Images of Destruction*. New York: Routledge & Degan Paul.

Relationships

Bireda, M. (1990) *Love Addiciton: A Guide to Emotional Independence*. Oakland, CA: New Harbinger Publications, Inc.

Bugen, L.A. (1990) *Love & Renewal: A Couple's Guide to Commitment*. Oakland, CA: New Harbinger Publications, Inc.

Carnegie, D. (1981) *How To Win Friends and Influence People*. New York: Simon & Schuster.

Kinghma, D.R. (1987) *Coming Apart: Why Relationships End and How To Live Through the Ending of Yours*. Oakland, CA: New Harbinger Publications, Inc.

McKay, M., M. Davis, and P. Fanning (1983) *Messages: The Communication Skills Book*. Oakland, CA: New Harbinger Publications, Inc.

McKay, M., R. Rogers, J. Blades, and R. Gosse (1984) *The Divorce Book: A Practical and Compassionate Guide*. Oakland, CA: New Harbinger Publications, Inc.

McKinley, R. (1989) *Personal Peace: Transcending Your Interpersonal Limits*. Oakland, CA: New Harbinger Publications, Inc.

Scott, G.G. (1990) *Resolving Conflict: With Others and Within Yourself*. Oakland, CA: New Harbinger Publications, Inc.

Viorst, J. (1987) *Necessary Losses*. New York: Simon & Schuster.

Williams, W. (1988) *Rekindling Desire: Bringing Your Sexual Relationship Back to Life*. Oakland, CA: New Harbinger Publications, Inc.

Relationship Audio Tapes

Assertiveness Training. Oakland, CA: New Harbinger Publications, Inc.

Becoming a Good Listener. Oakland, CA: New Harbinger Publications, Inc.

Effective Self-Expression. Oakland, CA: New Harbinger Publications, Inc.

Fair Fighting. Oakland, CA: New Harbinger Publications, Inc.

Making Contact. Oakland, CA: New Harbinger Publications, Inc.

Sexual Communication. Oakland, CA: New Harbinger Publications, Inc.

Relaxation and Stress Reduction

Adair, M. (1985) *Working Inside Out*. Berkeley, CA: Wingbrow Press.

Base, G. *Animalia*. New York: Harry N. Abrams, Inc.

Benson, H., and W. Proctor (1985) *Beyond the Relaxation Response*. New York: Berkeley.

Benson, H., and M. Clipper (1975) *The Relaxation Response*. New York: W. Morrow.

Birkedahl, N. (1990) *The Habit Control Workbook*. Oakland, CA: New Harbinger Publications, Inc.

Borysenko, J. (1990) *Guilt Is the Teacher, Love Is the Lesson*. New York: Warner Books.

Bricklin, M., M. Golin, D., Grandenetti, and A. Leiberman (1990) *Positive Living and Health*. Emmaus, PA: Rodale Press.

Carlson, R., and B. Shield (1989) *Healers on Healing*. Los Angeles: J.P. Tarcher.

Davis, M., E.R. Eschelman, and M. McKay (1988) *The Relaxation & Stress Reduction Workbook*. Oakland, CA: New Harbinger Publications., Inc

Davis, M. (1988) *Leader's Guide to Relaxation & Stress Reduction Workbook*. Oakland, CA: New Harbinger Publications, Inc.

Easwaran, E. (1981) *Meditation*. Petaluma, CA Nilgiri Press.

Flach, F. (1985) *Resilience: Discovering a New Strength in Times of Stress*. New York: Fawcett.

Gawain, S. (1982) *Creative Visualization*. New York: Bantam Books.

Gillespie, P., and L. Bechtel (1986) *Less Stress in 30 Days*. New York: New American Library.

Harp, D. (1990) *The New Three Minute Meditator*. Oakland, CA: New Harbinger Publications, Inc.

Hanh, T. (1976) *The Miracle of Mindfulness! A Manual on Mediation*. Boston: Beacon Press.

Hay, L. (1987) *Heal Your Life and Body*. Santa Monica, CA: Hay House.

Kabat-Zinn, J. (1990) *Full Catastrophe Living*. New York: Delacorte Press.

Luthe, W. (1969) *Autogenic Therapy*. New York: Grune and Stratton.

Matthews-Simonton, S., O.C. Simonton, and J.L. Creighton (1984) *Getting Well Again*. New York: Bantam Books.

Nuernberger, P. (1981) *Freedom From Stress: A Holistic Approach*. Honesdale, PA: Himalayan International Institute of Yoga Science and Philosophy.

Padus, E. (1986) *The Complete Guide to Your Emotions and Your Health*. Emmaus, PA: Rodale Press.

Pelletier, K.R. (1977) *Mind as Healer, Mind as Slayer*. New York: Delta.

Seigel, B. (1990) *Love, Medicine and Miracles*. New York: Harper & Row.

Seigel, B. (1989) *Peace, Love, and Healing*. New York: Harper & Row.

Taylor, D., and M. Rock (1987) *Gut Reaction: How To Handle Stress and Your Stomach*. New York: Berkeley.

White, J., and J. Fadiman (1976) *Relax*. New York: Dell.

Relaxation and Stress Reduction Audio Tapes

Applied Relaxation Training. Oakland, CA: New Harbinger Publications, Inc.

Autogenics and Meditation. Oakland, CA: New Harbinger Publications, Inc.

Body Awareness and Imagination. Oakland, CA: New Harbinger Publications, Inc.

Progressive Relaxation and Breathing. Oakland, CA: New Harbinger Publications, Inc.

Ten Minutes to Relax. volumes 1 and 2, based on *The Stress Reduction & Relaxation Workbook*. Oakland, CA: New Harbinger Publications, Inc.

Kabat-Zinn, J. *Mindfulness Meditation Practice Tapes* (2 tapes) which include a guided body scan meditation, a guided sitting meditation, and two sides of very slow and simple yoga meditation exercise. Write to: Stress Reduction Tapes, P.O. Box 547, Levington, MA 02173.

Relaxation Video Tapes

Seigel, B. *Innervision: Visualizing Super Health*.

A catalogue of books, audio tapes, video tapes, and workshops by Dr. Seigel and others whom he recommends is available by writing to ECAP, 1302 Chapel St. New Haven, CT 06511; or call 203-865-8392.

Relaxation: An anti-tension workout. CA: American Health. Karl Lorimar Home Video, 1986.

Self-Esteem

Branden, N. (1988) *How To Raise Your Self-Esteem*. New York: Bantam Books.
KcKay, M., and P. Fanning (1987) *Self -Esteem*. Oakland, CA: New Harbinger Publications, Inc.
Waitley, D. (1988) *Being the Best*. Chicago: Nightingale-Conant.

Sexual Abuse

Adams, C., and J. Fay (1989) *Free of the Shadows: Recovering From Sexual Violence*. Oakland, CA: New Harbinger Publications, Inc.
Bass, E., and L. Davis (1988) *The Courage To Heal*. New York: Harper & Row.
Davis, L. (1990) *The Courage To Heal Workbook*. New York: Harper & Row.
Finney, L. (1990) *Reach for the Rainbow*. Park City, UT: Changes Publishing.
Finney, L. (1990) *Reach for the Rainbow: Advanced Healing for Survivors of Sexual Abuse*. Park City, UT: Changes Publishing.
Forward, S., and B. Craig (1978) *Betrayal of Innocence*. Los Angeles: J.B. Tarcher.
Maltz, W. (1991) *The Sexual Healing Journey*. New York: Harper Collins.
Matsakis, A. (1991) *When the Bough Breaks: A Helping Guide for Parents of Sexually Abused Children*. Oakland, CA: New Harbinger Publications, Inc.

Sleep

Catalano, E. (1978) *Getting To Sleep*. Oakland, CA: New Harbinger Publications, Inc.
Trubo, R. (1978) *How To Get a Good Night's Sleep*. Boston: Little, Brown.

Substance Abuse

Beattie, M. (1989) *Beyond Codependency*. New Hork: Harper & Row.
Beattie, M. (1988) *Codependent No More*. New Hork: Harper & Row .
Schneider, J. (1988) *The Enabler: When Helping Harms the Ones You Love*. Oakland, CA: New Harbinger Publications, Inc.
Woititz, J. (1983) *Adult Children of Alcoholics*. Pompano Beach, FL: Health Communications.

Suicide

Beattie, M. (1991) *A Reason to Live*. Wheaton, IL: Tyndale House Publishers, Inc.
Hyde, M., and E. Forsyth (1986) *Suicide, The Hidden Epidemic*. New York: F. Watts.
Reynolds, D., and N. Farberow (1976) *Suicide Inside and Out*. Berkeley, CA: University of California Press.

Support Groups

Goodman, G., and M. Jacobs (1985) *Common Concern*: Program of tapes and booklets on developing a mutual support group. Oakland, CA: New Harbinger Publications, Inc.

Women

Boston Women's Health Collective (1976) *Our Bodies, Ourselves: A Book By and For Women*. New York: Simon & Schuster.
Chesler, P. (1973) *Women and Madness*. New York: Avon Books.
Dalton, K. (1980) *Once a Month: The Original PMS Handbook*. Oakland, CA: New Harbinger Publications, Inc.
DeRosis, H. (1976) *The Book of Hope: How Women Overcome Depression*. New York: Macmillan.

Lush, J., and Rushford, P. (1987) *Emotional Phases of a Woman's Life*. Old Tappen, NJ: Fleming H. Revell Co.

Scarf, M. (1980) *Unfinished Business: Pressure Points in the Lives of Woman*. New York: Doubleday.

Mental Health Organizations

Center for Community Change Through Housing and Support
University of Vermont
Psychology Department
John Dewey Hall
Burlington, VT 05405
802/656-0000

A National research, dissemination, and training organization focused on the housing and community support needs of people with psychiatric disabilities. The Center works with national organizations, federal, state, and local governments, service delivery agencies, and consumer and family advocacy groups to further the goal of full community participation for people with psychiatric disabilities and labels of severe and persistent mental illness.

Depression and Related Affective Disorders Association (DRADA)
Meyer 4-181
600 N. Wolfe St.
Baltimore, MD 21205
301/955-4647

Smooth Sailing is a quarterly newsletter published by DRADA and sent to all DRADA members. Call for information on membership and programs.

Lithium Information Center
Department of Psychiatry, University of Wisconsin
Center for Health Sciences
600 Highland Ave.
Madison, WI 53792
(608) 263-6171

The Lithium Information Center does computer searches on lithium information for a fee. Information is also available through the mail.

National Alliance for the Mentally Ill (NAMI)
2101 Wilson Blvd., Suite 302
Arlington, VA 22201
703/524-7600

An organization of over 100,000 people who have had mental disorders, and their family members, with chapters all over the country. Referral to the nearest group can be made by the national or state NAMI office. The organization has an excellent newsletter, and an annual convention in Chicago that offers speakers and workshops on all aspects of mental illness.

The Consumer Council is the consumer arm of NAMI and can be reached at the same address and phone number. They also have a newsletter, and you can get on that mailing list through the NAMI office.

The National Alliance for Research on Schizophrenia and Depression (NARSAD)
60 Cutter Mill Road
Great Neck, NY 11021

NARSAD raises and disributes funds for scientific research into the cause, cures, treatments, and preventions of severe mental illnesses, primarily schizophrenia and depressive disorders.

National Depressive and Manic-Depressive Association
53 West Jackson Suite 505
Chicago, IL 60604
A membership organization that provides direct support services to consumers and their families, legislation and public policy advocacy, litigation to prevent descrimination, education, and public awareness, and technical assistance to local affiliates.

National Institute for Mental Health
Information, Resources & Inquiries Branch, Room 15C-05
Office of Scientific Information
5600 Fishers Lane
Rockville, MD 20857
Provides an excellent list of free publications on depressive disorders.

National Mental Health Association
1021 Prince St.
Arlington, VA 22314
Information on available resources.

National Teleconference Project
Northeast Independent Living Center
130 Parker St.
Lawrence, MA 01843
Distributes monthly educational and advocacy information packets, and holds a monthly teleconference.

Reclamation, Inc.
2502 Waterford
San Antonio, TX 78217
512/824-8618
A national alliance of people who have experienced psychiatric disorders, working with them to help reclaim human dignity destroyed by the stigma of mental illness. Members receive a quarterly information newsletter.

Recovery and Re-Emergence
719 Second Ave. North
Seattle, WA 98109
A national organization of people who promote Re-evaluation Counseling (Co-Counseling) as a way to cope with mental and emotional problems.

Recovery, Inc.
802 North Dearborn St.
Chicago, IL 60610
A community mental health organization that offers a self-help method of training at weekly affiliate group meetings.

Organizational Newsletters

Caring and Sharing
Portland Tri-Counties DMDA
13720 S.W. Butner Road.
Beaverton, OR 97005

Constructive Action Newsletter

The American Conference of Thereutic Selfhelp/Selfhealth/Social Action clubs
710 Lodi St., B 1104
Syracuse, NY 13203
315/471-4644

Counterpoint
Westview House
50 South Willard St.
Burlington, VT 05401

Counterpoint is a newspaper put out by mental health consumers in Vermont. It features news about mental health consumers and their families.

Dendron News
454 Willamette, #219
P.O. Box 11284
Eugene, OR 97440
503/341-0100

An independent international nonprofit publication for people concerned about psychiatric oppression and exploring options for humane emotional support.

Newsletter
Depressive & Manic-Depressive Chapter of Topeka
Mental Health Association in Shawnee County
Box 675
Topeka, KS 66601

The Fine Line
The Alliance
26 Euclid Ave.
Syracuse, NY 13210

Manic Antics
111-A N. Kirkwood Road.
Kirkwood, MO 63122

Manic Blues
Manic-Depressive Self-Help Group of Hawaii
1164 Bishop St., Suite 124
Box 189
Honolulu, HI 96813

St. Louis Self-Help Center Newsletter
305 Sante Ave.
St. Louis, MO 63122

St. Louis Self-Help Center Newsletter contains articles and descriptions of mental health support groups that meet at the center.

Manic Depressive & Depressive Association, Inc.
P.O. Box 30886
Lincoln, NE 68503-0202

United Self-Help Newsletter
United Self-Help
277 Oahu Ave.
Honolulu, HI 96815
(808)926-0466

Coping with Depression & Manic Depression

A new videotape by Mary Ellen Copeland

Mary Ellen Copeland brings her book to life in this filmed workshop.

All the advice, suggestions, and techniques for self-help contained in her book are enriched with explanations and examples presented to a live audience.

Mary Ellen Copeland is engaging and entertaining. She inspires confidence that *you* can achieve real breakthroughs in coping with depression or manic depression. Condensed in this video are the fruits of years of research and hundreds of interviews with depressed persons.

Warm, helpful, and inspiring.

—— Order Form ——

Complete this form and return it to New Harbinger Publications, Inc., 5674 Shattuck Avenue, Oakland, CA 94609, or phone us at (800) 748-6273, or fax this page to (510) 652-5472.

Please send me _____ copies of *Coping with Depression & Manic Depression*

Your Name _____

Address _____

City, State, Zip _____

Telephone: Daytime, Mon.-Fri (_____)_____
             (In case we need to contact you about your order.)

Check for $29.95 plus $3.80 shipping (Californians add appropriate tax).
Charge to ☐ Visa   ☐ Mastercard

Expiration Date _____

Signature _____

Lifetime Guarantee: If not satisfied, return this tape at any time for a full refund, less shipping and handling.

Other New Harbinger Self-Help Titles

Couple Skills: Making Your Relationship Work, $12.95
Handbook of Clinical Psychopharmacology for Therapists, $39.95
The Warrior's Journey Home: Healing Men, Healing the Planet, $12.95
Weight Loss Through Persistence, $12.95
Post-Traumatic Stress Disorder: A Complete Treatment Guide, $39.95
Stepfamily Realities: How to Overcome Difficulties and Have a Happy Family, $11.95
Leaving the Fold: A Guide for Former Fundamentalists and Others Leaving Their Religion, $12.95
Father-Son Healing: An Adult Son's Guide, $12.95
The Chemotherapy Survival Guide, $11.95
Your Family/Your Self: How to Analyze Your Family System, $11.95
Being a Man: A Guide to the New Masculinity, $12.95
The Deadly Diet, Second Edition: Recovering from Anorexia & Bulimia, $11.95
Last Touch: Preparing for a Parent's Death, $11.95
Consuming Passions: Help for Compulsive Shoppers, $11.95
Self-Esteem, Second Edition, $12.95
Depression & Anxiety Mangement: An audio tape for managing emotional problems, $11.95
I Can't Get Over It, A Handbook for Trauma Survivors, $12.95
Concerned Intervention, When Your Loved One Won't Quit Alcohol or Drugs, $11.95
Redefining Mr. Right, $11.95
Dying of Embarrassment: Help for Social Anxiety and Social Phobia, $11.95
The Depression Workbook: Living With Depression and Manic Depression, $13.95
Risk-Taking for Personal Growth: A Step-by-Step Workbook, $11.95
The Marriage Bed: Renewing Love, Friendship, Trust, and Romance, $11.95
Focal Group Psychotherapy: For Mental Health Professionals, $44.95
Hot Water Therapy: Save Your Back, Neck & Shoulders in 10 Minutes a Day $11.95
Older & Wiser: A Workbook for Coping With Aging, $12.95
Prisoners of Belief: Exposing & Changing Beliefs that Control Your Life, $10.95
Be Sick Well: A Healthy Approach to Chronic Illness, $11.95
Men & Grief: A Guide for Men Surviving the Death of a Loved One., $11.95
When the Bough Breaks: A Helping Guide for Parents of Sexually Abused Childern, $11.95
Love Addiction: A Guide to Emotional Independence, $11.95
When Once Is Not Enough: Help for Obsessive Compulsives, $11.95
The New Three Minute Meditator, $9.95
Getting to Sleep, $10.95
The Relaxation & Stress Reduction Workbook, 3rd Edition, $13.95
Leader's Guide to the Relaxation & Stress Reduction Workbook, $19.95
Beyond Grief: A Guide for Recovering from the Death of a Loved One, $10.95
Thoughts & Feelings: The Art of Cognitive Stress Intervention, $13.95
Messages: The Communication Skills Book, $12.95
The Divorce Book, $11.95
Hypnosis for Change: A Manual of Proven Techniques, 2nd Edition, $12.95
The Chronic Pain Control Workbook, $13.95
Visualization for Change, $12.95
My Parent's Keeper: Adult Children of the Emotionally Disturbed, $11.95
When Anger Hurts, $12.95
Free of the Shadows: Recovering from Sexual Violence, $12.95
Lifetime Weight Control, $11.95
The Anxiety & Phobia Workbook, $13.95
Love and Renewal: A Couple's Guide to Commitment, $12.95
The Habit Control Workbook, $12.95

Call **toll free, 1-800-748-6273,** to order. Have your Visa or Mastercard number ready. Or send a check for the titles you want to New Harbinger Publications, Inc., 5674 Shattuck Avenue, Oakland, CA 94609. Include $3.80 for the first book and 75¢ for each additional book, to cover shipping and handling. (California residents please include appropriate sales tax.) Allow four to six weeks for delivery.

Prices subject to change without notice.